DATE DUE

Flag Burning and Free Speech

LANDMARK LAW CASES
&
AMERICAN SOCIETY

Peter Charles Hoffer
N. E. H. Hull
Series Editors

Titles in the series:
The Bakke *Case*, Howard Ball
The Reconstruction Election Cases, Robert M. Goldman
Flag Burning and Free Speech, Robert Justin Goldstein
The Salem Witchcraft Trials, Peter Charles Hoffer
The Reconstruction Justice of Salmon P. Chase,
Harold M. Hyman
The Struggle for Student Rights, John W. Johnson
Lochner v. New York, Paul Kens
Religious Freedom and Indian Rights, Carolyn N. Long
Marbury v. Madison, William E. Nelson
The Pullman Case, David Ray Papke
When the Nazis Came to Skokie, Philippa Strum
Affirmative Action on Trial, Melvin I. Urofsky
Lethal Judgments, Melvin I. Urofsky

ROBERT JUSTIN GOLDSTEIN

Flag Burning and Free Speech

The Case of *Texas v. Johnson*

UNIVERSITY PRESS OF KANSAS

Published by the University Press of Kansas (Lawrence, Kansas 66049), which was organized by the Kansas Board of Regents and is operated and funded by Emporia State University, Fort Hays State University, Kansas State University, Pittsburg State University, the University of Kansas, and Wichita State University

Library of Congress Cataloging-in-Publication Data

Goldstein, Robert Justin.

Flag burning and free speech : the case of Texas v. Johnson / Robert Justin Goldstein.

p. cm.—(Landmark law cases & American society)

Includes bibliographical references and index.

ISBN 0-7006-1053-7 (hbk. : alk. paper)—ISBN 0-7006-1054-5 (pbk. : alk. paper)

1. Johnson, Gregory Lee—Trials, litigation, etc.   2. Texas—Trials, litigation, etc.

3. Freedom of speech—United States.   4. Flags—Desecration—United States.

I. Title.   II. Series.

KF224.J64 G65 2000

342.73'0853—dc 21   00-041165

British Library Cataloguing in Publication Data is available.

Printed in the United States of America

10 9 8 7 6 5 4 3 2 1

The paper used in this publication meets the minimum requirement of the American National Standard for Permanence of Paper for Printed Library Materials Z39.48-1984.

CONTENTS

In 1991, the state of New Mexico unveiled a larger-than-life statue of the Spanish founder of the colony, Juan de Oñate. In 1598, Oñate marched up the Rio Grande to present-day Española (midway between modern Santa Fe and Taos) with over two hundred soldiers, missionaries, and settlers and coerced the Pueblo peoples into providing him with land, labor, and converts. Oñate and his successors then ruthlessly put down a series of Indian rebellions. In 1998, during the four-hundredth centennial of the founding of the colony, persons unknown among the descendants of the Pueblos celebrated the anniversary in their own way—by cutting off the left leg of the statue and hiding it.

The native protesters were engaging in an act of symbolic speech, defacing (or rather defooting) the statue to remind those who came to see it that there was another history of New Mexico that the statue and its inscription mischaracterized. Such acts of symbolic (that is, nonverbal) speech are as much a part of American history as the erection of historical markers and sculptures, but no case so focused the attention of Americans on the issues surrounding symbolic free speech as *Texas v. Johnson*, the so-called "flag desecration case."

Professor Goldstein is the nation's leading expert on the case, having devoted many years to studying, analyzing, and writing about it. In this superbly detailed and even-handed book, he traces the development of laws against flag abuse and court challenges to them, including the Vietnam War–era case of peacenik Abbie Hoffman's "flag shirt." He balances the veneration in which some laws and many people held the flag against what U.S. Supreme Court justice William Brennan called "[the] vital constitutional principle forbidding government censorship of unpopular political views." But was burning the flag protected by such vital principles, or did it go too far? Free speech, particularly political speech, is essential to an ordered liberty—without free speech we cannot protect any of our other liberties—but the courts have denied that the First Amendment protects all speech. Could the government punish flag burning on the grounds that desecration of a venerated object would offend observers and lead to more serious disorders? Courts in our country traditionally allow state and federal agencies great latitude in protecting public health, welfare, and order.

Gregory Lee Johnson was a member of a Maoist (pro–Communist Chinese) political organization, and the target of his protests on an August 1984 afternoon in Dallas was the Republican renomination of President Ronald Reagan. At the culmination of a series of "die-ins" and impromptu speeches, the group burned an American flag on the steps of the city hall. The protest led to a handful of arrests for disorderly conduct, and four protesters, including Johnson, were charged with desecrating the flag. He alone fought the charges through the state courts and all the way to the Supreme Court of the United States. He "totally rejected the system [of American government]" but used it to try to vindicate his and others' rights to free speech.

Professor Goldstein precisely and fully recounts the story of the trials, appeals, and final decision of the high court using actual testimony and oral argument, as well as interviews with Johnson, the lawyers, and the judges who heard the many rounds of appeals. The case, widely covered in the media from its inception, gained even more notoriety when Johnson retained William Kunstler, the most famous defender of radical causes in the second half of the twentieth century. Kunstler argued the case before the U.S. Supreme Court, and the author takes us inside the Court's secret deliberations to explain the reasoning of the justices. This is legal history firsthand and at its best.

The case also attracted the attention of leading politicians, becoming an issue in the 1988 presidential election. The victor, George Bush, subsequently embraced a number of patriotic initiatives, including one calling for an amendment to the United States Constitution to criminalize flag burning to overturn the Supreme Court's 1989 ruling upholding Johnson's right to burn the flag. On the floor of the House of Representatives, one congressman called the High Court's 5 to 4 decision on the case "treasonous," and national polls showed a strong majority for some sort of amendment. The second half of Goldstein's book traces the

{ *Flag Burning and Free Speech* }

reactions to the decision in and out of government and the attempts to draft and pass through Congress a bill and later an amendment to overturn *Johnson*. As of this writing, the Supreme Court rulings protecting symbolic free speech, including the destruction of flags, stand.

But the shouting is not over, for the anti–flag desecration amendment is not dead. Indeed, every year its advocates bring it up in Congress. Thus this volume in the Landmark Law Cases series is not only a historical survey, it is a guide to the ongoing debate—an essential guide, if legislators, jurists, students, and everyone else interested in free speech truly want to understand the issues that *Texas v. Johnson* raises.

On August 23, 1984, the *New York Times* published a six-paragraph article at the bottom of page 26, which reported on a disorderly protest in Dallas, Texas, during the Republican National Convention that was meeting there to renominate President Ronald Reagan. The article briefly mentioned in its lead paragraph that the demonstrators had "burned an American flag," but never elaborated on this reference, and mostly concentrated on their raucous march through Dallas, which included a variety of acts of petty vandalism. The article mentioned that ninety-nine of the demonstrators had been arrested for "disorderly conduct," and was accompanied by a photograph of an unidentified protester being led away by the police. That protester was later identified as one Gregory Lee Johnson. The original "disorderly conduct" charge lodged against him was shortly replaced by a new allegation—that he had burned the flag, in violation of a 1973 Texas law that made such conduct subject to a $2,000 fine and a one-year jail term.

From this small and obscure news acorn, a very large legal and political oak was to grow, spurring a controversy that has lasted for over fifteen years, especially in the wake of the Supreme Court's June 21, 1989, ruling in the case: in *Texas v. Johnson* the Court held that Texas could not, without violating the First Amendment, prosecute Johnson for burning the flag in order to express his political views. Subsequently, President George Bush endorsed a constitutional amendment to overturn the *Johnson* ruling, and although Congress refused to endorse such a measure in 1989, it did attempt to circumvent *Johnson* by passing the 1989 Flag Protection Act (FPA). After the Supreme Court struck down the FPA as unconstitutional in *U.S. v. Eichman*, proponents of a constitutional amendment were thwarted again in Congress in 1990. In 1995, 1997, and 1999, the revived amendment was endorsed by more than the needed two-thirds majority in the House of Representatives, but it was defeated in the Senate in 1995 and again in 2000.

The controversy over the Supreme Court's *Johnson* ruling, which reached true fever pitch in the summer of 1989, involved high emotions, complicated political maneuvering, arcane legal arguments, and debates about the fundamental meanings of democracy, patriotism, and the basic philosophy of the American political system. Rarely has a Supreme Court decision aroused so much public and political interest throughout the nation. The purpose of this book is to try to explain the historical background to the *Johnson* decision, the legal and philosophical arguments for and against it, and the political maelstrom it ignited and that, albeit at a considerably reduced level, still burns today. Because this book is directed at a general audience and because I have previously published more detailed and completely documented accounts of the flag burning controversy aimed at a scholarly audience, this work is not footnoted, but it is accompanied by a bibliographical essay directing those interested to primary sources and other published accounts.

As the flag desecration controversy (and this book) suggests, symbols can be extremely important to large numbers of people, so important that they may attract as much or more attention and emotion than arguments over more "concrete" matters. As these words are being penned (or, more accurately, word processed) in April 2000, two other highly symbolic disputes have occupied much media attention for months: whether the Confederate flag should continue to fly over the state capitol building in Columbia, South Carolina, and whether a six-year-old Cuban boy, Elián González, who survived a failed attempt by his mother to reach the United States by sea from Cuba, should remain in the United States or be returned to his father in Cuba. These controversies are, of course, very different. The Confederate flag dispute, like that over desecration of the American flag, is essentially purely symbolic, since flags are purely symbols, and the primary dispute is over what the flag represents—a proud southern heritage to some people (mostly whites), a legacy of slavery and discrimination to others (mostly blacks)—and therefore whether it should be honored by the state of South Carolina. Young Elián is obviously flesh and blood and, to his family at least, probably not a symbol at all, but his fate has clearly become so important to so many in both the United States and Cuba because he has become a symbolic representation of the political dispute between these two nations (the example of the statue of the Spanish founder of New Mexico discussed in the series introduction to this book provides yet another variant, since, unlike infinitely reproducible flags, many of which are privately owned, it involves a unique, publicly-owned object, but, if it may be literally "concrete," it is completely symbolic in function, unlike a live human being).

Like these other examples, but no doubt more so, the flag desecration controversy became so inflamed because the symbolic power of the American flag is so great, because it is so important to so many people, and because the issue became a symbolic part of a much broader dispute about the nature and direction of American politics and history; that is, the argument became not only a fight over a symbol but a symbolic fight over a symbol. Although the basic arguments of the differing sides in the flag desecration controversy will be discussed in detail and at length in the body of this book, in short, those who wish to ban flag "desecration" (a term that by definition applies only to consecrated, or holy, objects) view the flag as a unifying symbol that represents American democracy and freedom and that has become literally sanctified by history and, especially, by the fact that it has flown over so many battlefields where so many Americans have died. Such an object is essentially viewed as beyond ordinary rules and ordinary concepts of law.

Moreover, in the minds of many of those who wish to outlaw flag desecration, the entire issue has become symbolically identified with their broader social and political views, which, repeatedly during the over one-hundred-year history of the controversy, have often involved a perception that American traditions and identity, as symbolized by the flag, were under attack by various newly emerging forces that needed to be repelled. As documented in this book, during the origins of the flag desecration controversy around 1900 these forces included "new" immigrants (from southern and eastern Europe rather than the traditional immigrant source of northwestern Europe) and the emergence of trade unions and radical political viewpoints such as socialism. During the Vietnam War, or second major flag desecration controversy, the perceived threatening elements included the antiwar movement, black militants, and the eruption of an activist "counterculture." Prominent during the most recent controversy, triggered by the 1989 *Johnson* ruling, have been generalized fears of social and moral decay, as represented by such indicators as high rates of crime, drug use, and divorce and a general perception of lessened respect for tradition and authority in general. Put slightly differently, the target and fear of the recent antiflag desecration movement has essentially been that of a recurrence or institutionalization of aspects of the 1960s that conservatives and traditionalists hated at the time and still view with alarm and disgust. It is no coincidence that a 1998 book by Balint Vazsonyi, *America's 30 Years War: Who is Winning?* features a burning flag on the cover, since this image remains one of the most powerful mental memories of the Vietnam War era and the so-called "cultural war" that this period is said to have triggered. Only in this context of the broader symbolic importance of the recent controversy over flag desecration can one understand comments by those who favor a constitutional amendment to overturn *Johnson*, such as that by American Legion national commander William Detweiler, who told Congress in 1995 that his organization regarded flag burning as "a problem even if no one ever burns another flag," and that by Senate Judiciary Committee chairman Orrin Hatch, the leading Senate sponsor of the amendment and a failed contender for the 2000 Republican presidential nomination, who declared during the March 2000 Senate debate on the amendment that sending it to the states for ratification "would create the biggest debate on values this country has seen in years" and that "that alone would justify everything we are talking about today," since "tolerating desecration of the flag is silent acquiescence to the degeneration of the broader values which sustain us as a free and democratic nation, the ramifications of which are far more profound than mere symbolism."

Although I have tried to present both sides of the flag desecration controversy in a fair manner, no doubt my own views about this subject have influenced this book, and I feel it is only fair to my readers to let them know what my own bias is—not to try to convince those who disagree, but rather to alert them that they should be on their guard. In short, I believe that although flag desecration is usually a completely counterproductive activity that primarily alienates people, it nonetheless is a form of political expression and therefore must be constitutionally protected in a society that claims freedom of expression as its philosophical touchstone.

Those who advocate the criminalization of flag desecration make three basic arguments, none of which I find convincing. The first is that the vast majority of Americans are appalled by flag desecration and wish to outlaw such behavior. Most opinion polls suggest that about 70 percent or more of the population think the Supreme Court was wrong in *Johnson* and *Eichman*, and that flag desecration should be banned, even if it takes a constitutional amendment to do so. But we do not live in a *majoritarian* democracy, where the majority can impose its will about any subject at any time, but in a *constitutional* democracy, wherein certain rights are guaranteed to everyone no matter how unpopular they may be. As Supreme Court justice Robert Jackson wrote in the 1943 case of *West Va. School Board of Education v. Barnette*, in which the Court ruled that public school children could not be forced to say the Pledge of Allegiance and salute the flag if such violated their beliefs:

> The very purpose of a Bill of Rights was to withdraw certain subjects from the vicissitudes of public controversy, to place them beyond the reach of majorities and officials, to establish them as legal principles to be applied by the courts. One's right to life, liberty and property; to free speech, a free press, freedom of worship and assembly, and other fundamental rights may not be submitted to vote; they depend upon the outcome of no election.

All of us at one time or another hold very unpopular views. Which of us is willing to let our views be censored when they are unpopular?

Beyond the argument about the unpopularity of flag desecration, those who wish to outlaw it often argue that flag desecration is *conduct*, and not an exercise of speech or press, which alone are

{ *Preface* }   xv specifically mentioned in the First Amendment. The problem with this argument, even aside from the fact that the Supreme Court has been protecting symbolic expression for over sixty years, such as the right to wave red flags, is that carried to its logical conclusion, it would make it constitutional to forbid all forms of non-verbal communication, including pantomime, sign language, theater, music, spitting, and hissing. Indeed, such an interpretation of the First Amendment would make it legal to forbid waving the American flag—which was quite unpopular in the South for many years after the Civil War—but this would be an absurdity. Everyone knows that waving an American flag or a red flag is as purely expressive as is burning an American flag or a red flag— indeed, a pure symbol such as a flag has no other function and can *only* be used in a symbolically expressive way. We intuitively recognize the inherently expressive nature of flag desecration when it occurs in other countries, as when Americans hailed the desecration of national flags in Communist countries in 1989–1990.

Ultimately, the argument for banning flag desecration comes down to the position, as sketched out above, that the flag is special and that Americans have a special regard for it, because among other things, it represents freedom and the sacrifice of lives in its behalf; therefore, if necessary, a special exception to normal rules safeguarding freedom of expression to outlaw flag desecration should be made. As Chief Justice William Rehnquist declared in his *Johnson* dissent, this view holds that the flag "is not simply another 'idea' or 'point of view' competing for recognition in the marketplace of ideas" because "millions and millions of Americans regard it with an almost mystical reverence."

What's wrong with this argument, which basically holds that flag desecration is so offensive that normal constitutional rules simply shouldn't apply? Above all—and here is where the issue become highly symbolic to those who disagree—it is that in a system whose very heart is the protection of freedom of expression no exceptions can be made without severely damaging the basic principle upon which the system is founded, and that once such an exception is made the door is open to similar exceptions in the future. As Supreme Court justice Oliver Wendell Holmes once put it, the

{ *Flag Burning and Free Speech* }

whole point of providing a firewall of constitutional protection for free speech is not to protect popular speech, which never needs protection, but precisely to protect "the thought we hate." If the fundamental principles of democracy can be bent to exclude one object or one subject of discussion, there can be no principled legal barrier to extending such restrictions. But even if it were true that restrictions on freedom of expression could, in practice, be strictly limited to outlawing flag desecration, this still could not justify such a ban in a democratic country, where the fundamental principle of government is the right to peaceful dissent, even if expressed in an outrageous and offensive manner. As Reagan administration solicitor general Charles Fried, a well-known conservative legal scholar who lived under Nazi and Communist tyranny in Czechoslovakia, told the Senate Judiciary Committee (SJC) in 1990, "the man who says you can make [such] an exception" to the principle of freedom of expression "does not know what a principle is," just as the man who says, "Only this once let's make 2 + 2 = 5" does not understand logic or mathematics. In short, such an "exception" would destroy the principle itself.

The clearest evidence that those who seek to ban flag desecration really are seeking to outlaw certain *thoughts* is that the strongest backers of the constitutional amendment, American veterans' groups, regularly burn flags themselves in ceremonies that they deem a patriotic means of retiring worn flags. In short, they tell us, if you burn a flag with good thoughts in mind, it's fine; but if you burn a flag with bad thoughts in mind you should be jailed. *We don't jail people for having bad thoughts in a democratic country.* As Senator Howard Metzenbaum (D-OH) asked the SJC in 1989, "What is the value of patriotism forced by the threat of prisons? What example is more American, more faithful to American values? Jailing flag burners or tolerating them?"

The fundamental reason, then, why flag desecration should and must be protected is because otherwise the whole principle of democratic self-government that our system is based upon will unravel. Even if all the flags in the country suddenly magically disappeared, the nation will survive unharmed if it keeps its principles intact. But if the democratic principles that are supposed to

{ *Preface* }   xvii govern our political system are permanently, or even temporarily, limited, even if the number of flags is multiplied by three, our freedoms will have been irreparably damaged. Those who seek to ban flag desecration are making a fetish of the flag, confusing the flag that only symbolizes our freedoms with the substantive freedoms themselves. Did hundreds of thousands of American soldiers really give up their lives to protect a piece of cloth, or did they fight to protect a political system based on freedom, which the cloth only symbolizes, and whose symbolic value would itself be diminished if we jail people for damaging it? As *Chicago Tribune* columnist Stephen Chapman wrote in 1989, in response to the argument that we must ban flag desecration because American soldiers literally died to protect it, it seems unlikely that American soldiers would have "deserted in droves" during Vietnam if Congress had changed the design of flag. "What would they have said," he asked, " 'Sorry I don't mind dying for the red, white and blue, but getting killed for this purple and gold model is too much'?" In short, jailing people for desecrating the flag would be desecrating something far more valuable—the ideas that the flag stands for and the crown jewel of freedom of expression that is at the heart of our constitutional democracy.

Finally, flag desecration may serve socially useful purposes. Flag desecration is a desperate act, but I believe that in the past and certainly conceivably in the future there are times when such peaceful forms of desperate protest may be needed and useful. Had two hundred prominent Americans collectively burned flags to protest the forced expulsion and detention without trial or charges of over one hundred thousand Japanese Americans during World War II, or to protect the excesses of McCarthyism or the FBI, I can at least imagine that there is a small chance that American history might not bear those stains today. Similarly, if two hundred prominent Americans had burned flags to protest the deepening American involvement in Vietnam in 1965, perhaps there is a small chance that there might not be a wall today in Washington, D.C., with fifty-eight thousand names carved in it.

CHAPTER I

The Early History of the American Flag Desecration Controversy

---

The Pre–Civil War Cultural History of the American Flag

At least from the historical perspective of the year 2000, the American flag's role in the life of the nation before the Civil War was remarkably unimportant. Although the flag ultimately became a ubiquitous symbol of the United States, displayed widely in front of government buildings, private homes, and commercial enterprises and extensively used as a design springboard for clothing, advertising, and the widest possible variety of products, it attracted little interest or public display for over eighty years after it was first adopted as the symbol of a new nation by the Continental Congress on June 14, 1777. The government of the newly self-declared nation did not even bother to proclaim a new flag until a year after the Declaration of Independence, and no one seems to have taken much notice of it at its creation. Moreover, the flag's design was left so unclear or was so poorly known that it flew with widely varying arrangements, numbers and colors of stars and stripes. Reflecting its lack of general popularity, the American army did not fight under it for over fifty years and demand for flags was so low that no private company manufactured them until after 1845. Only the Civil War turned the flag into a widely beloved object of adoration (but only in the North).

The most important impetus for the creation of a new flag following the 1776 Declaration of Independence was apparently the communication of an American Indian, Thomas Green, who in early 1777 sent the Continental Congress "three strings of wampum to cover [the] cost" of an American flag, which he requested for the protection of Indian chiefs should they travel to meet with the Congress. On June 14, 1777, eleven days after Green's request was presented to the Congress, that body adopted a resolution that declared, "the flag of the United States be made of thirteen stripes, alternate red and white; that the union be thirteen stars, white in a blue field, representing a new constellation." This action, which occupied one sentence in the congressional proceedings, went unmentioned in the press until ten weeks later when the August 30 *Pennsylvania Evening Post* reported it.

The apparent general lack of interest in the new flag, compounded by the vague description of the arrangements of the stars in its canton as "representing a new constellation" and the (mostly informal, until 1818) addition of new stars and stripes as new states joined the Union, led to endless confusion about the flag's design. American emissaries abroad could not accurately describe it eighteen months after its creation—one said the flag consisted of "13 stripes, alternately red, white and blue"—and as late as 1847 the Dutch government politely inquired, "What is the American flag?" More than a dozen arrangements of the stars in the thirteen-star flag have been documented between 1779 and 1796, including the well-known circular arrangement, but also with stars in the shape of a cross, a straight line, and a square with four stars on each side and one in the middle. Almost every other aspect of the flag also appeared in at least some variations: the number of points in the stars, the color of the stars, and the color order of the stripes. Moreover, even though the 1777 resolution described the stripes as red and white, some flags had red, white, and blue stripes, including the flag flown by American sailor John Paul Jones during his famous Revolutionary War capture of the British frigate *Serapis*.

The number of stripes varied so widely as new states were admitted to the Union that in 1818 Congressman Peter Wendover complained to the House of Representatives that although a 1795 law that recognized the addition to the Union of Vermont and Kentucky directed "that the flag shall contain fifteen" stripes, the banner then flying over Congress had thirteen stripes, those at the nearby Navy Yard and Marine barracks each had "at least 18 stripes," and "the

{ *Flag Burning and Free Speech* }

flag under which the last Congress sat during its first session . . . from some cause or other unknown to me, had but nine stripes." Congress fixed the number of stripes permanently at thirteen in 1818, adding one new star for each state joining the union, but other aspects of the flag's design, including the arrangement of the stars, the color order of the stripes, and its length-height ratio, were only standardized by a 1912 executive order issued by President William Howard Taft.

In historical retrospect, far more significant than confusion about the flag's design was that before the Civil War the flag was not widely displayed and played only a minor role in the nation's patriotic oratory and iconography. The main function of the new flag until the Civil War was to designate American ships at sea and federal buildings rather than to serve as a general rallying standard. The flag was not flown over state and local government build-ings—not even schools—and, as the director of the Betsy Ross house in Philadelphia noted during the 1989–1990 flag desecra-tion controversy, "It would have been unthinkable to fly an Amer-ican flag at a private home."

Even as a utilitarian object, the flag's antebellum use was highly limited. Until the 1830s, for example, the American army primar-ily flew distinct regimental emblems, and the 1846–1848 Mexican War—which finally stimulated enough demand to make viable the establishment of the first full-time private flag manufacturer—was the first conflict during which American army units fought under the Stars and Stripes. The flag was at best a minor icon in the panoply of American patriotic symbols: far more popular were depictions and stories about George Washington, the American eagle (when John Frémont explored Indian territory in the 1840s he did so under an eagle flag), and "Columbia," a feminized rep-resentation of "Liberty" (as in the lady with the torch depicted today at the beginning of Columbia motion pictures). Although the War of 1812, which produced Francis Scott Key's "Star Span-gled Banner," and the Mexican War clearly boosted the flag's pop-ularity (during the latter, for example, newspapers wrote lurid accounts about flag raisings over the "halls of Montezuma"), text-books and even patriotic Fourth of July oratory rarely invoked the flag, and artifacts of popular culture, such as textiles, wallpaper, and china, used flag imagery far less than other patriotic icons. Thus, a 1997 book by historian Len Travers, *Celebrating the Fourth: Independence Day and the Rites of Nationalism in the Early Republic*, barely mentions the flag. "The Star Spangled Banner," set to the tune of an English drinking song, which eventually became the national anthem in 1931, was often parodied during the antebellum period with such alternative lyrics as, "Oh! who has not seen by the dawn's early light / Some bloated drunkard to home weakly reeling."

Perhaps the clearest sign of the flag's early insignificance was that American politicians did not begin to use flag imagery in their campaigns until 1840, when supporters of successful presidential candidate William Henry Harrison inscribed political slogans supporting their hero on the flag's white stripes, an innovation to be repeated in virtually all subsequent nineteenth-century presidential campaigns. In a few instances, nonmainstream political groups also employed the flag during the antebellum period, as when the anti-Catholic/anti-immigrant Know-Nothing movement of the 1840s adopted the flag (along with the eagle and George Washington) to represent their conception of the nation as rightly consisting of white Anglo-Saxon Protestants. On July 4, 1854, Boston abolitionists flew flags upside down and draped them in black to protest congressional enactment of the fugitive slave law (requiring the return of escaped slaves), while their leader, William Lloyd Garrison, burned a copy of the Constitution.

The Civil War and the Flag

Only the outbreak of the Civil War in April 1861, symbolically begun by Confederate troops firing on flag-bedecked Fort Sumter, South Carolina, transformed the Stars and Stripes into a true national icon (in the North). "Until now," a woman named Nancy Cunningham wrote in her diary, "we never thought about the flag being more than a nice design of red and white stripes." According to the leading nineteenth-century flag historian, George Preble, "When the stars and stripes went down at Sumter, they went up in every town and county in the loyal states," as the flag developed a "new and strange significance" and flags "suddenly blossomed" from "every city, town and village," including from churches, "colleges, hotels, store-fronts and private balconies." The demand for flags so outstripped supply that the price of flag bunting in New York jumped from $4.75 to $28.

The tattered remnants of the Fort Sumter flag became a major fund-raising device in the North: one hundred thousand people gathered on April 20 in New York City to view it, and the flag was subsequently transported from city to city and repeatedly "auctioned" at large rallies held for war relief. Throughout the Civil War, elaborate flag raising and flag presentation ceremonies (often involving flags especially sewn for military units by seamstress volunteers) were held before large crowds. At one ceremony, held in northwestern Pennsylvania in June 1861, Captain Asa Cory, leader of the volunteers, pledged to protect the flag, declaring, "Our Southern States have discarded this National emblem and insulted and vilified it; yet we trust it will ere long float again over a *united Union*." At another rally in Kalamazoo, Michigan, soldiers were presented with a flag containing the motto "Do Your Duty" stitched into the field of stars.

As the conflict raged, flag poetry, songs, and stories became increasingly popular. Thus, the popular northern anthem, "The Battle Cry of Freedom," included the line, "we'll rally round the flag, boys," while James Fields's song "The Stars and Stripes" maintained, with regard to the new Confederate flag, that "*Their flag* is but a rag—Ours is the *true* one / Up with the Stars and Stripes—Down with the new one!" Northern soldiers sometimes died seeking to keep the flag flying during battle and/or were awarded medals for protecting it from capture. Before the Confederate army captured one Union regiment, Union soldiers tore up their flag, burned parts of it, and divided the rest among themselves to keep it from rebel hands. Other flags had the locations of the battles they had survived stitched into their bunting.

In a number of instances in the North, the locations of businesses and individuals that failed to fly flags or were viewed as insufficiently patriotic were subjected to mob assaults, sometimes leading to hasty efforts by targets to obtain flags to display. In the South, the federal government threatened and took more formal action to suppress flag disloyalty. On January 29, 1861, more than two months before the war began, after word reached Washington that Louisiana officials were threatening to confiscate a federal revenue ship, President James Buchanan's treasury secretary, John Dix, telegraphed to a clerk in New Orleans, "If anyone attempts to haul down the American flag, shoot him on the spot." With the war's outbreak, scattered incidents of deliberate physical damage to the flag were reported from the South, including apparently the first protest flag burning in American history, at Liberty, Mississippi, on May 10, 1861. The most startling instance of official punishment for flag mistreatment occurred in New Orleans, where William Mumford was hung for treason on June 7, 1862, after a military court found him guilty of pulling down, dragging in the mud, and tearing to shreds an American flag that had been hoisted over the New Orleans mint amid the federal reoccupation of the city. Confederate president Jefferson Davis subsequently labeled Mumford's execution an "outrage" and "deliberate murder."

The Rise of the Flag Protection Movement

The flag's popular new status remained firmly entrenched in the North after the war's end, as was made clear by the flag displays and ceremonies connected with numerous historical commemorations, such as those celebrating the 1876 revolutionary centennial and the 1892 Chicago Columbian Exposition. But for citizens' daily lives, the flag's heightened popularity was most evident in its increasing appropriation for commercial purposes, as modern forms of advertising developed amid the nation's postwar economic expansion. Among the products and services that used flag symbolism to market themselves, according to various publications issued by "flag protection" groups which sprang up by 1900 to protest that such advertising usage degraded and "desecrated" the flag, were breweries, burlesque shows, doormats, pool rooms, chewing gum, whiskey barrels, patent medicines, trolley tickets, toilet paper, the costumes of prizefighters and Uncle Sam, and paper used to wrap fruit, cheese, cigars, and ham. Politicians also continued the pre–Civil War practice of printing their slogans (and sometimes their portraits) on the flag, a practice many veterans imitated by printing the names of their regiments and the battles in which they had fought across the flag's stripes.

In 1878, Representative Samuel Cox introduced the first congressional bill targeting such practices: it sought fines and imprisonment for anyone who "shall disfigure the national flag, either by printing on said flag, or attaching to the same, or otherwise, any advertisement for public display." A similar bill was passed by the House of Representatives in 1890 after a House Judiciary Committee report, "To Prevent Desecration of the United States Flag" (perhaps the first official use of "desecration" with regard to the flag), declared that the flag should "be held a thing sacred" and that to "deface, disfigure, or prostitute it to the purposes of advertising" was "a crime against the nation."

What will henceforth be termed the "flag protection movement," or FPM, blossomed after about 1890, spurred by Union veterans' organizations—especially the Grand Army of the Republic (GAR), which, of course, exempted "battle flags" from their attacks—and above all by patriotic-hereditary organizations such as the Sons of the American Revolution (SAR) and the Daughters of the American Revolution (DAR), which sprang up in large numbers after 1885. By 1898, organizations demanding that "flag desecration" be outlawed were so numerous that they agreed to coordinate their efforts by forming the American Flag Association (AFA).

The FPM vehemently denounced commercialization of the flag and other unorthodox uses of it as a prostitution of the emblem and maintained that such uses of flag imagery degraded its significance. Thus, when administrators of the California hall at the Chicago Columbian Exposition used a forty-foot flag to carpet a stairway during an 1893 reception, the DAR indignantly protested that the flag was being turned into a "footmat." The authors of an 1895 FPM pamphlet claimed that "The tender sentiment associated with . . . decent use of the national emblem is sadly marred when we see it shamefully misused as an apron on labor day parades, and as a costume to bedeck stilt walkers, circus clowns, prize fighters and variety players or gaiety girls." In a 1902 pamphlet, leading FPM spokesman Charles Kingsbury Miller (who, ironically, had made his fortune in the advertising industry) denounced the "clutch of sordid tradesmen" who had turned the flag into "an article of commerce" by using it as a "medium of deception and fraud to proclaim their defective merchandise, flimsy wares and adulterated goods." Such "unscrupulous" businessmen, Miller proclaimed, had "polluted" the flag, whose "sacred folds were never designed to be defaced with advertisements of beer, sauerkraut candy, itch ointment, pile remedies and patent nostrums, to serve as awnings, horse blankets, merchandise wrappers, pillow and footstool covers or as miniature pocket handkerchiefs, on which to blow noses, or with which to wipe perspiring brows." DAR Flag Committee chairwoman Frances Saunders Kempster similarly bitterly complained that the flag had been "contaminated by the greed of gain until it has been dragged down to the vilest associations" by those who had turned it into a transformer of "patriots' blood into traders' gold."

Although the original impetus to form the FPM was commercial use of the flag, its ire was also raised by incidents that resulted in damage to flags during their widespread use for partisan purposes. In 1896, such uses reached new heights when Republican candidate William McKinley's campaign distributed millions of flags and flag buttons as signs of support for him, even declaring October 31, 1896, as a national flag day in McKinley's honor, which was highlighted by a New York City parade of over one hundred thousand people featuring masses of flags. In perhaps a dozen or so incidents, supporters of Democratic candidate William Jennings Bryan reportedly vented their anger at slurs upon their loyalty made by McKinley's backers by tearing down or otherwise assaulting "McKinleyite" flags, even allegedly burning one such flag in Sedalia, Missouri.

Reacting to reports of these and similar incidents during the 1896 campaign and thereafter, in 1898 SAR Flag Committee chairman Ralph Prime (who also served as AFA president) denounced both those who used the flag for "selfish and unpatriotic" commercial advertising and those whose "partisan, political and unpatriotic sentiment" used the emblem for promoting political candidates. Similarly, FPM spokesman Miller wrote that the flag's "sacredness" had been equally abused by "avaricious tradesmen and crafty politicians." Ironically, perhaps, one of the clearest examples of such commercial use of the flag was its increasingly frequent appearance in Broadway musicals, including George M. Cohan's 1906 *George Washington, Jr.*, which featured the song known today as "You're a Grand Old Flag"—it had originally been called "You're a Grand Old Rag" but Cohan changed it after a theater critic complained that the original title constituted flag desecration. Cohan made use of patriotic symbolism so frequently and effectively during his shows that he once commented, "Many a bum show is saved by the American flag."

Although the original targets of the FPM—advertisers, political parties, and showmen like Cohan—were clearly mainstream elements in American society, new, far less mainstream targets soon emerged. These new targets consisted of perceived "un-Americans," such as so-called "new immigrants" from southern and eastern Europe (who by 1890 began far outnumbering those originating from the traditional northern and western European homelands of American immigrants), political radicals, and trade unionists. Gradually after 1900, and especially after the twin 1917 developments of American intervention in World War I and the Bolshevik revolution, the FPM began to focus almost exclusively on the alleged use of flags to express political protest by such forces, who were often indiscriminately lumped together as perceived threats.

For example, pamphleteer Miller warned in 1900 that the country had become the "international dumping ground" for "hundreds of thousands of the lowest class of immigrants" who swelled the "populace who abuse" the flag and posed a "menace to the nation," along with the "riotous elements of the labor organizations" and assorted and apparently interchangeable "Socialists, Anarchists, Nihilists, Populists, Tramps and Criminals." Two years earlier, Miller lamented that "we observe our flag no longer protected by the sentiment of a century ago, but treated with open disrespect," a development he attributed to "the multitude of uneducated foreigners who land upon our friendly shores" and to the "seeds of contempt" for the flag which had been "manifested in part by anarchy and murderous labor riots." He demanded that "desecration of the American flag be stopped by law, before our people discover that the clenched fist of lawlessness has become the mailed hand of defiance." Kempster, chair of the DAR Flag Committee, told her organization in 1899 that the flag needed protection against the "fomenter of sedition," the "anarchist" and the "children of those new to this country." AFA president Prime declared in 1912 that those guilty of "malicious outrages" against the flag had invariably been immigrants associated with "meetings and demonstrations of the labor movement," whose leaders were obligated to "eliminate from their membership from one end of the land to the other all flag desecrators and all anarchists of every name, style and sentiment."

Spokesmen for big business and major newspapers also frequently suggested that unions and strikers were anti-American elements who hated and desecrated the flag. Thus, John Kirby, a leading figure in the big business–dominated National Association of Manufacturers, condemned unions as "those who neither revere nor respect the flag of our country." In 1911 the bitterly antilabor *Los Angeles Times* faked photographs, which received national circulation, that claimed to show American Federation of Labor president Samuel Gompers (who opposed anything that might allow unions to be portrayed as radical) standing on an American flag at a Labor Day rally. The *New York Times* of July 16, 1913, declared that the "chief care" of patriots was that the flag be treated with "reverence" and therefore when "socialists, anarchists, syndicalists or other malcontents tear down our flag and trample it in our own territory, it is time to take action."

Many newspapers supported the FPM's primary goal of obtaining flag desecration laws and they often suggested that disloyal immigrants were to blame for incidents of desecration. Thus, a May 3, 1912, *Bakersfield Californian* editorial about an alleged flag desecration incident at a New York labor meeting declared that

{ *Flag Burning and Free Speech* }

those who "find the flag offensive . . . should be summarily sent to the land of their birth." The April 25, 1912, Everett, Washington, *Herald*, describing the flag as the "world's token of peace, political freedom, intelligent self-government and the highest and best effort of the human race to attain universal liberty and welfare," said that anyone who disagreed "should seek a country better to his liking." Given this repeated association of flag desecration with immigrants and "un-Americanism," not surprisingly the flag consistently played a major role in the growing pre–World War I "Americanization" movement, which sought to ensure that immigrants developed strong loyalties to their new homeland. Thus, at the elaborate conclusion of the Ford Motor Company's compulsory "English Melting Pot" school for immigrants, "graduates" dressed in native costumes descended into a great pot, only to reemerge wearing neat business suits and waving American flags.

After the 1917 Bolshevik revolution, "Communists" were added to the FPM's "usual suspects." For example, the United States Flag Association (a successor organization to the AFA, which gradually became moribund after about 1912) declared that "proper respect and reverence" for the flag was never "so vitally important as it is today" when "communistic and other anti-American propaganda" was allegedly flooding the country. During 1923 Flag Day celebrations, Secretary of Labor James Davis warned that "disrespect for the flag" constituted one of the "first steps" toward Communist revolution, and in 1927 Representative J. Mayhew Wainwright of New York, a leading proponent of flag desecration legislation, urged the House Judiciary Committee (HJC) to stem the "communistic and radical sentiment so prevalent" in the country.

By 1900, the constant linking of flag desecration with "un-Americanism," radicalism, and organized labor had become so common that many union members habitually began carrying flags at strikes and rallies to demonstrate their loyalty. For example, the *Coast Seamen's Journal* reported that at a 1901 Labor Day celebration in support of a San Francisco strike, "patriotism was the keynote" of a parade of twenty thousand workers, that "everywhere the nation's flag and the nation's colors were on view," and that "unionism that is founded on patriotism and order cannot be stamped out."

According to a scholar of "visual traditions" in Pullman, Illinois, workers "appropriated the flag as part of their everyday lives by displaying and photographing it in family and community celebrations of national holidays," above all as a "symbol of neighborhood solidarity and workers' desire for a freer life."

In several instances, trade unionists complained that their flagholders had been assaulted by police and soldiers during strikes. Thus, during a bitter 1913–1914 Michigan copper strike, workers invariably paraded behind flags and clashes with troops often resulted in literal battles for flags. During a 1914 Colorado coal strike, workers marched behind flags to protest the arrest of the well-known labor agitator Mother Jones, only to be attacked by mounted troops with guns and sabers drawn. This event led to headlines in the labor press such as "Woman carrying American flag knocked down with butt of gun and flag torn from her hands by militiamen." According to a history of Colorado labor, during a 1927 miners' strike, state police shot and killed five men who had been among "the front rank carrying American flags, as was customary."

Despite rhetoric that increasingly targeted political and labor radicals and "new immigrants" as the main flag desecraters, documented instances in which flags were either verbally attacked or physically damaged to express political dissent during the pre–Vietnam War era were relatively rare. Even verbal attacks on the FPM generally reflected less hostility to the flag than anger at those viewed as manipulating it for political ends such as silencing dissent and diverting public attention away from social and political injustices. For example, during the 1898 Spanish-American War, the conservative *Cigar Makers' Journal* complained that "anyone who differs" with those who sought "to foist imperialism and militarism" upon the nation were "now accused of being traitors and traducers of the flag." In 1900, President Ed Boyce of the radical Western Federation of Miners attacked employers who sought to "conceal yourselves under the folds of the stars and stripes to disguise your true motive." In 1903 a left-wing newspaper in Spokane, Washington, termed some employers "foul pirates" who sought to sail under the "fair" banner of the flag, and urged workers to "save it now from desecration, by taking it back from the

{ *Flag Burning and Free Speech* }

hands of the corporate freebooters and make it stand for what it was intended, 'life, liberty and happiness.' Socialism is the thing to stop flag desecrators."

Although physical flag desecration or verbal criticism of the flag by immigrants, unions, and political radicals were uncommon, by the time the United States entered World War I in 1917 these new targets had eclipsed the mainstream elements originally perceived by the FPM as the prime flag abusers, and such "un-Americans" have remained the usual flag desecration suspects ever since. Mainstream advertising and partisan political use of the flag, the original targets of the FPM, virtually ceased attracting their attention thereafter, although the flag desecration laws enacted in all of the then forty-eight states between 1897 and 1932 outlawed virtually all unorthodox flag use, including any association of flag imagery with advertising.

The Goals and Motivations
of the Flag Protection Movement

FPM organizations and spokesmen deliberately and systematically sought to create what amounted to a "cult of the flag" by ideologically transforming it into a sacred object to be treated only in a highly reverent manner. The very word "desecration" made clear that the flag was to be regarded as "sacred," since by definition only an object that has been religiously "consecrated" can be "desecrated." Unquestionably, the greatest long-term influence of the FPM was to link the flag and the sacred/religious, which is clear from the general acceptance of the term "desecration" to describe injury to the flag and from constant references to the "sacredness" of the flag that has permeated American political oratory for many years.

Explicitly religious references and comparisons to the flag were highly stressed in FPM rhetoric. GAR commander-in-chief William Warner told Union veterans in 1889 that schoolchildren's reverence for the flag should be like that of Israelites for the Ark of the Covenant, and a 1895 FPM publication declared that "the stars and stripes are heaven's benediction" and "its folds are sacred." In 1898, Miller wrote that the flag "should be kept as inviolate as was the Holy of Holies in King Solomon's temple," and referred to "those three sacred jewels, the Bible, the Cross and Flag," and AFA president Prime proclaimed that the flag should be maintained as a "sacred emblem, not to be used for any unholy or mercenary or partisan uses," but to be "kept pure by patriots." DAR Flag Committee chairwoman Kempster complained bitterly in 1899 that the flag, "christened and hallowed" by the "prodigal outpouring of noble blood," should be "held free and pure and sacred as the cross," but had been "contaminated by the greed of gain."

Miller most clearly summed up the FPM's viewpoint in a 1900 pamphlet that declared that the United States "must develop, define and protect the cult of her flag, and the symbol of that cult—the Star Spangled Banner—must be kept inviolate as are the emblems of all religions." In perhaps the ultimate logical conclusion to this conception, during the rising tide of patriotism and hysteria associated with American entry into World War I, in 1918 William Norman Guthrie published a pamphlet titled *The Religion of Old Glory*, which, along with attacks on racial miscegenation and calls for maintenance of the United States as a "white nation," described detailed religious ceremonies dedicated to flag worship. The book included an extensive ritual, "The Ceremony of Worship Unto Old Glory," which was performed at a New York City church in 1918.

To the FPM, the flag, like a true holy relic, literally had magical properties that could help civilize and transform "un-American" elements at home and abroad. At the 1898 national GAR encampment, held in the aftermath of the Spanish-American War and American colonization of the Philippines and Cuba, the GAR's chaplain-in-chief thanked God for supplying a flag "to carry forth for civilization and to make the nations which have been blackened by superstition and darkness, brighter and more beautiful." According to a 1911 claim by DAR Flag Committee chair Mrs. Jacob Dickinson, when the flag was "unfurled in the darkest savage districts of the far-off Philippines," its impact was "awesome," as it "seemed to present to them all that liberty and protection of person and property could guarantee to a dependent and benighted race." Members of the GAR's female auxiliary, the Woman's Relief Corps, maintained that the mere presence of flags in American schoolhouses marked "a grand step toward making brave, manly boys and womanly girls," and, upon immigrant children, its effect had "been to make them enthusiastic Americans." According to a GAR member speaking in 1892, if children learned "to add and subtract and multiply under that flag" they would "do it a great deal better." On rare occasions, even those typically sympathetic to the FPM suggested that such deification of the flag was turning the emblem into a fetish and obscuring its real meaning: thus, the *Grand Army Record*, a veterans' newspaper, lamented in 1894 that "all this blow and bluster about the 'Flag,' . . . is merely senseless bosh and mystifies rather than enlightens and educates unless the speaker . . . make[s] clear what the emblem represents and is used for."

As references to schoolhouse flags above suggest, the FPM not only promoted flag desecration legislation, but also fostered numerous other forms of flag homage. At its 1891 national encampment, GAR members began the practice of standing when the "Star Spangled Banner" was played, a habit that gradually spread among the general population. The GAR also specialized in holding elaborate ceremonies in which flags were donated to schools with the intent that henceforth they would fly them every day. In response to such pressures, during the 1890s the states first began to legally require that schools display the flag and conduct flag salute rituals. By 1908, according to the GAR, twenty-six states and territories either required or encouraged some form of regular school flag rituals. The GAR and other FPM organizations also enthusiastically sponsored numerous "living flag" displays created by children and others dressed in flag colors.

Before 1910 such flag rituals were almost exclusively northern events. Thus, in 1907 the GAR's national patriotic instructor reported that schoolrooms were displaying flags everywhere "with the exception of those in the south." No doubt this reflected the views of many southerners that the Stars and Stripes was a symbol of oppression, occupation, and defeat rather than liberty and celebration. Such feelings were probably exacerbated by the FPM's domination by northerners, including many veterans who had fought against the South during the Civil War, as well as by protests by Union veterans against all efforts to honor the Confederate flag. In 1887, for example, the GAR successfully led a campaign to overturn President Grover Cleveland's order to return captured Confederate battle flags still in War Department custody, a decision that led Senator Joseph Hawley of Connecticut to declare that the best way to deal with flags taken from "our misguided brothers and wicked conspirators" was to burn them, which provoked the GAR's head to famously thunder, "May God palsy the hand that wrote that order. May God palsy the brain that conceived it." This flag controversy was the leading newspaper story of the summer of 1887 and may have been decisive in Cleveland's 1888 electoral loss to Benjamin Harrison, a decorated Union veteran and GAR supporter. In 1890 the annual GAR convention demanded that display of the Confederate flag be outlawed as an "affront to patriotism" that "encourages disloyalty."

Unquestionably, the FPM was partly motivated simply by a growing sense of American pride and nationalism as the country developed into the world's leading industrial power and an increasingly important global political power during the late nineteenth century. During the Spanish-American War, passions were stirred by news accounts of the American flag replacing the Spanish banner in Cuba and the Philippines, and no one complained about desecration when Admiral George Dewey dragged a five-hundred-foot flag in the wake of his flagship returning from battle at Manila. During World War I, flag enthusiasm soared again, so much so that flag manufacturers tripled their prices (partly because of a price-fixing scheme that was uncovered by the Federal Trade Commission in 1917) and the military arranged massive "living flag" displays, including one with thirty thousand soldiers at Camp Dodge, Iowa.

Beyond pure pride and patriotism, the composition and rhetoric of the FPM clearly suggests that its leaders were also motivated by fears that "their" America and their long-established leadership positions were endangered by newly emerging forces that were perceived as threatening to the traditional social and political order. Big business, the propagator of flag advertising that was the FPM's first target, was originally the clearest threat to the traditional order to emerge following the Civil War. By the late 1890s, however, big business became displaced in the FPM's collective mind as primary threats to the flag and to the existing order by the far "stranger" new immigrants and ideologically much more threatening movements of labor and political radicals. Consciously or not, FPM backers clearly feared that "their" America was under a threat of dissolution by these new elements. Intuitively, they felt that one way to combat threats to the country's unity and to their own traditional leadership of the nation was to focus the nation's attention on love for the flag and a "return to traditional values"— a theme that would recur during flag desecration debates during the 1960s and 1990s.

The new perceived threats to the flag were the same forces that were blamed for the general turbulence that had rocked American society at least ever since the 1877 railroad strikes and riots, including subsequent labor-related crises such as the Haymarket affair of 1886, the 1892 Homestead Strike, and the Pullman Strike and mass unemployment marches of 1894. These disturbances had been accompanied by a sweeping industrialization and urbanization of American life, the rise of the modern labor movement, the emergence of vocal socialist and anarchist movements, and a vast increase in immigration from regions other than the traditional northwestern European sources. Collectively these developments transformed American society and politics in the post–Civil War period and inevitably created new social forces that threatened the role of precisely those traditional middle- and upper-middle-class elites of northwestern European ethnic heritage who led the FPM.

Under such threats, patriotic-hereditary societies such as the DAR and the SAR, which constituted one major FPM element, sought to assert their alleged special identity as the most "true" Americans by mining what historian Arthur Schlesinger Sr. has termed "the unearned increment of ancestral reputations," as well as asserting their traditional role as elites who had "formed the socially ambitious local gentry in many an American small town." They felt especially threatened by the new immigration, as well as other forces transforming American society, such as the massive industrialization that was creating new business elites seemingly overnight. Surely it is no coincidence that the SAR was organized in 1889 and the DAR the following year, just at the time when the size of the "new immigration" was becoming evident. Similarly, it is not surprising that one of the early pioneers of the FPM, a New York City auditor named George T. Balch, began urging flag rituals in the schools as early as 1890 as an explicit remedy for what he termed the "evils and dangers" posed by the "human scum cast on our shores by the tidal wave of a vast immigration." A ritual he proposed in 1895 had students declaring that "American principles, the American language and the American flag SHOULD BE SUPREME OVER ALL OTHERS," and he proposed completing a flag salute with the words, "ONE COUNTRY!—ONE LANGUAGE!—ONE FLAG!"—a slogan uncomfortably similar to Hitler's later "One people, one nation, one leader."

The second major force in the FPM, veterans' groups, and especially Union Civil War veterans' organizations such as the GAR—perhaps the most powerful lobby in the country with four hundred thousand members—were led by similar social strata. As Wallace Davies, a leading historian of veterans' and patriotic groups has noted, both viewed themselves as having a special charge and special right to define proper Americanism. By virtue of their physical defense of the Union, the Civil War veterans "thought that they had acquired a first mortgage upon the country," and the hereditary groups asserted their lineage to anoint themselves the "guardians of the American past and interpreters of its ideals." To a considerable extent, as historian Stuart McConnell has argued, what groups like those represented in the FPM sought to do was to "re-envision the nation as a place that was (or that should be) owned by people like themselves." It was only a natural progression from this conception that those who should control the nation should have the right to control the flag—and, if need be, to use the power of the state to punish those with differing ideas.

Not surprisingly, the exclusivist and nativist orientation adopted in regard to the flag by the clearly conservative but relatively mainstream groups that comprised the FPM were also adopted by groups much further on the right-wing fringes of American politics. For example, during the 1920s the revived Ku Klux Klan (KKK) proudly surrounded itself with flags as it proclaimed openly racist, anti-Semitic, and anti-Catholic views. The KKK's most prominent symbols were the Bible, the (often burning) cross, and the flag: on August 9, 1925, forty thousand Klansmen marched down Pennsylvania Avenue in Washington, D.C., carrying hundreds of flags behind a flag color guard. Gerald L. K. Smith, one of the most notorious racists and anti-Semites of the 1930s and thereafter, named his newspaper *The Cross and the Flag*.

CHAPTER 2

Flag Desecration Laws and Prosecutions, 1897–1980

Flag Desecration Laws, 1897–1970

FPM leaders vigorously lobbied at both state and federal levels for stringent laws against all forms of flag "desecration," maintaining that such action was needed to preserve the nation. Thus, in 1900 the vice president of a Spanish-American War veterans' group declared that flag desecration was a "crime more heinous in its ultimate effects than theft, arson or murder, as it strikes at the root of law, order and government," and FPM pamphleteer Charles Kingsbury Miller termed flag protection laws "essential to our welfare as a nation," as disrespect for the flag "may ultimately cause the government itself to tremble on its foundations," especially as it encouraged in the "leaders of mobs and misguided strikers" a general "spirit of lawlessness and license." According to FPM leaders, such threats to the stability of American society could be lanced by simply fostering—and if necessary, requiring—respect for the flag. In 1892, the head of the GAR proclaimed that if American schoolchildren were "imbued with a reverence for the flag and all it represents," then the "future of the Republic is assured." DAR Flag Committee chair Kempster declared in 1907 that flag protection legislation would deliver alike to the "illogical and visionary enthusiast," the "glib-tongued, blatant demagogue," the "crafty schemer," and the "malignant fomenter of sedition" the message to "Cease! Cease!"

Between 1897 and 1932, the FPM obtained flag desecration laws in all of the then forty-eight states. The laggard states, unsurprisingly, were mostly former Confederate states: the last state to pass a flag desecration law, in 1932, was Virginia, home of the Confederate capital, Richmond. Most flag desecration laws provided maximum penalties of thirty days in jail and a $100 fine, but a few were much harsher, including laws passed in Texas and Montana during World War I with maximum sentences of twenty-five years of imprisonment. Sixty years later, amid the spate of flag desecration incidents associated with protest against the Vietnam War, about ten states revised their penalties upward: for example, Alabama, Oklahoma, and Illinois increased their maximum punishments from thirty days of imprisonment and $100 fines to between two and five years in jail and $3,000 to $10,000 fines.

Although the laws varied somewhat, the vast majority had substantially identical provisions because they were generally based on a 1902 AFA model bill. The laws typically outlawed three kinds of activities: 1) placing any kind of marking, lettering, or pictures on the flag for any purpose, or displaying, selling, or distributing such altered flags; 2) using the flag or representations of the flag in any form of advertising, such as selling a product with a picture of the flag on it or depicting the flag in an advertisement; and 3) publicly mutilating, trampling, defacing, defiling, "defying," or casting "contempt," either "by *words* [emphasis added] or act," upon the flag. Most of the laws defined "flag" extremely broadly, typically including anything that even vaguely resembled a flag, including all objects "made of any substance whatever" and "of any size" that "evidently" purported to be the flag or included its colors and "the stars and the stripes in any number," such that a person seeing it "without deliberation may believe the same to represent" the flag.

Despite the phenomenal success of the FPM in state legislatures, it repeatedly failed to obtain passage of a federal flag desecration law, although such bills did pass one house of Congress (only) on nine different occasions between 1890 and 1943. Southern opposition, usually overtly based on the states'-rights grounds that flag protection was a local matter, was largely responsible for the failure to pass a general federal flag desecration law until 1968, when such a measure was finally enacted largely in response to a widely publicized April 1967 New York City flag burning during an anti–Vietnam War protest in Central Park. The 1968 law used the same definition of "flag" referenced above, but confined its reach to persons who "knowingly" cast "contempt upon any flag of the United States" by engaging in "publicly mutilating, defacing, defiling, burning, or trampling upon" it; no reference was made to advertising use or verbal criticism of the flag.

The congressional debate leading to the 1968 law reflected the first real national debate over flag desecration since the 1890–1920 period, and provided a preview of the controversy to follow in the wake of the 1989 Supreme Court ruling legalizing flag desecration in *Texas v. Johnson*. The essential argument in support of the bill was put forth by Representative Hale Boggs (D-LA), who maintained that flag desecraters were engaged in "outrageous acts which go beyond protest and violate things which the overwhelming majority of Americans hold sacred." Representative Edna Kelley (D-NY) termed flag desecration "a direct attack on the sovereignty" of the country and a "form of destruction of the basic values and principles of our government." Pennsylvania Supreme Court justice Michael Musmanno told the HJC during 1967 hearings that flag burners were "miserable wretches," "vile America-hating hooligans," and "treasonous" agitators "fit to conspire with Communists who would force our freedoms into the straitjacket of Bolshevistic dictatorship." Musmanno inadvertently explained not only why flag burning upset so many people, but also why those who opposed the bill viewed it as a direct attack on freedom of expression by asking, "How could demonstrations against American policy be more vividly and dramatically manifested than by burning the very flag of the United States?" Proponents of the bill, however, rejected the argument that flag desecration involved constitutionally protected "symbolic" expression on the grounds that the First Amendment explicitly referenced only "speech" and "press."

Opposition to the proposal was clearly viewed by most politicians as political dynamite. During the HJC hearings, over sixty congressmen supported it, but none spoke in opposition. The few congressmen who opposed it during floor debate or in dissent from the HJC majority report stressed a free speech argument:

HJC members John Conyers and Don Edwards protested that outlawing flag desecration would "do more real harm to the Nation than all the flag burners can possibly do" because it would stifle "the freedom to dissent," the "real 'evil' at which the bill was directed." Opponents also argued that although the bill sought to protect the flag's symbolism, it would reduce the substantive freedoms that the flag supposedly represented, and also that the entire controversy diverted attention from the nation's real, rather than symbolic, problems. Thus, *Commonweal* magazine asked sarcastically in October 1968, "Seeing as nothing can be done about the war in Vietnam or rampant racism here, why not at least begin with respect for the flag?"

The Vietnam War–era flag desecration controversy reflected a much broader debate about the nation's direction. As the war dragged on, protesters increasingly resorted to flag burnings and other unorthodox flag usage to protest the war and other aspects of American foreign and domestic policy, while backers of the war and others who were appalled at flag burnings and the general so-called "counterculture" responded by wearing flag pins in their lapels (including President Richard Nixon and the White House staff) and placing tens of millions of flag decals on their windows and cars. By 1969, flag patches, pins, and decals were appearing on police uniforms and cars throughout the country (often in technical violation of flag desecration statutes), even as police were arresting protesters for wearing flag patches on their jeans. *Reader's Digest* alone mailed out a reported 49 million flag decals in 1969; its "vice-president for flag production" explained that displaying them was "a way for the ordinary fellow who works all day, has saved a little money and who leads an ordinary life" to respond to "campus unrest, racial disharmony and all the other things that are wracking this country."

Clearly, the 1960s flag desecration controversy was only one manifestation of a much deeper division within the country, one that would subsequently be labeled the "culture wars" and that would provide a recurrent theme in American politics for the indefinite future. Just as the original 1890–1920 flag desecration controversy became so intense because the FPM associated attacks on the flag with a perceived general assault on the traditions and stability of American society, the Vietnam-era controversy became especially "inflamed" because for many Americans flag burning became a symbol of a whole constellation of events associated with the 1960s antiwar opposition, including the emergence of a counterculture and increases in violent crime, black militancy, and political radicalism, all perceived as threatening the value system and political structure of American society. Thus, Representative Richard Roudebush (R-IN), a leading sponsor of the 1968 law, termed the growing wave of domestic "anarchy and disrespect for law and order" as a key reason why the nation needed to preserve the flag's "respect and dignity." In a lengthy 1970 cover story, *Time* magazine lamented that the flag had "become the emblem of American's disunity" as the "defiant young blow their noses on it, sleep in it, set it afire or wear it to patch the seat of their trousers," whereas other Americans' response was to "wave it with defensive pride, crack skulls in its name and fly it from their garbage trucks, police cars and skyscraper scaffolds." A burning flag would remain for many Americans appalled by the 1960s counterculture the primary visual image of that period, and that indelible memory unquestionably heightened the massive adverse response to the Supreme Court's 1989–1990 rulings striking down flag desecration laws.

———

Flag Desecration Prosecutions, 1897–1974

During the period immediately following the passage of the first flag desecration laws in 1897, at least some of the states attempted to seriously enforce them against advertising and partisan political uses of the flag. For example, the *Chicago Inter-Ocean*, which had demanded in 1895 that the "most sacred of symbols" be used only "honorably and holily" as part of "our covenant with destiny," reported on October 20, 1899, that the 1897 Illinois law had "terrorized" Chicago, leading to over one thousand prosecutions in less than four months, and was already regarded "as one of the most odious" state statutes ever, as there was "not a person in

Chicago who is safe" since flag depictions in one illegal form or another "are really omnipresent in business places and homes." The July 22, 1900, *New York Times* reported that as a result of the 1899 New York state law police would "summarily" haul down all forms of flag advertising, that the police would "frown" on businesses that sought customers by "decorating their stores, factories and innumerable billboards with American banners," and that newspapers could not even "announce in red letters on a background of American flags the victories of our troops over the Chinese [during the Western suppression of the Boxer Rebellion there]."

These early prosecutions of mainstream flag uses were soon almost entirely replaced by prosecutions directed against only those perceived as political malcontents. This drastic reorientation can be clearly seen by contrasting the 1900 *New York Times* story just cited with a 1917 *Times* story published as the nation entered World War I, which quoted the New York City district attorney as announcing that "in such a time as the present, when the spirit of patriotism is everywhere apparent," the state flag desecration law "should not be construed too technically" with regard to any "proper [that is, patriotic] use" of the flag. By 1962, the American Law Institute (ALI), a nongovernmental organization of prominent judges, lawyers, and professors closely intertwined with the legal establishment, proposed in its Model Penal Code (MPC) that all restrictions on commercial usage be deleted from state flag desecration laws because "whatever may have been true [previously], it is scarcely realistic today to regard commercial exploitation of the national emblem or colors as a serious affront to popular sensibilities."

After 1910, the vast majority of reported flag desecration prosecutions were directed against perceived political dissidents. A search of the available, if unquestionably incomplete, newspaper and legal records indicates that between 1907 and 1964 at least five dozen flag desecration prosecutions were brought across the nation, of which about 80 percent were directed at perceived political dissidents; such prosecutions were especially concentrated during the 1914–1920 period associated with World War I and postwar tensions. At least half of the politically oriented prosecutions involved no allegation of *physical* flag desecration. For example, a Kansas City man was arrested in 1911 for cursing the flag; a Michigan striker was sentenced to thirty days of imprisonment (and severely beaten by deputies) in 1913 for "cursing the American flag and American government"; in April 1917 a Wisconsin man was fined $50 for "slurring" the flag; an Iowa man was arrested (and subsequently severely beaten by fellow inmates) for refusing to remove his hat when the flag passed by during a 1922 parade; and during World War II an Arkansas man was fined $50 and jailed for a day for calling the flag a "rag" without eyes, ears, or mouth and refusing to salute it when he was asked to do so as an apparent condition of obtaining relief supplies.

In the most severe flag desecration penalty in American history, E. V. Starr was sentenced to ten to twenty years of hard labor at a state penitentiary under Montana's draconian World War I law for refusing a mob's demands to kiss the flag (a favorite wartime vigilante punishment for the allegedly disloyal) and for terming it "nothing but a piece of cotton" with a "little paint" and "other marks" on it that "might be covered with microbes." In a 1930 incident with a similar flavor, two women administrators of a New York state Communist youth camp were jailed for ninety days each for "desecrating" a flag by refusing to hoist one at the order of a mob of seven hundred local residents and Ku Klux Klan (KKK) members who invaded their camp and then abducted them and brought them before a judge. Justice of the Peace William Westbrook told the two defendants that their sentences were a warning to "communists all over the United States that they could not trifle with the American flag or teach un-Christian doctrines."

As the *Starr* case and others discussed above suggests, official penalties for displaying insufficient respect for the flag were often supplemented by the unofficial sanctions of vigilantes, especially during the eras of the two world wars. During World War I, scores of suspected political dissidents like Starr were attacked by mobs that sought to compel them to kiss the flag, often while government officials looked the other way or even joined in. For example, during a large antiwar demonstration in Boston on July 1,

1917, mobs of soldiers and sailors forced hundreds of socialists to kiss the flag, while police stood by. During the period leading up to and including American involvement in World War II, about two thousand students who refused to salute the flag (mostly Jehovah's Witnesses acting out of religious conviction) were expelled from public schools, and in hundreds of incidents, mobs, often acting with official approval and participation, attacked Jehovah's Witnesses because their refusal to salute the flag was viewed as reflecting insufficient patriotism.

Among the two dozen or so prosecutions for *physical* flag desecration between 1907 and 1964, the only flag *burning* involved an eccentric socialist-pacific New York clergyman named Bouck White, who acted in concert with several supporters in 1916 as a protest against nationalism during the period of increasing tension leading to American entry into World War I. Along with two others, White was given the maximum penalty under New York's 1899 flag desecration law of thirty days in jail and a $100 fine by a judge who declared that he regretted lacking "the power to make this sentence a matter of years." Although all three were native-born Americans, he declared the sentence was designed to warn immigrants and others "that hereafter it must be 'hats off to the flag.'"

Other instances of prosecutions for physical flag desecration included the arrest of a New Jersey man in 1914 for throwing a flag to the ground and trampling it; World War I incidents included two New Jersey men charged with spitting on and cutting flags to pieces and two reported "Scandinavian" butlers arrested in New York for shooting holes in a flag; a left-wing speaker was arrested in Monticello, New York, in 1933 for blowing his nose on a flag and wiping his face and clothing with it; and an Italian alien was fined $50 in 1940 for flying a flag from an outhouse. Between World War II and the Vietnam War there were only a handful of such prosecutions (and arrests for "verbal" flag desecration seem to have disappeared): for example, in 1946 three members of a left-wing union were each jailed for ten days for using a flag as a receptacle for strike contributions during a May Day parade, and in 1951 two Illinois youths arrested for dragging a flag behind their car were ordered to recite the Pledge of Allegiance in court, to study a book on flag etiquette, and to attend public flag ceremonies.

By the mid-1960s, flag desecration prosecutions had become so rare that in 1966 the National Conference of Commissioners on Uniform State Laws (NCCUSL), a group of representatives of state governments, which in 1917 had recommended that all states pass flag desecration laws, withdrew its support for them on the grounds that they were "obsolete." Within a year of the NCCUSL recommendation, flag desecration erupted into the public arena once again, primarily as a result of the 1967 New York City flag burning discussed above. This and other flag desecration incidents spurred passage of the 1968 federal flag desecration law and led to many hundreds of flag desecration prosecutions between 1966 and 1975 (usually under the older state laws), although only about two dozen prosecutions were triggered by flag *burnings* as opposed to other unorthodox flag uses. The latter included "wearing" the flag or flag simulations, usually as a trousers seat patch, but also occasionally as a poncho, shirt, vest, and so forth; "superimposing" symbols, usually the "peace sign" (a trident surrounded by an oval) over the flag or a portion of it; and a wide variety of miscellaneous charges such as publishing a picture of a burning flag, driving a car painted with the flag's colors, pouring paint over a flag, and displaying a flag at half-mast in an inferior position to the United Nations flag.

Invariably, such prosecutions were brought only against "peace" demonstrators, but not against "establishment" and "patriotic" elements who also used the flag in unorthodox and often technically illegal ways. Thus, the *New York Times* reported in 1971 that the extremely broad flag desecration laws "have rarely been invoked against anyone except those who differ with prevailing ideas of patriotism," and that such targets were often "rebellious young people [arrested] for improper display of the flag on their clothing by policemen wearing flag patches or pins on their uniforms, while widespread commercial use of the flag is tolerated in advertisements and promotions." In a 1970 Topeka, Kansas, case, a judge dismissed the prosecution of a man who had displayed a "peace flag" decal on his car after his lawyer pointed out that city police cars bore flag decals "defaced" by a "love it or leave it" slogan. A young Pennsylvania man who was prosecuted for wearing a flag patch on his trousers was apparently well aware of the differential treatment meted out to those using the flag in unusual ways: although long-haired and "modishly" dressed when arrested, he appeared in court short-haired and conventionally dressed, but when the judge sentenced him to thirty days in jail and a $100 fine, he fainted and a wig hiding long, curly hair flew off his head.

The emotionalism surrounding the flag during the Vietnam War clearly sometimes influenced prosecutors, courts, and juries, especially in conservative areas such as Dallas, where the Supreme Court's 1989 *Texas v. Johnson* case would originate in 1984. Dallas grand juries often returned indictments in flag "wearing" cases, but refused to indict a bank that advertised using flag imagery in clear contravention of the state's World War I–era "Disloyalty Act," which authorized up to twenty-five years in jail for verbally insulting or physically damaging flags. In response to demands that he prosecute the bank, a Dallas assistant district attorney termed the issue "ridiculous" and "not in the spirit of the law." In a 1970 Dallas case in which David Renn was given ten years of probation for displaying a "peace symbol" flag, attorney Stanley Weinberg, who was to become Gregory Lee Johnson's original lawyer in *Texas v. Johnson*, recalled in a 1990 interview that he was told by a juror after the verdict that the jury wanted to acquit Renn "but for the fact that they were going to have to face the community, because they honestly didn't believe that he should have a prison sentence or a felony on his record because he was sincere." Renn's conviction was later overturned by the Texas Court of Criminal Appeals owing to prosecutorial misconduct, such as repeated references to Renn as a "hippie," "anti-Christ," and "communist."

The most severe penalty for flag desecration during the Vietnam War era was a four-year jail term meted out to Gary Deeds, nineteen, for burning a piece of flag bunting in 1970 in a Dallas city park. Deeds's lawyer, John Nelms, recalled twenty years later that the sentence was the "biggest shock that I've had as a trial lawyer." Nelms added, "If Deeds had done almost anything else, possession of drugs, stealing a car, burglarizing a house, anything but armed robbery or aggravated sexual assault or murder, he would have gotten probation. I never dreamed at any time up to the moment I heard that verdict in my ears that there was even a remote possibility that he would go to prison." Nelms added that because the case was well publicized, the jurors who "all had to go home to their own neighborhoods" didn't want to "see the people across the street or at the country club say, 'Why'd you let that little pinko commie off for?' There's that kind of pressure, very subtle, but it's there." The *Deeds* trial judge, John Vance, would later seek to uphold, both as an appellate judge and, subsequently, before the Supreme Court as elected Dallas County district attorney, the 1984 Dallas flag burning conviction of Gregory Lee Johnson.

The bitterness of the "war over the flag" during the Vietnam War era spawned a variety of bizarre court penalties. For example, Martha Meyers, an Arlington Heights, Massachusetts, high school senior convicted of flag burning, was sentenced in 1970 to carry a large fifteen-pound flag on a three-mile march through Cambridge, Massachusetts, as an alternative to serving six months in jail. Meyers was also banned from attending school by her local school board, although she was allowed to complete her work at home on condition that she abstain from attending graduation ceremonies. In Florida, a high school student convicted for wearing a "flag shirt" was sentenced to a ten-day term of raising the American flag in front of Titusville City Hall at 7 A.M., and when he failed to awake in time on the first day, the judge imposed the previously suspended sentence of twenty days in jail and a $100 fine.

––––––

Flag Laws and the Courts, 1900–1975

The earliest court rulings on the constitutionality of flag desecration laws, overwhelmingly used at first to prosecute commercial flag imagery, generally struck them down on the grounds that they improperly violated private property rights, had no valid state purpose, or both. Just when such rulings suggested their demise, however, in 1907 the Supreme Court upheld a flag desecration law in *Halter v. Nebraska*, an 8 to 1 ruling filled with patriotic oratory.

The Court declared that "every true American" had a "deep affection" for the flag" and therefore often "insults to a flag have been the cause of war, and indignities put upon it, in the presence of those who revere it, have often been resented and sometimes punished on the spot." Rejecting claims that flag desecration laws invaded personal property rights and that the state had no legitimate interest in protecting the flag from insult, the Court added:

> [A] State may exert its power to strengthen the bonds of the Union and therefore, to that end, may encourage patriotism and love of country among its people. . . . [L]ove both of the common country and of the State will diminish in proportion as respect for the flag is weakened. . . . [Advertising usage of the flag] tends to degrade and cheapen the flag in the estimation of the people, as well as to defeat the object of maintaining it as an emblem of national power and honor. And we cannot hold that any privilege of American citizenship or that any right of personal liberty is violated by forbidding the flag to be used as an advertisement on a bottle of beer.

Although the ruling did not address free speech rights (which was never raised by the defendants in any of the early cases which involved commercial use of the flag), *Halter* was so broadly worded that the Court clearly would have rejected any such claims (especially since before 1925 the Court consistently refused to extend free speech rights to individuals who challenged *state*, as opposed to federal, laws on the grounds that the First Amendment only barred *Congress*, and not the states, from infringing upon freedom of expression). If *Halter* seemed to permanently establish the constitutionality of flag desecration laws, however, major developments in Supreme Court interpretations of the meaning of the First Amendment beginning in the mid-1920s suggested that this might not be the case.

In *Gitlow v. New York* (1925), the Court reversed earlier holdings and now applied the First Amendment to state, as well as federal, restrictions on free speech. In *Stromberg v. California* (1931), the Court significantly broadened and liberalized its interpretation—and not just the jurisdictional reach—of the First Amendment.

Stromberg was the first case in which the Court made clear that protected expression extended to "symbolic speech" and was not restricted to traditional forms of "speech" and "press," the only forms of communication specifically mentioned in the First Amendment. *Stromberg* traced its origins to the 1919–1920 "red scare," when, amid absurdly exaggerated fears of an imminent Communist revolution, thirty-two states banned the display of red flags, which had become associated with socialism and communism. The California law had been used in *Stromberg* to prosecute a woman who had allegedly led children at a Communist youth camp in saluting a red flag while they pledged allegiance to "freedom for the working class." The Court overturned the conviction on the grounds that outlawing the peaceful display of a red flag solely for the purpose of signaling "peaceful and orderly opposition to government by legal means" violated a "fundamental principle of our constitutional system." In retrospect, *Stromberg* contained the seeds of the Court's 1989 *Texas v. Johnson* ruling, because it established the principle that peaceful expression using flags was constitutionally protected, a principle clearly applicable to flag desecration unless the Court were to hold that American flags were different than other flags or that peaceful physical or verbal assaults on flags should be treated differently than peacefully waving them.

In the 1943 case of *West Virginia Board of Education v. Barnette*, the Court made clear that general principles of constitutional law, at least in the First Amendment area, did apply to American flags. *Barnette* involved a challenge by Jehovah's Witnesses to the widespread requirements that public school children salute the flag and recite the Pledge of Allegiance or face expulsion. Citing *Stromberg* among other precedents, the *Barnette* Court struck down the requirements, holding that under the First Amendment, a child required by state laws to attend public schools could not be forced by public authorities "to utter what is not in his mind." Justice Robert Jackson declared:

The case is made difficult not because the principles of its decisions are obscure but because the flag involved is our own. . . .

Freedom to differ is not limited to things that do not matter much. . . . The test of its substance is the right to differ as to things that touch the heart of the existing order. If there is any fixed star in our constitutional constellation it is that no official, high or petty, can prescribe what shall be orthodox in politics, nationalism, religion or other matters of opinion.

Although *Stromberg* and *Barnette* dealt with flags, they did not directly address flag desecration, an issue that the Court never confronted again after *Halter* until 1969. In the meantime, however, the Court continued to broaden its rulings concerning the First Amendment with regard to dissenting political speech in general and "symbolic speech" in particular, in ways that further paved the road to its ultimate 1989 *Johnson* ruling, gradually expanding First Amendment protections for political expression to encompass virtually any point of view that stopped short of immediately inciting disorder. Essentially the only exceptions to protected political expression were direct, abusive personal insults that the Court, in *Chaplinsky v. New Hampshire* (1942) termed the equivalent of "fighting words" that "by their very utterance inflict injury or tend to incite an immediate breach of the peace," or words that were "directed to inciting or producing imminent lawless action" and were "likely to incite or produce such action" (*Brandenburg v. Ohio*, 1969). Such exceptions aside, the Court made clear that speech was protected even if it "induces a condition of unrest, creates dissatisfaction with conditions as they are or even stirs people to anger" (*Terminiello v. Chicago*, 1949) or included "vehement, caustic and sometimes unpleasantly sharp attacks on government and public officials" (*New York Times v. Sullivan*, 1964).

Additionally, the Court steadily expanded forms of symbolic expression that qualified for First Amendment protection. By 1969, protected symbolic speech included peaceful picketing in labor disputes, parading in support of civil rights, and the right of schoolchildren to wear black armbands to school to protest the Vietnam War. In the latter case, the Court made clear that such symbolic political speech, which it termed "closely akin to 'pure speech,'" was just as protected as traditional written or spoken expression, and therefore could not be restricted because it was viewed as offensive or posing a vague, potential threat to the peace.

Yet the Court never made precisely clear the boundaries of First Amendment–protected symbolic expression, and in some rulings it suggested that symbolic expression was not as completely protected as traditional forms of speech and press. For example, in the 1965 case of *Cox v. Louisiana*, the Court "emphatically" rejected the "notion" that the Constitution granted the "same kind of freedom to those who would communicate ideas by conduct such as patrolling, marching and picketing on streets and highways" as to "those who communicate ideas by pure speech." In *U.S. v. O'Brien* (1968), a ruling that would eventually prove of central importance to the 1989–1990 flag desecration controversy, the Court upheld a conviction for burning a draft card to protest the Vietnam War and declared, "We cannot accept the view that an apparently limitless variety of conduct can be labeled 'speech.'" Although the 1965 federal anti–draft card burning law had clearly sought to suppress a particularly widely publicized form of antiwar dissent, the Court upheld it on the strained grounds that it was intended to foster the effective functioning of the draft. In *O'Brien*, the Court held that restrictions on expression that also involved "conduct" could be upheld where the government regulation was within its "constitutional power" and furthered an "important or substantial governmental interest" that was "unrelated to the suppression of free expression," and "if the incidental restriction on alleged First Amendment freedoms is no greater than is essential to the furtherance of that interest."

The Court illustrated how it would apply the *O'Brien* guidelines in several later cases. In *Clark v. Community for Creative Non-Violence* (1984), the Court upheld a government ruling forbidding a group seeking to protest homelessness from camping overnight in a Washington, D.C., park, on the grounds that the *purpose* of the regulation was to avoid damage to the park and to keep it generally accessible rather than to suppress political viewpoints. However, in *Boos v. Barry* (1988), the Court overturned a law banning picketing outside embassies if the demonstrations sought to bring public "odium" or "disrepute" on the governments involved, since there the law's purpose was held to target particular forms of expression and was thus deemed "content-based," rather than only "incidentally" affecting expression in a "content-neutral" manner as in *O'Brien* and *Clark*. In *Boos*, the Court, applying the same approach that it would invoke a year later to overturn flag desecration laws, held that the regulated expression was the legal equivalent of "pure speech," and therefore the statute involved must be "subjected to the most exacting scrutiny" and could be upheld only if it was found "necessary to serve a compelling state interest," such as preventing a direct threat to the peace, as in *Chaplinsky* and *Brandenburg*. Translated insofar as possible into ordinary English, the key point in *O'Brien*, as it potentially applied to flag desecration, was that if the government acted out of purely suppressive *motivations*, the First Amendment would probably invalidate legislation, but if the government's *purpose* was nonsuppressive, then flag desecration laws would likely survive since the remaining *O'Brien* guidelines provided rather low legal hurdles.

Between 1969 and 1974, the Court overturned three flag desecration convictions, but did so on narrow grounds that evaded the fundamental constitutional question of whether physically damaging flags for the purpose of political expression was protected by the First Amendment. Especially since the Court subsequently refused to even consider numerous other flag desecration cases until 1989, it almost certainly deliberately sought to avoid squarely facing the issue for fear of provoking precisely the kind of political uproar that followed its 1989 *Johnson* ruling.

The first of these cases, *Street v. New York* (1969) stemmed from a 1966 flag burning by Sidney Street, a black World War II veteran, who was convicted under the New York law that banned casting "contempt" upon the flag "either by words or act." Although Street was clearly prosecuted for burning the flag in response to the shooting of civil rights activist James Meredith, rather than for any "words," testimony indicated that he had accompanied his action by proclaiming "if they let that happen to Meredith we don't need an American flag." During his trial and subsequent proceedings before two New York appeals courts that upheld his conviction, the focus was on whether flag burning was constitutionally protected, and his oral remarks attracted virtually no attention.

When the Supreme Court overturned Street's conviction 5 to 4, however, it held that Street might have been convicted solely for his words (which suggested the unlikely scenario that the jury would have acquitted him if the charge had been solely based on the flag burning). The Court declared that it had resisted the "pulls to decide the constitutional issues involved on a broader basis than the record before us imperatively requires," since any guilt finding solely based on Street's words was enough to overturn the conviction in the absence of any evident threat to the peace. The Court cited the 1931 *Stromberg* red flag case and the 1943 *Barnette* compulsory flag salute decision in declaring that "It is firmly settled that under our Constitution the public expression of ideas may not be prohibited merely because the ideas are themselves offensive to some of their hearers," even including opinions about the flag that were "distasteful," "defiant or contemptuous."

Supreme Court records and the recollections of Court clerks who served when *Street* was decided make clear that the case caused extraordinary turmoil within the Court. The Court's preliminary voting forecast a 7 to 2 ruling in Street's favor, but subsequently Justices Byron White and Abe Fortas changed their minds, resulting in the final 5 to 4 ruling. According to Supreme Court clerks, Justice Hugo Black, normally a staunch supporter of the First Amendment, who voted against Street from the beginning, told Chief Justice Earl Warren that if the conviction was overturned "next they'll be peeing on the flag," and Warren, who also consistently voted against Street despite his strong First Amendment record, told his clerks that his feelings about the flag were more important than normal legal considerations, since flag burning was "simply a wrong thing to do," and "Boys, it's the flag. I'm just not going to vote in favor of burning the American flag." Walter Dellinger, a Court clerk at the time of *Street* who testified before Congress in 1995 in opposition to a proposed constitutional amendment to outlaw flag desecration as a Clinton administration Justice Department official, recounted that Black and Warren were "so exercised" and "so angry and so amazed to find themselves" in the *Street* minority that he and other law clerks could overhear the two justices "shouting about flag burners" from behind the "heavy wooden doors" of a Supreme Court room where they were meeting privately to discuss the case.

In 1974, the Court overturned two more flag desecration convictions, but again avoided the fundamental issue of the constitutionality of forbidding physically damaging flags for the purpose of political expression. In *Smith v. Goguen*, the Court reversed the conviction of a Massachusetts teenager for "contemptuously" treating the flag by wearing a flag patch on his trousers on the grounds that the law was unconstitutionally vague. During the preliminary private Supreme Court conference on the case, Chief Justice Warren Burger strongly urged upholding the Massachusetts law because respect for the flag was important, since "We have little to cling to in this country when trouble brews." Justices William Douglas, William Brennan, and John Marshall took a radically different view, urging that the statute be struck down as violating the First Amendment, but they could not obtain a majority for this position. Ultimately, the majority held that because the Massachusetts law was so vague that it allowed "policemen, prosecutors and juries to pursue their personal predilections" and failed "to draw reasonably clear lines between the kinds of non-ceremonial treatment that are criminal and those that are not," there was no need to "decide additional [First Amendment] issues." In a dissent that would become subsequently important during the 1989–1990 flag desecration controversy, Justice Harry Blackmun seemed to maintain that the Massachusetts law was neither unconstitutionally vague nor aimed at punishing any particular expression, but simply and constitutionally sought to punish anyone who harmed the "physical integrity" of the flag for whatever reason.

In *Spence v. Washington*, another 1974 case, the Court reversed a Washington State conviction resulting from the prosecution of a man who had placed a "peace sign" with removable tape on a flag he had hung out of his apartment window. The *Spence* ruling, an unsigned, or per curiam, ruling, was extremely narrowly written and tightly tied to the specifics of the incident, but its key finding seemed to be that, even if the state had a constitutionally valid interest in "preserving the national flag as an unalloyed symbol of our country," no such interest could have been harmed here because, by using removable tape, Spence did not "permanently disfigure the flag or destroy it." (In a bitter dissent, Justice William Rehnquist suggested that, using this logic, Spence might have been constitutionally convicted if he "tore the flag in the process of trying to take the tape off.") A footnote to the majority opinion pointed out that the Washington law (which was entirely typical of state flag desecration laws), if "read literally," would ban veterans from attaching "battalion commendations to a United States flag" and forbid newspapers from publishing "mastheads composed of the national flag with superimposed print."

Spence included several points that would help pave the way for the Court's 1989 *Johnson* ruling. The Court rejected outright the heart of the Washington Supreme Court's earlier ruling upholding Spence's conviction, which declared that the availability of alternative means of expression such as written and oral speech could mitigate banning symbolic forms of expressing the same ideas. Moreover, the Court indicated that if Washington State had an interest in protecting the flag's symbolic value it was "related to expression," which suggested that flag desecration prosecutions were subject to a higher level of scrutiny than the relatively lenient *O'Brien* test (unless somehow the Court distinguished between temporarily and permanently altering flags). Also, for the first time, the Court provided a guideline for determining when symbolic conduct qualified as "expression," holding it did so when "an intent to convey a particularized message was present, and in the surrounding circumstances the likelihood was great that the message would be understood by those who viewed it."

Collectively, the Court's three rulings between 1969 and 1974 left the impression that it took an exceedingly dim view of flag desecration statutes but was unwilling to confront them head-on for fear of provoking a political firestorm, especially during an armed conflict abroad that had led domestically to the flag's becoming a primary weapon in the "culture wars." If the Court majority's apparent general disdain for flag desecration laws was implied, if

{ *Flag Burning and Free Speech* }

somewhat opaque, the fervent support for such laws by the Court's minority was crystal clear. The four minority justices in *Street* each wrote separate, bitter, emotional dissents that declared physical flag desecration laws constitutional; thus, Black exclaimed, "It passes my belief that anything in the Federal Constitution bars a state from making the deliberate burning of the American flag an offense."

In both *Spence* and *Goguen*, Justice Rehnquist, providing a preview of his embittered 1989 *Johnson* dissent, emotionally rejected the majority's views. He maintained that the government could constitutionally regulate even private use of the flag to protect its "character, not the cloth," as "an important symbol of nationhood and unity," without seeking to suppress free expression, just as it could legally restrict other property and expression rights with valid copyright, libel, perjury, and incitement to riot laws, as well as forbidding "the painting of public buildings." In *Goguen*, Rehnquist extensively quoted patriotic poetry and rejected what he termed the Court's "highly abstract, scholastic interpretation of the First Amendment," instead relying on the "deep emotional feelings" aroused by the flag in a "large part of our citizenry," a concept that "cannot be fully expressed in the two dimensions of a lawyer's brief or of a judicial opinion."

By overturning three flag desecration convictions in as many cases, while ducking and dodging to avoid confronting the fundamental constitutional issue that they raised, the Court inevitably fostered confusion and uncertainty in the lower courts, which were flooded with flag desecration cases during the Vietnam War. This confusion was only exacerbated by the Court's refusal to even hear more than a dozen other flag desecration cases between 1969 and 1988, leaving convictions standing in almost every instance, including six flag burning cases.

Essentially left legally adrift by the Supreme Court, lower court flag desecration rulings suggested massive judicial discretion, chaos, and contradiction. Some courts relied on the Supreme Court's 1968 *O'Brien* draft card burning case to bolster their contention that flag desecration laws were unconstitutional, but others leaned upon *O'Brien* to reach the opposite conclusion. In some cases, "wearing" the flag—for example, as a pants seat patch, a vest, or cape—led to convictions, but in others to acquittals. In Ohio, a state especially fertile in flag desecration prosecutions, an appeals court overturned a 1971 conviction for displaying a flag with the "peace symbol" replacing the field of stars on the grounds that the defendant had simply expressed his "aspiration for peace" and was therefore not engaged in a "contemptuous act," yet a municipal court the same year upheld a conviction for driving a truck decorated with a painted flag with a large face of Mickey Mouse replacing the stars. In another Ohio case, an appeals court upheld a conviction for wearing a flag patch sewn on a back pants pocket since this amounted to wearing a flag "over the anus . . . a part of the human body universally and historically considered unclean" and thus "a clear act of defilement." However, in 1972 the Ohio Supreme Court overturned the conviction on the grounds that no physical damage had been done to the flag, and, as a matter of anatomy, a patch over a pants pocket was not "over the anus." The Court declared that using the flag desecration law against clothing would raise the question, "Is a flag worn by a policeman over his heart, or on his sleeve, or on his helmet permissible, and the same flag worn by a student impermissible depending upon which part of his anatomy it is upon or near?"

Generally, when appellate courts upheld convictions, as the Texas Court of Criminal Appeals did in 1971 in the *Deeds* case discussed earlier, they cited the state's interest in preserving the peace and protecting the flag as a symbol of the nation and held that such purposes did not conflict with First Amendment rights because they were not motivated by seeking to suppress dissent. However, about 60 percent of all Vietnam-era flag desecration convictions that were appealed were eventually overturned in the lower courts—although far less frequently in flag *burning* cases than in flag "clothing" or "peace symbol" prosecutions. Following the lead—or rather the refusal to lead—of the Supreme Court, however, generally such lower court reversals were based on narrow grounds that did not confront fundamental First Amendment issues. Many flag desecration convictions were overturned on the grounds that no physical desecration had occurred, no "contempt"

{ *Flag Burning and Free Speech* }

of the flag had been expressed, no breach of the peace had been threatened, or even that no real "flag" had been involved. For example, in 1973 the Iowa Supreme Court overruled a conviction for displaying a "peace symbol" flag on the grounds that it posed no threat to the peace, since although someone might have been "so intemperate as to disrupt the peace because of this display," if "absolute assurance of tranquillity is required we might as well forget about free speech." The conviction of the well-known "yippie" activist Abbie Hoffman for wearing a "flag shirt"—to which Hoffman had responded, "I regret that I have only one shirt to give for my country"—was overturned by the District of Columbia Court of Appeals in 1971 on the grounds that his store-bought shirt had never been a flag.

By 1974, lower courts in eight states had struck down flag desecration laws themselves—not just individual convictions—in whole or in part, but again usually without reaching fundamental First Amendment issues. Thus, a federal district court struck down the North Carolina law in 1971 primarily on the grounds that its typically all-encompassing definition of "flag" was "a manifest absurdity" and "simply unbelievable," and that "read literally, it may be dangerous in North Carolina to possess anything red, white and blue." The court added, "It seems to us that red, white and blue trousers, with or without stars, are trousers and not a flag, and that it is beyond the state's competence to dictate color and design of clothing, even bad taste clothing."

Between 1974 and 1979, with the end of American involvement in Vietnam, flag desecration incidents virtually disappeared. Yet the intensity of emotions still associated with flag burning was clearly demonstrated by the reaction to an apparent attempt by a man and his son to burn a flag in the outfield of Dodger Stadium during a baseball game between the Dodgers and the Chicago Cubs in Los Angeles on April 25, 1976. Cubs center fielder Rick Monday became a national hero for grabbing the flag away after the would-be flag burners doused it with lighter fluid, but before they could immolate it. As the father and son were arrested, the crowd gave Monday a standing ovation and burst into "God Bless America." After the game, Monday was picked as grand marshal of Chicago's annual Flag Day parade, the Cubs held a special "Rick Monday day," President Gerald Ford and baseball commissioner Bowie Kuhn congratulated him, and the Illinois legislature passed a special resolution of commendation. *The Sporting News*, in its report on the incident, said that Monday was "Francis Scott Key, Betsy Ross, Verdun and Iwo Jima—all wrapped up in one fleeting moment of patriotism."

Flag Desecration Laws, 1970–1980

Between 1970 and 1980, almost twenty state legislatures significantly revised their flag desecration laws in the first major overhaul of such statutes since their original enactments between 1897 and 1932. These revisions deleted provisions that outlawed ubiquitous, but never prosecuted, commercial use of the flag, and they often also deleted other long-standing provisions that were widely viewed as unconstitutional in light of the Supreme Court rulings in *Street*, *Goguen*, and *Spence*, such as bans on verbal disrespect for the flag. Thus, at least eleven states passed laws—modeled on the 1968 federal law—similar to Missouri's 1980 statute, which, in its entirety, read, "Any person who purposefully and publicly mutilates, defaces, defiles, tramples or otherwise desecrates the national flag of the United States or the state of Missouri is guilty of the crime of flag desecration."

At least another eight states passed revisions based on the ALI's 1962 Model Penal Code, which proposed that flags and other objects regarded with "veneration" by the public be protected against anyone who "intentionally defaces, damages, pollutes or otherwise physically mistreats" them "in a public place and in a way in which the actor knows will outrage the sensibilities of persons likely to observe or discover his actions." Among these states was Texas, in its 1973 venerated objects law, which also sharply reduced the penalty for flag desecration from the existing maximum of twenty-five-years of imprisonment—the harshest in the nation by far—to a far more typical maximum of one year in jail and a $2,000 fine.

Although the revised state laws sought to respond to court rulings which cast doubt on the constitutionality of previous statutes, they ultimately proved to be more constitutionally troublesome than their predecessors. By eliminating references to commercial use of the flag they clearly targeted *only* acts of political dissent and therefore amounted to the type of content-based discrimination that Supreme Court rulings had strongly suggested by 1970 would violate the First Amendment in cases involving symbolic speech. For example, in *Schacht v. U.S.* (1970) the Court struck down as unconstitutional content-based discrimination a federal law that banned the unauthorized use of military uniforms in stage productions *only* when such use "tended to discredit" the military. Moreover, statutes based on the 1962 MPC, which focused on whether observers of flag desecration were "offended" or "outraged," were on especially weak constitutional grounds because the Supreme Court had repeatedly made clear by 1970 in *Street* and other rulings that the criminality of political expression could not be based on such considerations (even aside from problems of vagueness inherent in criminalizing conduct based on the actor's ability to "know" that his conduct would "offend" or "outrage" others). Ironically, even the ALI concluded when it finally published an explanation of the MPC in 1980 that intervening Supreme Court rulings had probably rendered its "venerated objects" proposal unconstitutional, at least with regard to flags. The ALI noted that its "essential rationale" was to "prevent outrage to public sensibilities," but that the "only state interest" justifying criminal punishment for citizens who damaged their own flags was "directly derivative from the communicative aspect of the actor's conduct," and that "at best" its text was of "doubtful constitutionality" in light of *Street, Spence,* and *Goguen.*

CHAPTER 3

The Texas Flag Burning Trials of Gregory Lee Johnson, 1984–1988

The Revolutionary Communist Party and Flag Burning, 1979–1984

The 1984 Dallas flag burning that led to the Supreme Court's 1989 ruling striking down flag desecration laws in *Texas v. Johnson* was one of a series of flag burnings organized between 1979 and 1984 by a small Maoist organization, the Revolutionary Communist Party (RCP). During this period, the RCP lionized what it termed the "glorious achievements" of the late 1960s so-called Great Proletarian Cultural Revolution of Mao Tse-tung's China, which in the West was viewed as a chaotic, brutal wave of massive, indiscriminate terrorism and purges directed against all traces of Western influence. The RCP also identified itself with a wide variety of other political postures that seemed deliberately designed to repel mass public opinion in the United States in an apparent attempt to appeal to deeply alienated urban and minority youth. Thus, the RCP supported the Iranian students who seized the American embassy and burned American flags in Teheran in November 1979, and by the late 1970s advocated violent revolution in the United States (and virtually every other country around the world). The RCP limited its activities to oral and written agitation, however, along with a series of "propaganda by the deed" type of incidents, which mostly involved petty vandalism, clashes with the police, and flag burnings.

In a 1999 interview, New York lawyer Ron Kuby, who helped his law partner William Kunstler defend Gregory Lee Johnson before the Supreme Court in 1989, stressed that the RCP "never engaged in acts of armed struggle against the government, physical confrontation with the state," but instead organized

> more passive action which in no way conformed with their public appearance, peppering their speech with four letter words, every other word was "the fucking fascist state" or "shit this," almost sort of a caricature of the American working class they were trying to imitate. They were incredibly antagonistic in appearance and public persona and would pick symbolic acts that were calculated to outrage people. They thrived on confrontation with the police and the establishment, thereby trying to set themselves up as a model of militancy to attract youth.

In late 1979, apparently inspired by the Iranian students, the RCP's newspaper, *Revolutionary Worker (RW)*, began to glorify flag burning. For example, the February 1, 1980, *RW* published pictures of miniature "flag burning kits," including a pack of matches, a small paper flag, and an RCP button, and urged its readers to "burn the flag, then pin it proudly on your chest." Presumably acting under such inspiration, RCP members were implicated in at least eight flag burnings between 1979 and 1984, but they generally attracted only local media attention and most Americans were undoubtedly completely unaware of them. Prosecutions ensued in at least five of the flag burnings, and as a result almost a dozen people spent a total of about ten years in jail for actions the Supreme Court would ultimately declare in *Johnson* were protected by the First Amendment.

The only RCP flag burning during this period, aside from the 1984 Dallas incident, that attracted any significant media coverage led to convictions and eight-month jail terms for two RCP members, Teresa Kime and Donald Bonwell, under the 1968 federal flag desecration law, for a 1980 incident outside the Greensboro, North Carolina, federal courthouse. The Supreme Court's October 18, 1982, 8 to 1 refusal to hear their appeal attracted considerable press attention; although dissenting justices rarely publicly protest in such instances, Justice William Brennan published a blistering dissent that largely prefigured his majority opinions in 1989 and 1990 that struck down flag desecration laws in the *Johnson* and *Eichman* cases.

Brennan declared that the 1968 law, which banned acts that cast "contempt" upon the flag via physical "desecration" of it, disregarded the "vital constitutional principle forbidding government censorship of unpopular political views." Brennan maintained that, under *O'Brien*, since the defendants were engaged in expressive conduct and their actions "impaired no non-speech related governmental interest," the case was governed by the 1969 *Street* decision protecting the right to voice even "defiant or contemptuous" views about the flag. Brennan termed the law "flagrantly unconstitutional on its face" because its "contempt" provision left people legally free to engage in flag desecration for any reason, "except for the purpose of stating a contemptuous political message about the flag and what it stands for," and thus "everything it might possibly prohibit is constitutionally protected expression."

The 1984 Dallas Flag Burning Arrest
of Gregory Lee Johnson

The event that led to the Supreme Court's 1989 *Texas v. Johnson* ruling occurred on August 22, 1984, as the climax to a raucous demonstration protesting the impending renomination of President Ronald Reagan by the Republican National Convention then meeting in Dallas, Texas. According to contemporary newspaper accounts and unchallenged testimony during the subsequent Dallas trial and conviction of Gregory Lee Johnson for flag desecration, Johnson was part of a group of about one hundred demonstrators who marched over a mile for about two hours through downtown Dallas in stifling one-hundred degree heat that early afternoon, committing numerous acts of petty vandalism before burning a flag in front of Dallas City Hall. At his trial, Johnson, a member of the Revolutionary Communist Youth Brigade (RCYB), the RCP's youth group, described the protesters as including "anarchist youth, some Revolutionary Communist Youth, such as myself, some people who are religious pacifists, some people who just hate Reagan." Newspaper and film accounts of the protest indicate that almost all of the demonstrators were young and unconventional in appearance, including bare-chested men and some protesters wearing such badges of nonconformity as Reagan or pig masks, shaved heads, Mohawk haircuts, and long hair. A *Chicago Tribune* reporter described them as "largely punk rockers and disheveled-looking, long-haired folks," and the *Los Angeles Times* quoted one "well-dressed woman" as saying, "They looked awful," to which her daughter added, "Horrible."

According to newspaper reports and trial witnesses, the protesters made about ten stops along their route, where they listened to anti-Reagan speeches and sought to enter a variety of businesses, including banks, a department store, and several Dallas corporate offices, to protest their alleged involvement in various alleged misdeeds, including environmental pollution and the exploitation of poor countries. The protesters repeatedly held "die-ins" to portray the effects of nuclear war, chanted obscenities such as "Fuck America," pounded on windows with their fists, overturned newspaper racks, and spray-painted building walls and windows. Inside the exclusive Nieman-Marcus department store, protesters chanted "Eat the rich, feed the poor" to astonished shoppers, and, the *Los Angeles Times* reported, "nervous store salesmen swiftly covered an ornate chess set" when the protesters began chanting, "Let's go shopping!" At the Republic National Bank the protesters tore up and threw deposit slips on the floor; at the Le Relais restaurant they helped themselves to food from diners' plates; at the Sheraton-Dallas Hotel they tore down a Republican banner and kicked trash cans through the lobby; at two sites they uprooted potted plants; and at the Mercantile National Bank they pulled down and seized one or more American flags.

Damage caused by the vandalism was minor, no one was injured, and the large number of uniformed and undercover Dallas police who accompanied the protest made no arrests during the march. Dallas city spokesman Gail Cushing told reporters that police "felt they might cause a much more difficult situation to control" if they tried to break up the demonstration, especially since "the demonstrators were not injuring anybody." Police spokesman Ed Spencer said that the police "couldn't amass enough officers in one place to make the arrests until the protesters slowed down long enough for the police to surround them." He added that although the risk to public safety posed by such police action "would have been taken" if physical assaults were being committed, "these were property crimes."

The final destination of the marchers was Dallas City Hall, where at approximately 2:15 P.M. an American flag was burned inside a circle of demonstrators. Although a number of passersby gathered to watch the protest, no disorders accompanied the flag burning, during which some of the protesters spit on the flag and chanted, apparently from an RCYB flyer handed out during the march, "Red, white and blue, we spit on you. / You stand for plunder, you will go under." Other songs on the sheet included "Reagan, [Democratic presidential nominee Walter] Mondale, which will it be? / Either one means World War 3," "Ronald Reagan, killer of the hour / perfect example of U.S. power," and "1, 2, 3, 4, We don't want your fucking war / 5, 6, 7, 8, Organize to smash the state."

After the flag burning, many of the protesters jumped into the city hall fountain to cool off. About thirty minutes later scores of Dallas police, some on horseback, surrounded and arrested, without any resistance, about one hundred demonstrators (many of whom were still in the fountain). All demonstrators were charged with "disorderly conduct," a class C misdemeanor carrying a $200 fine. Many of those arrested were allowed to make brief statements to the press, and a man later identified as Gregory Lee Johnson was recorded shouting, "You can see here some shining examples of American democracy." Johnson was formally charged at about 5 P.M. with "disorderly conduct," for "using abusive, obscene language in a public place causing a crowd to gather." All of the disorderly conduct charges were soon dropped, but new charges were placed against Johnson and eight other protesters. In a 1990 interview, Dallas assistant district attorney and chief felony prosecutor Michael Gillett, who, as chief of the misdemeanor division in 1984 prosecuted Johnson for flag desecration, declared that "those that were committing offenses that the police could identify were filed on, and those that the police couldn't identify weren't filed on."

Four of the protesters against whom new charges were brought, including Johnson, were alleged to have committed the class A misdemeanor offense of "desecration of a venerated object" in connection with the city hall flag burning, dragging the flag on the ground before the burning, and a virtually unnoticed second flag burning that had occurred during the march outside the Nieman-Marcus department store. According to Dallas police records and information provided by Gillett in 1990, of the four persons charged with flag desecration, two (a woman who identified herself as Denise Williams, twenty-one, of San Francisco, charged in the city hall burning, and a man who identified himself as Kent Dewayne, twenty-one, of Buffalo, New York, charged for dragging a flag on the ground) failed to appear for trial and forfeited bonds, and a third, Mathew Michael Dodt, twenty-seven, of Austin, pled guilty on July 29, 1986, in connection with the Nieman-Marcus flag burning and was given a ten-day jail term.

The original disorderly conduct charge brought against Johnson was replaced at 2:18 A.M. in the early morning of August 23 with the "venerated objects" or flag desecration charge, invoking the 1973 Texas law that outlawed intentionally physically mistreating a "state or national flag" in a manner "that the actor knows will seriously offend one or more persons likely to observe or discover his action." Johnson eventually became famous because only he, of the four protesters charged with flag desecration, showed up in court to fight the charges, eventually all the way to the Supreme Court.

According to published material and information provided by Johnson in a 1990 interview, he was born in Richmond, Indiana, on October 25, 1956. Among the factors he cited as having "shaped or pushed me in the direction of a revolutionary way out of this system" were the jailing of his father for theft when he was two years old and being exposed to American racism and to anti–Vietnam War sentiment within the military when he lived on army bases in the South and in West Germany. According to Johnson, while selling the military newspaper *Stars and Stripes* at age twelve on an army base in West Germany, he engaged in many discussions with soldiers who viewed American intervention in Vietnam as a "war of aggression." He declared, "I owe a lot of my thinking to a whole generation of radical GIs who went against the masters of war." Johnson related that after returning to the United States in 1971 he decided he was "for revolution and not for reform" after reading a book by a black militant that he found in his Tampa, Florida, high school library. When he came into contact shortly thereafter with the RCYB, he recalled, he felt that "I'd been looking my whole life for something like that."

Johnson enrolled at the University of South Florida (USF) in Tampa in 1976, where he was apparently influenced by a professor who was an RCP member. Someone who knew him at USF described him to a reporter in 1989 as "very committed, very sincere, very committed to fighting for justice for the downtrodden," as well as a good speaker with "leadership qualities, in quiet ways." During his period at USF and after moving to Atlanta around 1980, Johnson became increasingly involved with the RCYB. According to a Tampa newspaper, he was arrested there almost twenty times during protests, and according to information introduced at his Dallas trial, he was arrested and convicted about six times in Atlanta between 1981 and 1984 on relatively minor charges such as "refusal to disperse" and trespassing, all apparently in connection with RCP protests. Johnson received a total of about $200 in fines and served nine months in jail for the Atlanta arrests. In a 1990 interview, Johnson's ACLU attorney, Doug Skemp, characterized him as a "real rabble rouser" and a "national protester for a long time" who "never backs away, goes to court, when he gets time [in jail], he doesn't run."

In the 1990 interview, Johnson said he quickly developed enormous respect" for the RCYB because "they were revolutionary" and favored "actively preparing" to "bring down the system," ultimately through armed "war between two sections of the people." He added that he especially admired the RCYB because the organization looked for inspiration to the Chinese Cultural Revolution. Johnson conceded that there were "excesses" during the Cultural Revolution, but maintained that its Western portrayal as essentially consisting of massive terror and repression was a "very crass distortion," because only the "capitalist roaders that want to open up China to being carved up by foreign imperialism" suffered, and "for the basic people in society" there was "an incredible flowering of debate" and "the greatest freedom of expression in an unprecedented way," as "peasants out in the field" laid down their tools and discussed "philosophy, literature, art, international politics." Asked his views concerning the applicability of principles of the Chinese Cultural Revolution to the United States, Johnson stated, "I'm not a civil libertarian," and that, for example, racist flyers should be banned immediately and that after a successful RCP revolution "we're going to deal resolutely" with the leaders of racist organizations and with the "heads of the major instruments of the state apparatus of the overthrown bourgeois state." He added, however, with regard to ordinary "people in society who have wrong ideas" about things like racism, misogyny, and chauvinism, "we're not going to resort to handcuffs and jails" but would "rely on struggle and debate and persuasion" since "they've been brainwashed with this 'America uber alles' stuff."

Johnson said that the RCYB sees the American flag as "representing an imperialist system which dominates and exploits large sections of the world," and whose "crimes committed against the people of the world exceeded even what the Nazis were capable of," with American "wars of aggression" and Central Intelligence Agency–organized revolts having led to "six million" deaths. Therefore, he continued, the RCYB "welcomes every defeat that the U.S. suffers in the world," such as the Iranian holding of American hostages, and seeks to use such events "to hasten the day when we can actually bring down the empire." In the United States, "freedom of speech only exists for the powers that be," Johnson maintained, but it was a "joke" for the "oppressed" who "don't have access to the media" and had been "bombarded for the last 10 years with nauseous American nationalist patriotism" in an attempt to rewrite the history of the Vietnam War and "turn it into a noble effort instead of a genocidal war of American aggression."

Johnson denied "actually" igniting the flag that was burned in Dallas in 1984. When asked if he had poured lighter fluid on it, he responded, "Those who say don't know, those who know don't say, but I didn't actually ignite it." When his Dallas trial began in December 1984, Johnson issued a press release over the RCYB's signature that denied the flag burning charge, but emphasized his full support of the August 22 events, terming it "great to see the American flag go up in flames, a symbol of international plunder and murder reduced to ashes."

In the 1990 interview, Johnson defended flag burning as a symbol of "total rejection of the system" and a "powerful political statement" that speaks with "international communicability, it crosses language barriers." According to Johnson, the power of flag burning is demonstrated by how "relentlessly and feverishly" the government has sought to suppress it, as well as by the fact that whenever people around the world "rise up and want to make a statement of strong hatred and contempt for U.S. imperialism and the capitalist regimes that back up brutal dictatorships, they burn the flag." In response to the suggestion that flag burning primarily alienates people, Johnson argued:

> You cannot bring about any radical change, any real fucking change, any revolutionary change, without bringing forth a radical right-wing reaction. You can be overwhelmed with the majority of Americans, that's always used to bludgeon you down, any time you begin to raise your head, they go, "The majority thinks another way," and you're supposed to go, "Oooh, oooh, I guess I'm weird." The majority of people at one time supported the Vietnam war or slavery, or McCarthyism or the incarceration of Japanese-Americans [during World War II], but that was wrong.

The key issue involved in the flag burning controversy, Johnson argued, was that of "forced patriotism" as the government seeks to "bind people together" in preparation for "new acts of aggression internationally."

The 1984 Dallas Flag Burning Trial of Gregory Lee Johnson

On August 24, the day after he was charged with flag desecration, Johnson was released from jail on a $200 cash bond, which a friend apparently posted, as police records indicate he had only $62.15 when arrested. His case was postponed several times, partly because he suffered a broken nose during an apparent altercation in San Francisco in early November, before coming to trial as docket number MA8446013-H/J before Dallas County Criminal Court judge John Hendrik on December 10, 1984. Hendrik, a Dallas native born in 1945, worked as a Bible and Fuller Brush salesman before spending nine years in private law practice after graduating from the University of Texas Law School in 1971, followed by his election to a judgeship in 1980. An extremely friendly, gregarious, and strikingly young-looking man, Hendrik was a longtime Republican activist with a reputation for being politically conservative but fair to all sides during trials.

Johnson's jury consisted of one man and five women (in Texas a six-person jury is used for misdemeanors), five in their thirties and the other fifty-two years old, all of whom indicated a Christian religious preference on their juror information cards. Two of the jurors were secretaries, one listed her occupation as homemaker, one was a tax accountant, one an educational consultant, and the remaining juror a "customer engineer" for IBM. On December 13, after four days of testimony, Johnson was found guilty. A few hours later, the same jury, after hearing thirty minutes of additional testimony and arguments under Texas's so-called "bifurcated" procedure, in which penalties are determined separately after a finding of guilt, assessed the maximum punishment of a year in jail and a $2,000 fine, without probation.

Johnson was represented without charge by two ACLU attorneys, Stanley Weinberg, fifty-five, a former reporter who grew up in the Bronx and obtained his law degree from Southern Methodist University in Dallas, and Doug Skemp, thirty-four, a law graduate of Baylor University in Waco, Texas. Weinberg, the lead attorney, was then president of the Dallas ACLU chapter. During 1990 interviews, both attorneys made clear that they viewed flag desecration, both personally and professionally, as constitutionally protected expression. Weinberg declared, "I doubt if I'll ever get a case again involving as important an issue" and termed the Texas venerated objects law "bad on its face," especially because of the vagueness of its "serious offense" clause. According to Weinberg, in the case of a flag burned in a deserted forest, the clause would make commission of an offense dependent on whether there was a "forest ranger up on top of a mountain fifty-five miles away with a high-powered telescope, who saw a puff of smoke and happened to see what he thought was a flag." Weinberg summed up his legal strategy at Johnson's trial as the "age-old" defense posture that "#1 the law was not good and he had every right to do this thing, but #2 he didn't do it."

Skemp declared that flag burning "upsets me a lot, it really hurts me," but "there's only one thing that hurts me more, to send someone to jail for doing it." Imprisoning flag burners, Skemp maintained, "lessens the meaning of the Constitution," because "the true test of what our flag means and what it stands for is that we can withstand criticism. Once we cease to have the right to burn it, to me it doesn't become much more than a piece of cloth." Skemp added that by prosecuting Johnson, "we kind of play into his hands" by bolstering his view of the United States as a repressive nation," but "we prove Gregory Johnson wrong by letting him do what he did."

Both lawyers recalled a considerable amount of friction with Johnson, aggravated by Johnson's absence from Dallas during most of the preparatory period and his desire to publicize and politicize the case to further the RCP's agenda. During the Dallas trial, they recalled, Johnson distributed press releases, held several news conferences during trial recesses, and frequently engaged courthouse visitors in political debates, although his lawyers wanted to focus on the legal issues. Weinberg remembered feeling that by politicizing the case Johnson risked not only getting convicted but "bopped into the maximum sentence," but "nothing I'm going to do could control him."

One particular bone of contention was Johnson's insistence on wearing to court each day a T-shirt emblazoned with the words "Revolutionary Communist Youth Brigade" that featured the silhouette of a man carrying a rifle. According to the lawyers, Johnson often tried to direct his own defense, and at one point, Weinberg recalled, he became so aggravated at Johnson that "I just flat turned around and told him, 'Shut the fuck up and sit down,' whereupon Johnson looked at me and said, 'Mr. Weinberg, I'm exercising my First Amendment rights.'" Weinberg added that thereafter Johnson "shut up and let me try the case," and that "Johnson is not really that unlikable once you get rid of the theatrics and the rhetoric. He's not bad, but, representing him, he didn't make himself lovable and nobody expected him to." Skemp noted that since he and Weinberg "never got a dime" for their representation, Johnson "didn't have anybody else who was going to do it for our price."

Johnson's trial was almost totally ignored by the national media, but it received heavy coverage in the Dallas press. Weinberg recalled "class after class after class [of high school students] coming up there" on field trips to watch the trial, until "there wasn't enough room in the courtroom" and "daily coverage, newspapers, TV, radio, there was a lot of attention paid to it." Skemp recalled Johnson as a "pretty cynical guy" who was "out for every bit of publicity he could get," and "loved every minute of the attention" and wouldn't have "missed this for all the money in the world," but also someone with "genuine feelings about the way the country ought to be run. I'm not going to say he wanted publicity personally for himself, I give him the benefit of the doubt and would say he wanted it for the issue."

Dallas was represented at Johnson's trial by Michael Gillett, a graduate of the University of Texas Law School, whose reputation, like most Dallas prosecutors, was that of a conservative "law and order" man and whose 1990 vita boasted that as a prosecutor he has obtained "in excess of 100 life sentences." During a 1990 interview, Gillett recalled that as chief of the misdemeanors division in 1984 he supervised about fifty employees and about fifty thousand cases a year, and viewed the *Johnson* trial as a "major case and as a result I chose to try it myself." He compared the march that preceded the flag burning as "kind of like a bunch of termites tearing up everything in their way." Gillett termed the flag burning "not speech" but "conduct," and added that, even if it was considered speech, it was no more constitutionally protected or worthwhile than going "into a theater and hollering fire" or "lewd comments made to a woman in a public place," especially because flag burning "went towards breaches of the peace." Even "an expression of an idea," Gillett maintained, must be "balanced" against the public's right to "order, decency and morality," and "if the majority doesn't have the right to legislate against that," he asked, doesn't that violate "what this country is about?" Gillett declared that "most Americans would feel the same way I feel, and that is, if you don't like the country, you know, pack your bags."

The four-day trial filled over eight hundred transcribed pages, but hardly any of it dealt with whether Johnson burned a flag in Dallas on August 22. The vast majority of evidence introduced by Gillett focused on the generally disorderly nature of the demonstration and Johnson's alleged leadership role in it, but the evidence about Johnson's role in the flag burning was thin, strongly contested, and largely circumstantial. During a pretrial hearing, Gillett implicitly conceded that the case against Johnson for personally burning the flag was not strong by arguing that throughout the march Johnson was "there and part of it and verbally encouraging it and participating in it," and that even if events occurred during the protest, "that the Defendant physically himself did not do," such as "spray painting the walls," because he was present "our theory is that by his conduct and participation that he would be responsible for acts of co-conspirators and was acting as a party by aiding and encouraging this type of conduct."

This argument was based on Texas's so-called law of parties, which, as Judge Hendrik charged the jury, holds that "a person is criminally responsible for an offense committed by the conduct of another if, acting with intent to promote or assist the commission of the offense, he solicits, encourages, directs, aids or attempts to aid the other person to commit the offense." During his closing argument, Gillett declared that although the prosecution believed that Johnson had burned the flag, Johnson was "guilty as sin as far as the law of parties is concerned." During a 1990 interview, Hendrik declined to say whether he thought Johnson had personally burned the flag, but emphasized "there wasn't any question" that Johnson had been "aiding, abetting or encouraging" the flag burning and therefore was clearly guilty under the law of parties.

Johnson was probably harmed most severely by the introduction of police and television videotapes of the demonstration, which Hendrik allowed, along with other testimony about the general events of August 22, over vigorous and repeated defense objections. The tapes depicted bizarrely dressed protesters engaged in spray painting, window pounding, and "die-ins," although, aside from one fleeting scene that showed Johnson making obscene gestures with his hands, they failed to show his personal involvement in the flag burning or any of the other activities portrayed. No photographic evidence bearing on who had burned the flag was ever introduced, aside from several ultimately inconclusive photos produced by the defense that seemed to show Johnson standing outside the circle when the flag was supposedly burning within it.

Even Gillett conceded during pretrial proceedings that the photographic evidence was unclear, when, in response to Hendrik's comment that after viewing the tapes Johnson might plead guilty, he responded "these tapes are not quite that good, judge." But the tapes were played repeatedly during the trial and the jury asked to see them again during their deliberations. In 1990, six years after the trial, juryman Rex Skelton (the only juror willing to be interviewed) volunteered that "what really influenced everyone the most was the tapes," and that although he "personally didn't have any doubt" that Johnson was involved in the flag burning, "what really ruined" Johnson was the pictures of the demonstration's "physical destruction of the properties. Although that was not the issue, when they're sitting there ripping things apart, that's what set everybody [that is, the jurors] wrong. That had quite a bit to do with it." Skelton added that he was negatively affected by Johnson's "total defiance of anything and everything that anyone else was thinking" and that he "didn't like the T-shirt," although such considerations had "no impact on his decision."

In a 1990 interview, Judge Hendrik volunteered to provide a copy of the tapes and agreed that they had had "a big impact" and "made most people pretty upset" because they were "pretty incendiary, if you pardon the pun." Weinberg argued in his 1990 interview that Dallas "had nothing to prosecute" Johnson on, especially because the tapes showed only a "bunch of extraneous things but nobody saw Johnson take part in any activity of damaging property," with "not a bit of film of the burning of the flag." He said that after Johnson's conviction "they told me in the jury room that there was a serious question in some of their minds as to being absolutely sure than Johnson did it," but "with the law of parties in there they could go ahead" and convict.

The major witnesses for the prosecution were two Dallas vice squad officers, Terri Stover and Ronald Tucker, who had infiltrated the August 22 protest as undercover agents dressed in blue jeans and tennis shoes. Both testified that they viewed Johnson as a leader of the demonstration, based on Stover's recollection of seeing him using a megaphone and on both of their recollections that Johnson had frequently engaged in what appeared to be a key role in "talking," "yelling," and "chanting" remarks such as "Fuck you, America" and "Screw everybody." They also testified that after other people stole an American flag from the Mercantile Bank that Johnson had been given it and stuck it under his shirt; and that, according to Stover, he had banged with his fists on a window at the Diamond Shamrock building and had participated in a "die-in" at the Southwestern Bell building, during which he "rolled on his back and was shooting the finger with both hands, saying 'Fuck America.' "

Although Stover testified that she did not see who burned the flag at city hall, Tucker testified that he had clearly observed Johnson burn the flag with a cigarette lighter after dousing it with lighter fluid. The only corroborating testimony came from Evelyn Olsovsky, a Dallas city security guard, who reported she had seen Johnson burn the flag from her vantage point inside city hall. Her account was severely compromised, however, because she claimed that Johnson had burned the flag "out in the open" and "all by himself"; every other witness for both sides testified that the flag burning was cut off from general view by a large circle of protesters. Two defense witnesses testified unequivocally that Johnson, who had short, dark hair on the day of the protest, could not have been the flag burner because they saw the flag burned by a person with long blond hair. Johnson himself did not testify during the guilt-innocence phase of the trial, but he denied burning the flag both during a five-minute closing argument Hendrik permitted him to deliver and in direct testimony during the trial's penalty phase.

Aside from stressing Johnson's alleged leadership role in the protest, the prosecution repeatedly sought to highlight his radical political views and to appeal to the jury's sense of patriotism. Gillett especially focused on Johnson's T-shirt, drawing the attention of witnesses and the jury to it on at least six different occasions. At one point, he even asked Johnson to "move out your hands, please," so that it could be more easily viewed. Urging the jury to give Johnson the maximum sentence, Gillett asked them to ponder what "this man with a gun on his chest" might have done had a passersby who had scooped up the ashes of the burned flag physically attempted to stop the flag burning.

When Johnson took the stand to plead for probation during the penalty phase of the trial, Gillett concentrated almost exclusively on bringing out Johnson's political radicalism. Johnson eagerly facilitated this task by expressing his view of the United States as an imperialistic power whose self-proclaimed devotion to democratic principles were false, as evidenced by his trial for burning the flag when, according to Johnson, his real offense was being "unpatriotic."

Noting that Johnson had declared in a press release that the flag burning for which he was being prosecuted was "great," Gillett asked Johnson if he felt the same way about seeing "deposit slips torn up that weren't yours, . . . a flag that was taken that wasn't yours, spray painting on property that wasn't yours, plants uprooted?" Johnson responded that his "big crime" was "talking about Ronald Reagan's candidacy" and that he could not "respond to the question as you've structured it because it puts forward a view of simple vandalism, frankly, and I think it guts the political heart out of like what was really going on that day and that's what's most disturbing to you," because the demonstration had shattered "your puffed-up confidence" that "these youth that you were relying on to be like cannon fire, to be shot out of a missile, would dare to come here and hold a protest challenging this whole future." When Gillett asked Johnson if he had chanted "Fuck you,

America," during the protest, Johnson conceded he had, but declared that such remarks were not directed at "average people" but instead at the "multi-death corporations" who "carry out plunder and corporate rape of the third world, and they were directed at the U.S. government, which is a utensil or an apparatus to assist in that."

Their exchange also included the following, in which Johnson reflected the RCP's view of Russia as a reactionary "revisionist" regime that had betrayed Communist ideals:

Q. Do you like the American Flag?

A. No, I do not. . . . I challenge anyone who upholds the patriotism of that flag to tell me how in the final analysis that doesn't boil down to wanting to maintain a privileged position over the people of the world. . . .

Q. Do you think the American flag represents anything good at all?

A. We've already been over that. If you want me to state repeatedly for the record, "No," and I think it's an honor to be compared to the Iranian people who, in 1953, the United States had put a bloody dictator in power, then people want to know why the Iranian people use the American flag to carry trash in. If somebody installed a dictator in your country, what would you do with the flag of the country that installed that dictator? . . . I'm not going to sit up here and especially at times like these in history when the government is crying out for the allegiance, the blind patriotic allegiance of millions [and] say, "America number one," which is what you want to hear and I think it's disgusting. . . . You're going against your so-called First Amendment . . . by saying that you can protest just as long as you bow down before the American flag. . . .

Q. Mr. Johnson, let me ask you this: If you don't like the country and you don't like the flag . . . why you just don't move to Russia? . . .

A. I don't consider it [Russia] to be any sort of society that people in the world who are striving for a future without oppression should look to for guidance. . . . If anything I think that there are more similarities between the United States and the Soviet Union. They mutually possess over 50,000 nuclear weapons. . . . I don't know these things aren't as of strong concern to you. What's more of concern is that the people here blindly and obediently follow and look brightly into the mushroom clouds and march off, and I suspect if you were in the Soviet Union, you would be guilty of doing the same thing: blindly following the government of the Soviet Union. . . . We have an enormous responsibility to work for a future that is free of the madness. . . . We have a responsibility, so for me to just move, to leave, would be an abdication, I think, of that responsibility.

Q. So you just want to stay here and work burning up American flags, huh?

A. That's a rather vulgar way of expressing it. . . . And I didn't actually do it. . . .

Q. [D]idn't you say it was great to see the American flag go up in flames?

A. And reduced to ashes, yes. . . .

Q. There's something real dangerous about you, isn't there?

A. To you and your society, to your system, not to the people. . . . [E]ventually the situation will arise where millions of people will be confronted with the alternative of either fighting in a third world war or fighting to overthrow the system that exists. . . .

Q. What's the rifle up in the air on your shirt stand for?

A. It stands for revolution.

Q. Well, why the gun?

A. Because it's going to take violence.

Q. So you do advocate violence?

A. Not individual violence.

Q. Oh, just as a group?

The prosecution's closing appeals to the jury, by Gillett and his colleague Randy Kucera, were filled with appeals to the jury's patriotism and references to Johnson's radicalism. Thus, Kucera referred to the information "flashed across the defendant's chest [on his T-shirt]," and declared that Johnson was the "leader" and the "instigator" of a "group of anarchists" who had sought to frustrate the effort of patriotic citizens of Dallas to make their city "sparkle in the national limelight" of the Republican convention. Gillett urged the jury to give Johnson the maximum punishment because he was "creating a lot of danger for a lot of people by what he does and the way he thinks," and had committed a deed that was "serious" and "offensive" as "far as every American is concerned and when you go back into the jury room you represent each and every one of them and don't forget it." At one point Gillett exclaimed, "You know what's fantastic, watching a baby being born, not our flag being burned." He told the jury that even if "you can't change [Johnson's] thinking," they should make clear that if anyone in Dallas burned the flag "that represents the things we love," the "full force" of the law would deliver the "message" to Johnson and "others like him, 'No more. We won't have it.'"

Weinberg maintained in his closing argument that Johnson was really being tried for "his politics," because he refused to respond to the state by "clicking [his] heels and automatically obeying." He added that even if Johnson had burned the flag the Constitution protected even "nasty speech" and "symbolic action" that speaks "louder" than words, and therefore an acquittal would demonstrate not only "reasonable doubt" about Johnson's guilt but that "the First Amendment is alive and well in Dallas."

Although the overwhelming focus of the trial was on the events of August 22, Weinberg's stress on the First Amendment reflected the defense's intent that, if Johnson were convicted, subsequent appeals would focus on the constitutionality of flag desecration laws. During both pretrial proceedings and the trial itself, the defense repeatedly but unsuccessfully sought to have Judge Hendrik stop the prosecution on the grounds that the Texas venerated objects law posed an unconstitutional threat to freedom of speech, but this argument was primarily designed to establish the groundwork for subsequent appeals, as trial court judges rarely attempt to establish fundamental constitutional precedents. Such precedent would be especially unlikely in the *Johnson* prosecution, given the conservative politics of Dallas, the controversial nature of the issue, the Supreme Court's repeated ducking of the First Amendment issues involved, and especially because in the 1971 *Deeds* case, the Texas Court of Criminal Appeals, the state's highest judicial authority in criminal cases, had upheld the state's flag desecration law. That defense arguments concerning constitutional issues were addressed largely to future appellate judges was made clear when, in response to Gillett's complaint that he could not "hear anything that's going on" as Weinberg was urging that Hendrik void the law, Hendrik responded, "It's not going to make any difference. It's for the record."

Despite Hendrik's refusal to halt the trial on constitutional grounds, Johnson's lawyers, both to build a record for later appeals and in hopes of finding a sympathetic jury response, stressed that Johnson had not burned the flag beyond any "reasonable doubt," but in any case the flag burning had been intended to express a political point of view and therefore was constitutionally protected. Thus, in his opening remarks, Weinberg declared, "There are two defendants in this case: Mr. Johnson and the First Amendment." During pretrial proceedings, Weinberg also stressed the allegedly defective nature of the "seriously offend" provision of the Texas law, an argument that would subsequently assume considerable importance. He complained that the provision made the law deeply flawed, because whether or not an action was "even a crime or not" depended on the "very subjective" reactions of unknown persons and "whether or not anybody is going to observe it or not," so that Johnson could not adequately defend himself because he was never told whom he supposedly knew would be seriously offended, for example, if these persons were "hidden behind a bush."

Interviewed in Dallas in 1990, when the flag desecration controversy sparked by *Johnson* was raging nationally, Judge Hendrik and the various lawyers all retained strong feelings about the issue and strong memories of the six-year-old trial that had touched it all off. They generally agreed that Johnson was hurt by his political views and by the conservative nature of Dallas politics, although, not surprisingly, there was disagreement about other aspects of the trial. Asked if he felt the controversy had become "blown all out of all proportion" by 1990, Gillett responded, "I think if you ask the surviving family members of every person who has been lost in a war defending the rights of this country, they're going to tell you that it is important." He added, "I don't think it's going to end until the law, either through statute or constitutional amendment, prohibits the burning of the flag" and "it wouldn't bother me in the least to have a constitutional amendment." Gillett said that Johnson's attorneys had done a "good job," but Johnson had "obviously hurt" his position by wearing the RCYB T-shirt and by expressing a "political philosophy I don't think most Americans agree with."

Johnson's lawyers were considerably less charitable about Gillett: Weinberg characterized Gillett as "forceful," "outraged," and engaging in the kind of "typical overkill" that Dallas prosecutors were "notorious" for in an attempt to get an "emotional response" from the jury. Skemp said Gillett was "self-righteous, sarcastic," and playing the role of a "true patriot" defending the country against what he portrayed as Johnson's "pure nihilism." Skemp added, however, that Gillett was sincerely "deeply upset" about the flag burning and also wanted to "make a real issue" of the incident because the flag "is very dear to him," since Gillett is "just a real law and order kind of guy." Skemp said that Johnson's trial statement that Gillett would have been a loyal policeman even in a totalitarian regime was "so true. If you look at Gillett he'd be a patriot wherever he was born."

Weinberg lamented that the defense had taken the posture of, "Come on folks, this is the fundamental bedrock principle of our government," but it was "outrage which carried the day, which is no surprise in Dallas." Skemp similarly stated that although Johnson had been "quite effective" as a witness, "the jury didn't seem to care." According to Weinberg, Johnson was "fairly toned down" as a witness and bested Gillett during their confrontation because he was "cooler than Gillett" and "made points back that Gillett, in the fervor of getting after the guy, couldn't respond to." Judge Hendrik shared the defense contention that Johnson bested Gillett in debate because "he knew his position better than Mr. Gillett knew his" and because Gillett resorted to the "tired and worn out cliché" of suggesting that Johnson leave the country if he didn't like it. "That was kind of the level of Gillett's debate," Hendrik said, adding, "I had to lower his debate score considerably" for using it.

Hendrik, who was interviewed in his chambers, which were decorated with classic illustrations by French caricaturist Honoré Daumier lampooning lawyers and judges, said that Johnson impressed him as "pretty serious" and "fairly committed" in his testimony rather than "an exhibitionist" who was "just playing games," as had been his first impression, and that Johnson's tale of seeing his father jailed at a young age and "hearing a little bit about his background made me understand that's why he might not be in love with the American system." Had the sentencing been up to him, Hendrik indicated that he would have given a lower fine and slightly lesser jail term than the maximum penalty dictated by the jury. Hendrik reported that his impression, based on Johnson's T-shirt and general demeanor, was that Johnson would have been "very disappointed" if he had been acquitted, because his attitude was that "he couldn't get a fair trial, that the whole system stinks and he had no chance." Hendrik said he did not think the T-shirt made any difference because just sticking to "the facts of case" was enough to "appeal to the community's feelings" and "anyone doing the same thing would have been found guilty" and would receive "close to the maximum [penalty] from any average Dallas County jury," given the "very staunchly conservative" nature of Dallas political attitudes.

Hendrik said that he never seriously considered declaring the Texas law unconstitutional because the case Johnson's lawyers presented for that was only a "50/50 proposition" and trial court judges are generally "a little hesitant to declare a state law unconstitutional" unless the authority was "clear." Hendrik added that, in all candor, "there's no doubt" that "any judge who's elected [as are all judges in Texas] would have to think long and hard" before declaring a flag desecration law unconstitutional, and that, based on conversations with other judges, "I know" that when dealing with controversial issues "most of the judges regularly pay attention" to public opinion and either "give it a whole lot of weight or not depending upon how courageous they are or how strong they feel about the individual position." Hendrik recalled thinking that because of the potential constitutional issues involved, the case would "very likely" get into the federal courts, although not to the Supreme Court, because "except maybe for *Roe v. Wade* [the 1973 ruling legalizing abortion] this is probably the only misdemeanor in the history of Dallas County to get to the Supreme Court."

Hendrik said that he "personally had no problem at all" with the Texas law, which he termed "a perfectly good law." He added that "the Supreme Court was wrong [in *Johnson*] and I'm in favor of a constitutional amendment to change it." Hendrik conceded that there were "elements of expression" in flag desecration, but he maintained that outlawing such behavior would not "be a significant limitation on free speech" because "people can express their ideas and opinions without burning the flag" and because flag burning was an "extremely violent, very provocative" attempt to "cause trouble" and to "show the utmost disrespect for the American system" that "is pretty close to treason." He compared speaking against the flag and burning it to the "difference between saying we ought to have a revolution and buying a machine gun" and termed flag burning "very much a revolutionary act that goes beyond just a theoretical discussion."

————

Legal Arguments During Appeals
of the *Johnson* Case, 1985–1988

As Gregory Lee Johnson went free on a $750 cash appeal bond shortly after his December 13, 1984, conviction, the lawyers for both sides began preparing appeals documents. Between the original trial and the June 21, 1989, Supreme Court ruling that would declare that the Texas venerated objects law had been unconstitutionally used to prosecute Johnson in violation of his First Amendment rights, the case was heard by two intervening Texas appeals courts. Because the fundamental arguments of the two sides changed relatively little during the five years of Texas and Supreme Court appellate litigation (even though the lawyers did), the legal briefs they submitted during this process will be consolidated here before returning to a chronological account of the legal history of *Texas v. Johnson*.

Although the fundamental constitutional issues raised by Johnson's prosecution were relatively minor and formal sideshows during his Dallas trial, they moved to the forefront during the appeals litigation. Dallas's legal representatives essentially conceded during the appeals process that the Dallas flag burning contained communicative aspects that raised First Amendment considerations, but they repeatedly maintained that Dallas had legitimate interests that overrode any constitutional protections that Johnson may have been entitled to. Johnson could still heap "abuse on the flag either verbally or in writing," Dallas argued, and was thus forbidden only from engaging in "flagrant acts of flag desecration," which were outlawed in a "content neutral" manner, whether committed "out of treason or patriotism, love or hate." Because the Texas law was aimed at reaching "only the non-communicative aspects" of destructive conduct regarding the flag, Dallas maintained, it met the Supreme Court's 1968 *O'Brien* test, which required only that the state demonstrate an "important or substantial interest" that was furthered by its statute that was "unrelated to the suppression of free expression." Dallas added, however, even if flag desecration was found to be clearly expressive under the Court's 1974 *Spence* test, which appeared to require a higher level of governmental justification, Texas had two "compelling state interests" that superseded any First Amendment rights Johnson might have claimed. These were the same two interests that had been repeatedly cited by courts that upheld flag desecration convictions during the Vietnam War, including the Texas Court of Criminal Appeals in its 1971 *Deeds* ruling: the right to prevent breaches of the peace and the right to protect the flag as a symbol of national unity.

Arguing that flag desecration could be outlawed as a measure to maintain the peace, Dallas maintained that the city hall flag burning had created a "potentially explosive" situation that could have provoked an "immediate physical reaction" from people who gathered to watch the incident. Dallas maintained that Johnson's "gang of protesters" had created an "inherently inflammatory situation" when they "invaded several businesses, damaged and destroyed chattels [properties] real and personal and chanted inflammatory slogans such as 'Fuck you, America' before burning the flag" before a "sizable crowd" on "public property during a time of increased public attention and presence." Dallas added that the Supreme Court's 1907 *Halter* decision upholding flag desecration laws and that of numerous courts during the Vietnam era established that the state had a legitimate interest in "preventing" disturbances, that the Dallas flag burning had threatened "imminent public unrest" at the "climax of a turbulent, destructive and potentially violent demonstration," and that it that it was "merely fortuitous that no undue public disorder or unrest actually" followed.

Dallas argued that it had an additional "substantial and compelling interest" in protecting the flag as a "symbol of national unity," and that because Texas had not sought to deny Johnson the right to publicly dissent through "legitimate protest activities," but only to ban him from using the flag for "physical destruction," the state could properly punish him for "trying to destroy the flag as a symbol revered by the vast majority of Americans." Such physical assaults, Dallas argued, were dangerous because they could damage the flag's ability to "survive" and "serve as a symbol of nationhood and unity" in a manner that was "qualitatively different from any other symbol that this nation uses to express its existence." Protection of the flag's symbolism, Dallas argued, reflected the nation's justifiable concern with "self perpetuation and self preservation," as toleration of public flag desecration could do "great harm" to the flag's effectiveness in providing a "rallying point for the people's support of our country in time of peace and war" and providing a "visible representation of the stability and strength of our country."

Johnson's lawyers consistently stressed a free speech argument in their briefs. They maintained that Johnson had been prosecuted in violation of the First Amendment—and of the free speech clause of the Texas Constitution—because the flag burning had "occurred as a symbol" during a "political protest demonstration" that clearly met the *Spence* test of "expression" because it sought to "convey a particularized message of dissatisfaction" with the Reagan administration and took place amid "recognized protest activity." They stressed that the combination of the "serious offense" provision of the Texas law and the state's focus on its need to protect the symbolic value of the flag made clear that Texas's primary interest was to suppress unwelcome political expression, a purpose they argued was squarely in conflict with the First Amendment and numerous Supreme Court decisions. They maintained that the Texas law was clearly directed against expression rather than conduct and was not "content neutral," because it sought to protect only "one view" of the flag as a representation of "nationhood and national unity" against other views, such as those held by Johnson," which viewed the flag as standing for "oppression or imperialism."

"Whether one is compelled to respect a flag by saluting it or by observing a series of taboos concerning its use of misuse," they continued, "the compulsion is viewpoint-based and presumptively unconstitutional in a society which declared itself dedicated to political toleration." Moreover, they added, as far back as the 1931 *Stromberg* ruling striking down red flag laws, the Supreme Court had repeatedly made clear that the "absence of words in no way diminished First Amendment protection" for political speech, a shield that was especially important because flag burning was a particularly powerful form of dissent precisely since its nonverbal nature "cuts across language barriers" worldwide in an "age of broadcast media, sound bites and instantly-transmitted television images."

Aside from a frontal First Amendment assault on the Texas law, Johnson's lawyers concentrated on the "seriously offend" provision of the statute. They maintained the provision was unconstitutionally vague because it failed to adequately inform potential violators exactly what conduct was forbidden and also encouraged "arbitrary and erratic arrests and convictions" by the police and courts. They contended that the "seriously offend" provision could "chill" even protected speech because, by making violation of the law dependent on "what onlookers might think" rather than on clearly defined conduct, it might lead individuals to avoid "all conduct disrespectful of the flag in the fear that it might cause some observer a degree of displeasure that could, conceivably, be described as serious offense."

Johnson's lawyers also rejected the contention that Texas was justified in enacting the law as a means against a generalized threat of breach of the peace. They argued that the Supreme Court had made clear in its 1941 *Chaplinsky* and 1968 *Brandenburg* rulings that laws outlawing expression that might cause "serious offense" but not necessarily a violent reaction were unconstitutional, since political expression could only be restricted when direct personal insults or other direct provocation to imminent violence were involved. Finally, Johnson's attorneys argued that because Judge Hendrik had told the jury that Johnson could be found guilty under the Texas law of parties either for burning the flag or encouraging others to burn it, the jury might have convicted Johnson solely for his verbal statements in violation of the Supreme Court's 1969 *Street* ruling.

In response to Johnson's lawyers' emphasis on the allegedly unconstitutional vagueness of the "seriously offend" provision of the Texas law, Dallas's attorneys maintained that the term was not vague at all, but outlawed only acts of physical flag abuse likely to outrage onlookers. They maintained that the law's application did not "depend upon a vague notion of the sensibilities of persons likely to observe the actor's conduct," which could make even a "relatively innocent touching" or merely "reckless or negligent handling" of the flag actionable, but extended only to "flagrant abuse of the flag" designed to "seriously offend" the "shared norms that society holds relative to treatment of the flag." In response to the "law of parties" argument suggesting that Johnson might have been convicted solely for his words, Dallas maintained that the "State's evidence," and the "overall theory of the State's case," which "was obviously believed by the jury," was that Johnson had "committed the offense acting alone."

The Legal History of *Texas v. Johnson* on Appeal in Texas, 1985–1988

Shortly after Johnson's conviction on December 13, 1984, his ACLU attorneys filed papers requesting the Court of Appeals for the Fifth District (Dallas) to hear his case, a right of appeal guaranteed to all persons convicted in Texas of criminal offenses. Following the formal notification by the court on May 8, 1985, that the case would be heard, Johnson's lawyers filed their appeal brief in what was titled *Johnson v. Texas*, case 05-85-00318-CR, on July 8, 1985. Dallas responded in September 1985 with a brief written by John D. Nation, the deputy head of the Dallas district attorney's appellate division, the office that represented Dallas in all criminal appeals.

Nation, a 1979 graduate of Bates College of Law (University of Houston), who had worked as a staff attorney in the Texas appellate courts and for the Dallas County district attorney before being appointed to his position in 1984, helped to supervise about twenty other attorneys and determined which attorney would handle each of the five hundred to seven hundred cases that Dallas litigated annually on appeal. In a 1990 interview Nation, who left the district attorney's office for private practice in 1987, recalled that he typically rated cases on a "legal difficulty" scale of one to six and that because the *Johnson* case rated at "about a five" and because it was of considerable public interest and involved his own constitutional law specialty, he assigned it to himself, a step he typically took in fewer than twenty cases annually. Nation recalled, "I knew from the day I took it that this was going to be in the Supreme Court one way or another."

Compared to Mike Gillett and Kathi Drew, the two Dallas prosecutors who, respectively, handled the case before and after he did, Nation gave the impression of having considerably less emotional investment in the issue. For example, Nation readily conceded, referring to the "seriously offend" clause, that the Texas law was "inartfully" and "unfortunately drawn," and he suggested that Johnson was "prosecuted probably because he was the most visible person" in the protest rather than because he had "necessarily personally burned the flag."

Nation readily conceded that flag burning was a form of expression rather than conduct, since "there isn't any point in denying the obvious, it's a politically motivated free speech issue." However, he added, "there's a limit past which you cannot go and Johnson went past that limit. My position was that he could do anything he wanted to up to burning the flag." Nation declared that he didn't think that flag burning "was going to bring the government crumbling to its knees," especially since Johnson "probably causes more Republican votes than anything else," but that he feared that over the long term "having the ultimate symbol of our country treated that way" would pose a serious threat to national morale and unity. According to Nation, "If you allowed obvious and repeated acts of destruction of our ultimate symbol, you're going to incrementally destroy whatever it is that keeps us together" and

> you will definitely have a big problem if you should need national unity in some future emergency. There are some things you can't be big about, there are some things that if you want our country worth living in, that you do put a stop to. America did not get to be the world power it is now with the national attitudes we have today. If this is the kind of country that Gregory Lee Johnson envisions, then we might as well give it up.

On September 26, 1985, oral arguments on Johnson's appeal were heard by a three-judge panel of the thirteen-member Dallas Court of Appeals. The presiding judge was John Vance, the trial court judge in the 1970 *Deeds* flag burning trial. Weinberg, Skemp, and Nation recalled in 1990 interviews that slightly under one hour of oral argument was heard virtually without interruption by the judges. Skemp recalled concluding from the silence that greeted the defense arguments, which he termed "really not normal at all," that "they aren't even interested in what we have to say" and "they were not going to get into any kind of argument with these kooky civil liberties lawyers." Nation suggested that the lack of questioning simply reflected that the judges "knew we had a lot of ground to cover," but he added that "the Dallas Court [of Appeals] is pretty conservative on crime issues, so they didn't have a prayer of winning in that forum." Weinberg recalled Johnson attended the oral argument dressed in "some rag-tag, jungle gym type thing with a bandanna on his head" and seemed pleased with what he viewed as a "very strong defense and thereafter never said anything nasty to me. He was surprised, he thought [because of past tensions between them] that I was not going to do something to represent him. I'm a defense attorney. I represent my clients."

On January 23, 1986, the appeals court issued a unanimous decision written by Vance that sustained Johnson's conviction. Although the court conceded that Johnson's flag burning constituted "symbolic speech" and thus qualified as a form of "constitutionally-protected free speech" under the Supreme Court's 1974 *Spence* test, it accepted Dallas's position that Texas's interests in "preventing breaches of the peace" and protecting "the flag as a symbol of national unity" justified any "infringement of Johnson's constitutional rights." Citing the 1971 *Deeds* decision of the Texas Court of Criminal Appeals, Vance wrote that flag desecration was so "inflammatory" that Texas could forbid it, even without any showing of resultant actual "imminent public unrest," and that the state additionally had a "legitimate and substantial interest in protecting the flag as a symbol of national unity." The court further rejected complaints that the Texas law was vague and overbroad, as well as the law of parties issue, holding that the evidence adequately demonstrated Johnson's "guilt as a sole actor."

On March 26, 1986, Weinberg and Skemp filed a petition for discretionary review (PDR) requesting that the Texas Court of Criminal Appeals hear their appeal from the appeals court ruling. On March 1, 1987, the court agreed to grant PDR in the case, which now became *Johnson v. State*, docket number 0372-86. In a 1990 interview, Court of Criminal Appeals judge Charles Campbell, who wrote the court's ultimate 1988 decision overturning Johnson's conviction on First Amendment grounds, explained that at least four of the nine Criminal Appeals judges must agree before the court grants PDR, and that only about 10 percent of the twelve hundred to fourteen hundred PDR petitions annually presented are accepted. Campbell said that granting PDR did not necessarily indicate that at least four of the court's judges disagreed with Vance's opinion, but rather "because it was a constitutional issue and specifically because it was a First Amendment issue I think you're going to find that appellate judges enjoy looking into First Amendment issues and researching and writing about them, so there is an interest separate and apart from all other considerations about why you grant review." Weinberg recalled in 1990 that he was not surprised that PDR had been granted, since the case was a "sexy issue, the kind you can sink your teeth into" and "you couldn't let a constitutional issue go by." Skemp agreed with Weinberg in a 1990 interview, adding that the "only reason I could think that they wouldn't [grant PDR] was that they just didn't want to touch it politically because they run for office." Both defense lawyers said that they had felt enormously encouraged by the concession by the Dallas Court of Appeals that in principle Johnson's flag burning was an exercise of "constitutionally-protected free speech." Thus, Skemp recalled feeling that the court's ruling was hopelessly illogical because "they said on the one hand this is protected speech and on the other hand made an exception that engulfed that whole area of speech," thereby creating "an exception that is larger than the rule itself."

On April 9, 1987, Weinberg and Skemp filed their brief with the Court of Criminal Appeals. Dallas responded on June 1, 1987, with a brief that was officially filed, as always, under the name of the Dallas County district attorney, John Vance, who, in a bizarre twist, had been elected to that post shortly after writing the very lower court ruling that he was now urging be upheld. The brief was primarily written and researched by Assistant District Attorney Kathi Drew, who had just replaced Nation as deputy chief of the appellate division. Drew, a longtime Republican activist who had several times been named "Woman of the Year" by the National Young Republicans, graduated from the Southern Methodist University Law School in 1977 and began working for the Dallas district attorney's office in 1981, after working as an attorney for several Texas courts.

In a 1990 interview, Drew recalled being puzzled about the grant of PDR "because I felt with *Deeds* there was nothing to be decided. I couldn't imagine the court ruling in favor of Johnson." Drew said she had no doubts about the wisdom or validity of the Texas venerated objects law, although she recalled feeling hindered in taking over Nation's entire duties and caseload upon his resignation "sort of by right of inheritance" simultaneously with the PDR decision, because she had never handled a First Amendment case, had no previous knowledge of the Johnson affair, and had only a couple of months to file her brief. Drew, unlike Nation but like Gillett, said she personally viewed flag desecration not as expression but as "conduct," and recalled feeling "very angry" that she could not argue this position because she was "hampered" by the Court of Appeals ruling, which clearly labeled such acts as "expression," leading her to conclude "after a great deal of soul searching and an incredible amount of advice" that the higher courts were "very unlikely to back off" on this point.

Drew declared, "I just find it very difficult to believe that the First Amendment was done to protect a destructive act, even if you accept that it is an act with expressive content. It seems to me that this [Supreme Court *Johnson* ruling] is the first time that this doctrine has been extended to something that is actually destructive in nature and I see it as really quantitatively different than any other type of symbolic speech that's protected." According to Drew, the flag is a "special" and "unique entity" that "really belongs to the nation as a whole" and therefore deserves protection even if an "extra category" of law, created if necessary by a constitutional amendment, was required. Asked what damage to the flag's symbolic value was caused by flag burning, Drew responded, "The act of burning a single flag is not inconsequential" because "anytime you have a symbol, the symbol's viability only lasts as long as it remains untarnished and the symbol can lose its meaning over a period of time through neglect, through abuse, through acts of destruction."

During the September 16, 1987, oral argument before the Texas Court of Criminal Appeals, Skemp recalled, in a 1990 interview, that after Drew quoted the court's opinion in the 1971 *Deeds* case to support her position, Judge Sam Houston Clinton, a former ACLU lawyer, "just looked at her, there's these nine judges and they are all sitting up high, he just looked up and down, looked at everybody and said, 'I sure hope we've done a little growing up since then.'" Drew, noting Clinton's ACLU background, recalled, "I wasn't the least surprised by his particular views," but added that, otherwise, "I had no indication that the court would reverse in this case." Charles Stanfield, an assistant to Judge Campbell, said in a 1990 interview that the oral argument was the first he had heard since joining the court, and termed it of "high quality," with attorneys on both sides "extremely well prepared." Stanfield added that, not knowing then how rarely First Amendment cases came before the court, he had felt "it was terribly exciting and I was just delighted to have a job where every week we were going to be deciding First Amendment issues."

On April 20, 1988, the court's 5 to 4 decision, written by Campbell, declared that the Texas venerated objects law had been unconstitutionally used to prosecute Johnson by violating his First Amendment right to engage in peaceful symbolic political protest. Rejecting its own *Deeds* analysis as inadequate in light of subsequent Supreme Court decisions, notably *Spence*, the court endorsed the Court of Appeals opinion that Johnson had engaged in "symbolic speech," but rejected that court's conclusion that Texas had interests compelling enough to justify overriding his constitutional rights.

The court rejected Dallas's asserted interest in outlawing flag desecration to protect the peace on the grounds that "there was no breach of peace" in the Johnson incident and that by banning all flag desecration that caused merely "serious offense," the Texas law outlawed "protected conduct which has no propensity to result in breaches of the peace." The court relied heavily on the Supreme Court's 1943 *Barnette* compulsory flag salute case in also rejecting the state's claimed interest in preserving the flag as a symbol of unity as inadequate to justify abridging Johnson's First Amendment rights and in constructing the heart of its analysis:

> Recognizing that the right to differ is the centerpiece of our First Amendment freedoms, a government cannot mandate by fiat a feeling of unity in its citizens. Therefore, that very same government cannot carve out a symbol of unity and prescribe a set of approved messages to be associated with that symbol when it cannot mandate the status or feeling the symbol purports to represent. If the state has a legitimate interest in promoting a State approved symbol of unity, that interest is not so compelling as to essentially license the flag's use for only the promotion of the governmental status quo.

The court added, citing *Barnette*, that for Texas to legally override Johnson's First Amendment rights to promote national unity it would have to demonstrate that Johnson's action posed a "grave and immediate danger" that the flag would lose its ability to "rouse feelings of unity or patriotism" and become devalued "into a meaningless piece of cloth. We do not believe such a danger is present." Therefore, the court declared that the Texas law was unconstitutional when "used to punish acts of flag desecration when such conduct falls within the protections of the First Amendment." The court declined to address the question of whether Texas could prosecute flag desecration that did "not constitute speech under the First Amendment," declaring instead that "our holding that the statute is unconstitutional as applied to this appellant renders a facial determination [as to the constitutionality of the statute itself] unnecessary." Having overturned Johnson's conviction on the basis of the First Amendment to the federal Constitution, the court did not address whether the law might also violate the free speech clause of the Texas Constitution.

In his 1990 interview, Judge Campbell said that the five-judge majority originally intended to declare the law facially unconstitutional on First Amendment grounds, and that the narrower ruling striking down the law only as *applied* to political protesters was written to obtain the pledged support of a sixth judge who subsequently reneged on his agreement and voted against the redrafted opinion. Stanley Weinberg, Johnson's lawyer, reported in a 1990 interview that court sources had told him that the court majority decided to avoid addressing the law's legality under the Texas Constitution specifically to reserve the right to strike it down on such grounds if the Supreme Court overruled its decision on federal constitutionality (the Supreme Court cannot overrule decisions of state courts concerning interpretations of state constitutions).

Campbell explained that he became the author of the ruling by pure chance, because the court assigns the writing of opinions to judges by having them draw "little plastic balls" with numbers on them even before the majority position of the court is established on a case, leaving it up to the "winner" to try to rally other judges to his opinion. Campbell, who was interviewed attired in shorts and a T-shirt on a hot spring day in the court's conference room in Austin, wryly recalled, "I'm the lucky fellow who drew Gregory Johnson." He added that after reading the briefs, hearing oral argument, and researching the case with Stanfield's help, he concluded that "Supreme Court precedent in this area was crystal clear, and to write it in any other way was just to completely ignore precedent with everything the Supreme Court has ever said about the First Amendment. As a judge, what I feel about the law personally cannot enter into how I interpret it from an objective standpoint."

Campbell said that he was particularly influenced by the 1943 Supreme Court *Barnette* ruling outlawing compulsory school flag salutes and by two "pretty clear" 1974 Supreme Court precedents overturning flag desecration convictions. According to Campbell, the *Johnson* conviction "just was not that different from the *[Spence]* peace symbol on the flag or the *[Goguen]* flag sown on the seat of the pants," because although the Supreme Court had not specifically decided any case "where there had been complete destruction of the flag, there was no way to distinguish it, unless you just wanted to make up some kind of magical distinction without a difference. It didn't seem like a tremendously difficult issue to address."

Campbell declared that flag burning is "symbolic speech" just as much as "putting the peace symbol on the flag. Gregory Johnson was symbolically disagreeing with his government, which I think the First Amendment gives him the right to do. He doesn't have to stand out there and shout. He can express it through symbolic means and that's what he was doing." Campbell added that, even aside from the fundamental First Amendment issues involved in the case, he "certainly" agreed with those who viewed the Texas venerated objects law as "terribly worded and just loaded with problems." In answer to those who argued that flag desecration would tarnish the value of a symbol that was critical to maintaining national unity, Campbell responded that the "symbol itself stays in place" despite the destruction of individual flags. He added that "if the sense of national unity is so fragile" that destroying some flags would endanger it, "then maybe the symbol of national unity is not that important anyway. If it's as strong as I think it is, it's not going to diminish national unity at all."

Campbell said that after Stanfield drafted an opinion under his direction and circulated it to the other judges, "It was not easy at all" to obtain majority support for his position, and discussions within the court were "heated, no doubt about it." He made clear that the "heated" discussions included concerns about possible adverse political consequences for the careers of the court's elected judges: "We discussed it and I'm not going to say that we didn't because that would be fudging the truth. I was aware that it was gonna cause me some problems with the veterans' groups and folks like that. We discussed it and finally I decided that it was written correctly, that it was the correct interpretation of the law."

Campbell added that some elected judges have "got their finger up in the air trying to figure out which way the wind is blowing all of the time," and that pressures in that direction can be especially strong for judges on the Court of Criminal Appeals, because they must run in statewide elections that require raising large sums of money, but "most of our constituents [that is, those most directly affected by the court's rulings] are locked in the penitentiary and don't make much money." But, he concluded, "One of the things that you better be aware of before you ever come up here is that you're going to have cases like this, and if you're not prepared to decide them honestly then you probably shouldn't be in this building, probably you ought to be looking for a job somewhere else."

According to Campbell and others involved in the case, the ruling attracted substantial press coverage and considerable adverse reaction in Texas, but the response was far less than that provoked in Texas and across the nation by the 1989 Supreme Court ruling upholding its decision. According to Campbell, public reaction was "heavier than in any case" in his eight years on the court, and it "was all of one mind," with "hundreds" of letters and phone calls and not "one single letter" supporting the ruling. Some of the letters were "abusive and threatening," he recalled, "although only in the sense of 'You can forget about being reelected next time, Charley,' that kind of thing, not physically threatening, certainly abusive in the sense that 'You're wacko, a communist.'" Nonetheless, only seven months after the April ruling, Campbell was re-elected to his judgeship.

Like the Supreme Court ruling that endorsed it a little over a year later, the Texas Court of Criminal Appeals decision was based on the narrowest possible 5 to 4 margin, and it stunned many observers—again, exactly like the subsequent high court ruling—because it was based squarely on fundamental First Amendment considerations the courts had usually avoided in flag desecration cases, because it came from a court that had a general reputation for highly conservative decisions, and because two of the judges in the majority, Campbell and Bill White, were widely viewed as extremely conservative. In 1990 interviews, Dallas prosecutor Drew recalled being "flabbergasted" by the ruling from an "extremely conservative" court; former prosecutor Nation termed it "very much unlike" the court's track record; Johnson's lawyer Weinberg declared, it "just surprised the heck out of me"; Judge Hendrik, the original trial court judge, declared that he was "quite a bit surprised" at the ruling, but added that although he disagreed with it, the decision "had to increase my respect" for the court because it "took a bit of political courage" to issue it; and Doug Skemp, Johnson's other lawyer, expressed the same view in far earthier terms: "It took a lot of balls for them to do what they did."

Drew's "flabbergasted" reaction was reflected in a brief she filed on behalf of the Dallas district attorney on May 3, 1988, asking the Court of Criminal Appeals to rehear the case, which concluded that "public burning of a United States flag simply cannot constitute protected speech, be it 'symbolic speech' or not," and that the state "must be permitted to regulate in this area." However, on June 8, 1988, the court, by 5 to 4, declined to reconsider its decision, leaving Dallas with the sole recourse of appealing to the United States Supreme Court. On July 26, Dallas filed with the Supreme Court a petition for a writ of certiorari, or agreement to hear the case on appeal, which the Supreme Court grants only when at least four of its nine justices agree to hear a case. The stage was now set for the flag desecration controversy to return to the national arena for the first time in over fifteen years.

{ *Flag Burning and Free Speech* }

CHAPTER 4

The Supreme Court and *Texas v. Johnson,* Fall 1988–Spring 1989

The Supreme Court Decision to Hear *Texas v. Johnson*

Dallas's petition for certiorari, officially made in the name of the state of Texas, was docketed upon its receipt by Supreme Court officials on July 27, 1988, as *Texas v. Johnson,* No. 88-155. During the Court's 1989–1990 term, it would receive about 5,000 requests to hear cases, and grant but 122 of them. These figures are somewhat misleading, however, because about 60 percent of all requests for certiorari are so-called "pauper's petitions," usually made in longhand by incarcerated criminals with normal filing fees waived, and the Court grants far less than 1 percent of such requests, partly because most of them do not raise significant questions of constitutional law. The "paid" petitions, like that of Texas, filed by lawyers and accompanied by a $200 filing fee, are accepted at a considerably higher, if still long-shot, rate of about 3 percent.

Texas faced an additional hurdle that almost prevented the Court from even considering its petition and therefore could have aborted the entire 1989–1990 flag desecration controversy. Under its 1988 rules, after the Texas Court of Criminal Appeals overturns a lower court decision on constitutional grounds, it allows seventy-five days for the Supreme Court to decide whether to hear an appeal before directing the original trial court to void the conviction and thus terminate the case. When the Supreme Court failed to rule on the certiorari petition within the requisite period following the Texas court's refusal to reconsider its ruling, the Criminal Appeals judges issued a formal directive to Judge Hendrik on September 8 to carry out its decision. However, before Hendrik—who was sympathetic to the appeal and was apparently dragging his feet—carried out the order, the Supreme Court justices began to informally discuss *Johnson*. Although Justice White had refused on September 1 to order the Texas court to delay its directive to Hendrik, according to an October 7 memorandum to Chief Justice Rehnquist from Justice John Paul Stevens, four of his colleagues, the minimum needed, had "indicated an intention to vote to grant cert" in *Johnson* and he therefore agreed to "make a fifth vote to grant Texas's application for a stay" of the order. This minidrama ended on October 11 when Rehnquist ordered the Texas court to stay its order until the Supreme Court had formally made its now-preordained decision to grant certiorari, which was reached and publicly announced on October 17.

The Supreme Court generally does not explain why it decides to hear cases, and especially since in *Johnson* it granted certiorari and then subsequently upheld the Texas court, some observers criticized it for needlessly provoking a national uproar when it could have simply let the Texas ruling stand. For example, in his book *The Rehnquist Court*, scholar Stanley Friedelbaum notes that *Johnson* provoked serious attempts to amend the Constitution that might have led to "an attenuation of expressive liberty," and termed the decision to hear the case a potentially "costly and ill-advised venture" because "it is difficult to detect any constructive rationale in support of a full-scale judicial foray when the goals sought by a majority had been attained [in the Texas court ruling]." Similarly, Supreme Court reporter Richard Carelli asked, in the aftermath of *Johnson*, "Why did they take it? The Court could have denied cert with the same effect."

Such comments assume that when the Court granted certiorari a five-man majority had already decided to uphold the Texas court ruling. At the time of the certiorari announcement, however, most observers concluded exactly the opposite: that the Supreme Court took the case because it wanted to overturn the lower court. This analysis reflected the general consensus that the Rehnquist Court was more conservative than the Warren and Burger Courts—which had overturned three flag desecration convictions between 1969 and 1974—and took note that although agreeing to hear

Johnson, in which a lower court had *overturned* a conviction on constitutional grounds, the Court had repeatedly refused since 1974 to hear appeals in flag desecration cases that almost invariably involved lower court rulings *upholding* convictions in flag burning cases. Moreover, Supreme Court justices tend to vote to hear cases especially when they view them as incorrectly decided below. In public statements, for example, Chief Justice Rehnquist has said that "there is an ideological division on the Court and each of us has some cases we would like to see granted," and the "most common reason" Supreme Court justices "vote to grant *certiorari* is that they doubt the correctness of the decision of the lower court." In the 1995 term, the Court affirmed lower court holdings in only 32 percent of cases in which it granted certiorari and decided with full opinions.

Since the vast majority of certiorari petitions are rejected without any serious consideration by the Court—almost 90 percent are denied unanimously and without discussion—one or more justices undoubtedly took an interest in *Johnson* at an early stage. Given Rehnquist's unusually important influence over the Court's certiorari agenda in his role as chief justice and his record in enthusiastically supporting flag desecration laws in his *Goguen* and *Spence* dissents, Rehnquist was probably the moving force in the Court's vote to hear *Johnson;* this speculation is supported by the 1999 recollection of a Court clerk who served in 1988–1989 who recalled that one of Rehnquist's clerks had vigorously lobbied other clerks to urge "their" justices to grant certiorari.

Even Texas Court of Criminal Appeals judge Campbell said in a 1990 interview that he had interpreted the certiorari decision as portending a reversal of his opinion: "I didn't see any reason why they would want to grant cert and then turn around and affirm me for Christ's sake, because the law was so crystal clear. Usually when the Supreme Court grants cert in a case like that it's because they're going to signal a new direction. I thought that they had decided that they were gonna change the rules and reinterpret the whole concept of what speech was under the First Amendment." Contemporary analyses of the certiorari announcement generally shared Campbell's view: civil liberties lawyer Martin Garbus predicted that the Court would find Johnson guilty by a 6 to 3 vote that would "seriously impair the right of free speech" and "stand as a precedent for years," and Dallas Civil Liberties Union president Joe Cook termed the certiorari decision "part of the [Court's] creeping fascism." Johnson himself told a reporter, "I don't really think they took the case so they could rule in my favor."

The 1993 release, shortly after the death of Justice Thurgood Marshall, of his previously secret Supreme Court records make clear that those who viewed the certiorari decision as signaling the Court's inclination to reinstate Johnson's conviction were almost certainly correct. Marshall's papers reveal that the certiorari vote was 5 to 4, with the justices generally regarded as conservative (Rehnquist, White, Sandra Day O'Connor, Antonin Scalia, and Anthony Kennedy) voting to hear the case, and the relatively liberal justices (Brennan, Marshall, Blackmun, and Stevens) voting in the negative. That Rehnquist was so publicly on record in his 1974 *Spence* and *Goguen* dissents as viewing flag desecration laws as constitutional, whereas Brennan had made equally clear in his 1982 *U.S. v. Kime* dissent that he held a strongly opposite viewpoint, further bolsters this interpretation. Moreover, Marshall's records reveal that his clerk recommended that he vote against granting certiorari because the lower court had "properly struck down the application" of the Texas law in its ruling.

Soon after the Court's October 17 certiorari announcement, Johnson decided to change lawyers, apparently in hopes of increasing the public and political profile of the case. On November 6, he wrote Weinberg to express "sincere gratitude" to Weinberg and Skemp for their "dedication" and "enormous amount of work," but added that "because of the nature and magnitude of this case and its national significance," he had retained the assistance of New York civil liberties lawyer William Kunstler. Kunstler, one of the founders of the Center for Constitutional Rights (CCR), an organization dedicated to providing legal defense without charge in civil liberties cases, was perhaps the most famous "radical" lawyer in the country.

Kunstler's reputation had been especially forged by his flamboyant defense of the so-called Chicago Seven, political radicals who had been charged with interstate conspiracy to provoke rioting at the 1968 Democratic National Convention, as a result of which he had been condemned to over four years in jail for contempt of court before the sentence was overturned on appeal. Earlier, Kunstler had been decorated for his World War II combat service in the Philippines, earned a law degree from Columbia University, defended civil rights workers in the South during the 1960s, and served as a legal consultant to Martin Luther King Jr. Kunstler told a reporter in 1989 that until his defense of the Chicago Seven, he had been a "traditional civil-rights attorney" who "believed in the system," but "after Chicago, it totally changed. I now see the legal system as an enemy." Attorney Gerald Lefcourt, who also represented "radical" clients during the 1960s, told a journalist in 1989 that Kunstler, who represented clients for the CCR without compensation in about 60 percent of his practice in the late 1980s, was always eager to represent the most unpopular defendants: "If a black guy was charged with rape in South Dakota of a white woman and a mob was out there ready to lynch him, Bill would be on the next plane."

According to 1990 and 1991 interviews with the key participants, Johnson was drawn to Kunstler by the latter's high media profile and obvious fondness for publicity, and his willingness to conduct the type of public, political defense that Johnson wanted to complement the lower-profile, legal defense required in the courtroom. Skemp recalled that "all of a sudden we heard from Johnson that he hired Kunstler," and "the deal was" that Johnson "wanted to raise money and he wanted to do these high-powered things and Kunstler was going to help him do it." Weinberg recalled that Johnson's decision "didn't really bother me that much," but added that he did regret "not being able to have that one little wonderful moment of glory up in front of the Supreme Court." Kunstler recalled, "I didn't know who [Johnson] was" and knew "absolutely nothing about the case" when he received a telegram from Johnson in November, but his impression was that Johnson hired him because "I'd be better known than the Texas attorneys who did a very good job for him. Also the CCR had the funds to take the case and publicize it and I think he probably thought his politics and my politics were a bit closer than the Texas lawyers." Kunstler added that Johnson didn't want his lawyers to "handle the matter as if it were a stinking fish that we didn't really want to soil our hands with," but wanted "enthusiasm about the act [of flag burning] itself," and that his taking the case involved the understanding that CCR lawyers "would address meetings, would speak in universities, would accept speaking engagements" about it, and "would not take public positions that would in any way interfere" with Johnson's "own political feelings."

Johnson declared that although his Texas attorneys "really need to be commended" for a "very, very good job," he decided to retain Kunstler because "this was an enormously important case and Kunstler is known throughout the world for representing radical causes." Asked if differences with the Texas attorneys had played a role in his decision, Johnson would only say that "the struggle with a client-attorney relationship has got to be, if not, you're just like the guy who goes to the doctor and says, 'Do whatever you want with me, doctor.' I always play an active role in the defense. I think political people should. For that matter, there's been discussion and struggles with my new attorneys."

Although Kunstler became the public face of Johnson's defense, the vast majority of the legal research and writing that ensued was carried out by CCR attorney David Cole, thirty, who had won numerous controversial civil liberties cases since graduating in 1984 from Yale Law School. In a 1990 interview, Kunstler, then seventy and sporting flowing gray sideburns, a booming voice, and a brash public persona, described Cole, who conveyed a modest, gentle style in speech, dress, and aura, as an "absolutely brilliant brief writer." Comparing himself to puppeteer Edgar Bergen's famous wooden friend, Kunstler added, "Cole did three-fourths of the brief. I was like Charlie McCarthy—he handed it to me [for presentation at oral argument] and said 'Go!'" In a common assessment of Cole, Paul Hoffman of the ACLU Foundation of Southern California told a reporter in 1989 that Cole was the "most brilliant young civil rights attorney in the country."

In a 1999 interview, Cole recalled that when he began working on the case in late 1989, "I had very little doubt that the Supreme Court would say, 'You can't throw people in jail for burning the flag.' I felt this was the clear direction of prior flag cases." Cole added that had he known of the certiorari vote lineup he would have concluded differently, namely that the more conservative justices "thought they had the votes to say you couldn't burn the flag." Cole recalled that in writing his brief he tried to present the Court with a "number of ways in which this case could be resolved in our favor without reaching the ultimate question as to whether flag burning was protected by the Constitution," such as noting the "particularly vulnerable" language of the Texas statute and the argument that Johnson might have been convicted for his words alone, because in previous cases the Court "did not necessarily want to confront the issue." He said that therefore, although he "always thought we would prevail," the Court's ultimate embrace of the "central issue" in striking down flag desecration laws used to prosecute political dissenters "surprised me," as did the "narrow margin" of the Court's 5 to 4 vote on Johnson's behalf.

In another 1999 interview, Kunstler's law partner, Ron Kuby, who acted as liaison with the RCP, recalled Johnson as "personally a lovely guy, committed and thoughtful and intelligent and brave." Kuby added that Johnson and other RCP members who worked on the case "were respectful of the lawyers but not deferential to them" and that "all the men and women of the RCP were wonderful, wonderful people to work with. They were passionate, dedicated, devoted, thoughtful, the kind of people you'd want to help build a new country." According to Kuby, the relationship with the RCP was "a much closer collaborative effort than you tend to see between lawyers and clients, and it was a tribute to the intelligence and knowledge of the clients that they could work with some of America's best civil rights lawyers and contribute meaningfully." In a 1991 interview, Kunstler similarly described the relationship between the defense lawyers and Johnson as "friends and colleagues as well as attorneys" and a "real working relationship," in which Johnson had "input" and the right of final approval of the Supreme Court legal brief.

Other Flag Controversies, Fall 1988–Winter 1989

Although typically a Supreme Court decision to simply hear a case attracts little media attention, the Court's October 17 announcement was given wide and prominent coverage, including a front-page story in the *Washington Post* and lengthy articles in many other leading newspapers. This unusual coverage reflected the fact that another highly contentious and symbolic political dispute concerning the flag had already become a central issue in the 1998 presidential contest owing to Republican candidate George Bush's repeated references to a hitherto obscure veto cast in 1977 by Democratic candidate Michael Dukakis, when he was governor of Massachusetts, of a law requiring public school teachers to lead daily recitations of the Pledge of Allegiance. Thus, in reporting the Supreme Court's decision to hear *Johnson,* United Press International declared that "debate over the sanctity of the American flag" had "moved from the campaign trail to the Supreme Court," and the *Washington Post* said that the Court had acted "at a time when the flag has become a potent symbol in the campaign for president."

Dukakis's veto, which was later overturned by the state legislature, was based on legal advice from both the Massachusetts Supreme Judicial Court and the Massachusetts attorney general that the law was unconstitutional under the Supreme Court's 1943 *Barnette* ruling banning compulsory flag salutes in the public schools. Bush effectively impugned Dukakis's patriotism by repeatedly referring to the veto, for example coupling the veto with allegations that Dukakis was "soft on crime" by declaring, "I simply can't understand the thinking that lets first-degree murderers" out of jail "so they can rape and plunder again and not be willing to let the teachers lead the kids in the Pledge of Allegiance." At one point Bush asked, "What is it about the American flag which upsets this man so much?" Much like the McKinley campaign of 1896 that had helped fuel the original flag protection movement, Bush surrounded his campaign stops and advertisements with flags, as well as habitually leading his audiences in mass recitals of the Pledge of Allegiance and even visiting a flag factory.

Bush stressed the Pledge of Allegiance issue so much, in a campaign largely devoid of other issues, that *Time* magazine declared in early October that "Five weeks after the Republican convention, the public can be certain of [only] two things about George Bush: he loves the flag and he believes in pledging allegiance to it every morning. But some voters may wonder what he would do with the rest of his day if he became president." A *New York Times* reporter wrote that whereas Bush asked "from sea to shining sea" why Dukakis vetoed the 1977 bill, Dukakis responded by citing *Barnette*, giving an "answer that was scholarly, cogent and politically devastating."

Because, by general consensus, Bush effectively used the flag controversy (for example, a postelection survey indicated that about 40 percent of all respondents said that the Pledge of Allegiance issue had been "very important" to them in determining their vote), memories of the uproar, together with the impact of Bush's so-called "thirty-second negative ads" attacking Dukakis as soft on crime, would remain for a long time in politicians' minds and strongly affect their subsequent reaction to the Supreme Court's 1989 *Johnson* decision. Even before the 1988 campaign was over, Democrats were already reacting to the Pledge of Allegiance issue by trying to cut their political losses: the Democratic-controlled House of Representatives decided to begin each session with a joint recital of the Pledge of Allegiance, and by the end of his campaign Dukakis began surrounding his own campaign rallies with flags and leading them in recitals of the Pledge of Allegiance.

Shortly before the March 21, 1989, Supreme Court oral argument on *Johnson*, yet another heated dispute over the flag erupted, centering on an art exhibit at the School of the Art Institute of Chicago (SAIC). The controversial exhibit, by black student "Dread" Scott Tyler, twenty-three, was part of a large art display by minority students that opened on February 17. Tyler's exhibit featured a wall-mounted photographic collage of flag burnings and flag-draped coffins, together with a flag placed on the floor and a ledger attached to the wall under the collage in which visitors were asked to record their responses to the exhibit title, "What is the Proper Way to Display the American Flag?" Veterans' groups were outraged that the flag was placed so that patrons seemed invited to walk on it to write in the ledger, and the exhibit set off weeks of protests in Chicago. A demonstration on March 12 by five thousand people forced the closing of Michigan Avenue, a major downtown artery, to traffic and attracted eleven Chicago aldermen, ten state legislators, and a variety of other politicians who lent their support.

SAIC was forced to spend $250,000 for extra security in connection with the demonstrations and the exhibit, which drew record crowds that eventually became so large that SAIC officials limited visitors to eight minutes. According to a 1990 interview with SAIC president Anthony Jones, during the course of the exhibit SAIC received many letters and phone calls that "were very, very violent and dangerous" and "I had to pull the female staff off the telephones because the level of sexual vulgarity and violence was so outrageous that they were very, very upset. There were people who had guns and knives and bomb threats and death threats and everything you could think of."

In response to the exhibit, the Illinois legislature amended the state flag desecration law to ban putting the American flag on the floor and also reduced funding for SAIC and the Illinois Arts Alliance, which had supported the SAIC's right to display the exhibit, to $1 each from previous levels, respectively, of $65,000 and $20,000. On March 16, the Chicago City Council also outlawed placing flags on the floor as part of a broader ordinance that banned displaying "any article or substance" bearing a representation of the flag (which was supported by council members who were wearing flag buttons and lapel pins).

The SAIC exhibit also evoked responses on the national level. On March 15, President Bush termed it "disgraceful," although he added that he was "very wary" of criminally punishing people for such displays, since "I'm always worried about the right of free speech." On March 16, only two days before the exhibit closed and five days before Supreme Court oral argument in *Johnson*, the Senate voted 97 to 0—without hearings and after only fifteen minutes of debate— to amend, for the first time, the 1968 federal flag desecration law to include outlawing maintaining a flag on the floor, in response to a measure introduced by Senate Republican leader Robert Dole and cosponsored by thirty-six other senators. Subsequently, a provision banning flags on the floor was included in the Flag Protection Act of 1989, which Congress passed in October in an attempt to overturn *Johnson* as an alternative to a constitutional amendment.

Just as much of the news coverage of the Supreme Court's October 1988 decision to grant certiorari in *Johnson* had been greatly fostered by and linked with the politicization of the flag during the 1988 presidential election, the Chicago controversy and the imminent Supreme Court oral argument were often discussed together in the media and clearly spurred increased news coverage of both. For example, on March 13 the *Los Angeles Times* ran parallel lengthy stories on the two controversies. Johnson, who had been touring the country during the winter of 1988–1989 seeking to bring attention to his case, told a reporter that until the Chicago controversy erupted "we had difficulty getting a lot of interest." Johnson and Tyler, the artist at the center of the Chicago uproar, quickly perceived the publicity advantage gained by linking the two cases: they appeared together, along with Kunstler, on several radio and TV shows, and issued statements in support of one another. For example, Johnson declared that "suppression of antipatriotic art and speech go hand-in-hand with enforcement of respect for the flag and compulsory loyalty to the government it symbolizes," and characterized the "attack" on Tyler and "the threat of the Supreme Court to reinstate my conviction" as representing "desperate steps" by a "sick and dying empire desperately clutching to its symbols."

The Bush administration also linked the two flag desecration controversies. In response to calls by veterans' groups and congressmen for toughened flag desecration legislation and prosecutions in response to the Chicago flag exhibit, the White House and the Justice Department both indicated an inclination to await a ruling in *Johnson* before taking any action. Thus, in a White

House–cleared response to a query from Senator John McCain, the Justice Department advised that "before deciding whether any amendments" to the 1968 federal flag desecration law "are warranted, we should await the Supreme Court's decision in *Texas v. Johnson*," since the Court's ruling "may not only determine whether the statute is constitutional as it currently exists, but it may also provide important guidance in determining the extent to which such behavior towards the flag may be constitutionally proscribed." In a letter to an Illinois veterans' group, the Justice Department similarly suggested that it would hold off in further federal flag desecration prosecutions while awaiting *Johnson*. Assistant Attorney General Edward Dennis advised that since the enactment of the 1968 law, "judicial decisions" had made its enforcement "more difficult," since "a number of cases" had determined that "activities that may be considered to be desecration of the flag to many Americans" are "protected by the First Amendment," and federal prosecution was "precluded" where "an acquittal of a defendant is likely, especially if the basis for such an anticipated acquittal appears to be the defendant's free exercise of judicially recognized constitutional liberties." Dennis added that "current enforcement" was "further complicated" because the Supreme Court "has before it a flag desecration case in which the exercise of free speech is a key issue." The White House insisted, in the words of an April 18, 1989, memo written by Patricia Bryan, associate legal counsel to President Bush, that such letters include "strong language condemning desecration of the American flag as unpatriotic."

———

Oral Argument Before the Supreme Court in *Texas v. Johnson*, March 21, 1989

The Supreme Court heard an hour of oral argument in *Johnson* on March 21, 1989. Dallas Assistant District Attorney Kathi Drew, making her first appearance before the Court, began her presentation by declaring that "for purposes of this argument today," Texas would "assume" that Johnson's flag burning constituted "symbolic speech." She then began to summarize Dallas's long-standing argument that the state had interests that overrode Johnson's First Amendment rights, but was unable to elaborate her position before she was bombarded with extremely hostile questions from two of the Court's leading conservative justices, Scalia and Kennedy. Brennan, Blackmun, and Marshall, who were widely expected to disagree with her, remained silent as Scalia rejected Drew's position that flag desecration would harm the flag's symbolic value and Kennedy made clear that he would have difficulty accepting her position that flag desecration was "speech" yet not constitutionally protected. Both suggested that they viewed the Texas law as an unconstitutional "content-based" restraint on dissident speech, and their questions seemed replete with incredulity at Drew's arguments and with suggestions that she was attempting to draw arbitrary and meaningless distinctions, such as arguing that the government could constitutionally ban flag desecration but not outlaw destruction of other symbols like the Constitution or Stars of David.

The official Court transcript includes the following dialogue between Drew and her primary antagonists:

DREW: We believe that preservation of the flag as a symbol of nationhood and national unity is a compelling and valid state interest. . . .

SCALIA: Now, why does the . . . defendant's actions here destroy the symbol? His actions would have been useless unless the flag was a very good symbol for what he intended to show contempt for. His action does not make it any less a symbol.

DREW: Your Honor, we believe that if a symbol over a period of time is ignored or abused that it can, in fact, lose its symbolic effect.

SCALIA: I think not at all. I think when somebody does that to the flag, the flag becomes even more a symbol of the country. . . . [Y]ou not just want a symbol, but you want a venerated symbol, and you don't make that argument because then you're getting into a sort of content preference. But I don't see how you can argue that he's making it any less of a symbol than it was.

DREW: Your Honor, I'm forced to disagree with you. . . . Texas is not suggesting that we can insist on respect. We are suggesting that we have the right to preserve the physical integrity of the flag so that it may serve as a symbol because its symbolic effect is diluted by certain flagrant public acts of flag desecration. . . .

KENNEDY: What is the juridical category you're asking us to adopt in order to say we can punish this kind of speech? . . . [T]here's just a flag exception of the First Amendment?

DREW: To a certain extent, we have made that argument in our brief. . . .

SCALIA: Could Texas prohibit the burning of copies of the Constitution, state or federal?

DREW: Not to my knowledge, Your Honor.

SCALIA: Well, how do you pick out what to protect? I mean, you know, if I had to pick between the Constitution and the flag, I might well go with the Constitution. . . .

DREW: Texas in this area . . . has made a judgment that certain items are entitled to more protection. . . .

SCALIA: But we up to now have never allowed such an item to be declared a national symbol and to be usable symbolically only in one direction, which is essentially what you're arguing. You can honor it all you like, but you can't dishonor it as a sign of disrespect for the country. . . .

DREW: Not at all. We are in no way arguing that one cannot dishonor the flag or that one cannot demonstrate disrespect for the flag. . . . What we are arguing is that you may not publicly desecrate a flag, regardless of the motivation for your action.

SCALIA: Well, one hardly desecrates it in order to honor it. I mean, you only desecrate it in order to show your disagreement with what it stands for, isn't that right? So, it is sort of a one-way statute. . . .

DREW: Not necessarily.

SCALIA: Will you give me an example where one—somebody desecrates the flag in order to show that he agrees with the policies of the United States. . . . (General Laughter)

DREW: I think it is possible . . . that an individual could choose to burn a flag as an honor for all the individuals who died in Vietnam. . . .

SCALIA: Your statute would cover that example? . . .

DREW: Yes, it would, Your Honor, because it does not go to the motive of the actor. . . . I'd like to turn very briefly, if I may, to the breach of the peace interest. We do feel that preventing a breach of the peace is a legitimate state interest. . . .

SCALIA: I suppose . . . if that theory alone is enough to support the statute . . . you could have such statutes for Stars of David and crosses . . . or whatever might incite people. . . .

DREW: [T]here are other sections of this statute where other items are protected, specifically public monuments, places of burial and worship. I don't believe that anyone could suggest that one may paint swastikas on the Alamo. . . .

KENNEDY: [B]ut that's because it's public property. . . .

DREW: I think the flag is this nation's cherished property, . . . And you protect the flag because it is such an important symbol of national unity. . . .

SCALIA: I never thought that the flag I owned is your flag. (General Laughter)

Kunstler, representing Johnson, maintained that the Texas law was clearly unconstitutional because it targeted expression and because Dallas had failed to present a convincing argument that its interests should override Johnson's free speech rights. When Justice Stevens, a World War II veteran, asked Kunstler if he believed the federal government had "any power at all to regulate" how the flag was "displayed in public places," Kunstler replied, "I don't think so," as he did not see "any state interest whatsoever." Stevens responded, "I feel quite differently," and, according to observers, his body language suggested that he was strongly offended. In a 1998 book, Edward Lazarus, who was a clerk during the 1989–1990 Supreme Court term, remembered Stevens's demeanor at oral argument as being "infuriated" at Johnson and "uncharacteristically testy" with Kunstler; in a 1999 interview, Kunstler's partner, David Cole, recalled that Stevens "visibly turned red and was clearly quite angry" at Kunstler's response.

{ *The Supreme Court and* Texas v. Johnson }   95

Cole said that Kunstler's response was "clearly the wrong answer," because Kunstler should have replied that the government did have an interest that "justified spending money to educate people about the flag," but "not the kind of compelling interest" that "justified throwing people in jail for burning the flag." Kunstler himself said in a 1991 interview that before oral argument he would have predicted a 9 to 0 Supreme Court vote in his favor because "the precedents were so clear," but that after Stevens's "very hostile question" he concluded that "I didn't have Stevens at all." Kunstler added that thereafter he still anticipated a "8 to 1 or 7 to 2" victory, and that the ultimate 5 to 4 decision for his position "really kind of shocked me," an impact he attributed to his failing to foresee that "feeling about the flag was so intense," even among Supreme Court justices, "when it came to actually burning the flag."

Kunstler's original expectation of a 9 to 0 victory was always unrealistic because Rehnquist—whom Kunstler termed a "vile human being" in the 1991 interview—was always a certain vote against Johnson. Rehnquist strongly challenged Kunstler at oral argument on several points, especially with regard to his claim that the Supreme Court's 1943 *Barnette* ruling striking down compulsory flag salutes in the public schools had already settled the flag desecration controversy. But their exchanges were relatively gentle. Kunstler joked at one point, "I don't know if I've convinced you," to which Rehnquist responded, to general laughter, "Well, you may have convinced others." In another exchange, Rehnquist said, "I don't think we're going to reach eye to eye on this," to which Kunstler replied, "I have that distinct feeling."

The official transcript includes the following remarks by Kunstler and Rehnquist:

> KUNSTLER: [T]his particular [Texas] act that we're concerned with . . . singles out communicative impact for punishment. . . . With reference to the nationhood and national unity, . . . I thought *Barnette* set that to rest. I thought that when Justice Jackson said that if there is any fixed star in our constitutional constellation, it is that no official, high or petty, can prescribe what shall be orthodox in politics, nationalism—

REHNQUIST: Well, the facts of *West Virginia v. Barnette* were quite different from this. There the students were required to salute the flag.

KUNSTLER: And here . . . people are required not to do something. . . . And I think that's a comparable situation. We can't order you to salute the flag, we can't order you to do all these obeisances with relation to the flag. . . .

REHNQUIST: Well, to me they're quite different. . . . [I]t seems to me one could quite easily say, you can't do one but you can do the other. . . .

KUNSTLER: With reference to breach of the peace, . . . [i]f you're going to forbid flag desecration, the threat of violence has to be so imminent that it really reaches clear and present danger proportions. . . . The statute here . . . doesn't say imminent breach of the peace at all. It just says "likely" or "might" or "The actor could reasonably believe that someone might be seriously offended by it." . . . The protest in this case did not lead to violence. . . . nor does the record reflect that the situation was potentially explosive. One cannot equate serious offense with incitement to breach the peace. . . . On vagueness and overbreadth, I think the vagueness is apparent. . . . What does "serious offense" mean? What is "unserious offense" as against "serious offense"? . . . You don't even know what physical mistreatment means in the statute. Does physical mistreatment mean wearing it, twisting it, burning it? It's just an undefinable statute. . . .

I think it's a most important case. I sense that it goes to the heart of the First Amendment, to hear things or to see things that we hate test the First Amendment more than seeing or hearing things that we like. It wasn't designed for things we like. They never needed a First Amendment.

Although most predictions published before oral argument had suggested that Johnson's conviction would be reinstated, press commentary thereafter shifted sharply, clearly reflecting the surprisingly hostile nature of the questions put to Drew by Scalia and Kennedy. For example, the *Baltimore Sun*'s veteran Supreme Court reporter Lyle Denniston, in a commentary appearing in *Harper's* magazine (which published an almost complete transcript of the oral argument, a virtually unprecedented indication of how much interest the case had aroused), characterized Drew's arguments as "weak" and noted that, at least on the "face of this case and from the way the justices framed their questions," most readers were likely to "quickly conclude that a decision against Texas is inevitable." Johnson declared on the evening of the oral argument that "things went excellent" and that the Court had made a "very cold, calculated decision" that "to try to ram this down people's throats was gonna be just too politically explosive and costly."

Drew and Kunstler indicated in interviews in 1990 and 1991, respectively, that not surprisingly they had come away from the oral argument with very different perspectives. Drew said, "I felt very good about what I had done," and termed reports such as that in *Harper's*, which suggested she had lost the case, as "not particularly fair." According to Drew, Kunstler had followed "no pattern to his argument whatsoever," but had simply "sort of stood up and rambled. Now I'm not the impartial observer, but this [Kunstler] is a living legend before the Supreme Court and I was really surprised that he had approached it light-heartedly." According to Kunstler, "Drew was not very strong as an arguer. She tried, but I guess this was her first argument and she had a tough row to hoe."

―――――

The Supreme Court Decision in *Texas v. Johnson*

According to the files of two Supreme Court justices, when the Court met in private conference on March 24, three days after oral argument, their preliminary vote indicated probable 7 to 2 support for upholding the ruling of the Texas court. Brennan, Marshall, Blackmun, Scalia, Kennedy, and O'Connor indicated that they would vote to uphold the lower court ruling (although O'Connor indicated her vote was "tentative"), and Stevens said he would "pass" but suggested in his remarks that he was leaning toward the majority position. Only Rehnquist and White indicated solid opposition to Johnson's case. The discussion of *Johnson*, like most Court conferences, essentially consisted of short statements of each justice's views rather than any meaningful discussion (according to one calculation, because of the Court's workload, each case is allotted less than thirty minutes at conference). Thus, when Brennan was asked by a journalist after his 1990 retirement from the Court whether he and Rehnquist had ever had a substantive face-to-face discussion about *Johnson*, he responded, "No. Contrary to belief, there's very little face-to-face debate." Justice Scalia has said, "To call our discussion of a case a conference is really something of a misnomer. It's much more a statement of the views of each of the nine justices, after which the totals are added and the case is assigned [for writing opinions]."

As chief justice, Rehnquist spoke first at the conference. He said that he still endorsed his 1974 *Spence* dissent (which White had joined), because "flag burning and fighting words may be punished constitutionally." Brennan, as the most senior associate justice, spoke next, declaring that the Texas law was unconstitutional because, in the words of a memorandum prepared for him by a clerk, it sought to punish political speech solely "because it might bring offense." Brennan noted that Drew had conceded that the Dallas flag burning constituted "symbolic speech," but he rejected her contention that Texas had overriding interests. As his clerk stated, "the state's argument rests on the idea that the government may punish those who show disrespect for the flag and who might offend others by doing so," but Supreme Court precedents dictated that "the government may not command respect for its institutions by punishing those who do not conform" and that "speech may not be restricted solely because of its communicative impact." Moreover, Brennan added, the "seriously offend" language of the Texas law was unconstitutionally vague because it failed to adequately inform citizens as to what conduct was illegal.

The remaining justices spoke in order of seniority. White maintained that to uphold the Texas court would run the First Amendment "into the ground," but Marshall indicated that he believed the case was controlled by the Court's 1974 *Spence* ruling overturning a flag desecration conviction. Marshall presumably followed the general guidance provided by a clerk's memorandum, which argued that the Texas law was unconstitutional because it was a "content-based regulation aimed at expressive conduct without any compelling [overriding] state interest" that was "unrelated to the expression," and also because the "seriously offend" language was unconstitutionally vague because it provided "no guidance" as to its meaning. Marshall's clerk accurately predicted that Rehnquist and White would be persuaded by the argument that the flag's symbolic representation of "national unity" needed to be protected, but he incorrectly suggested that "maybe even Blackmun" would accept this argument. In fact, Blackmun, speaking next, agreed with Marshall that *Spence* "governs here" in what he termed "another emotional case." Blackmun added that "First Amendment law" required affirming the lower court ruling since "this is expressive conduct and Texas relies on nothing not expressive" to override Johnson's rights.

Stevens said he was "going to pass," but his comments suggested that he intended to vote against Texas, although on "vagueness" rather than free speech grounds because Johnson was "not being punished" for his "message but his manner of communicating it." O'Connor said that although Texas maintained the Court should "carve out" an exception from the First Amendment to uphold the state law, "this is core speech for political purposes" and "our cases require" upholding the lower court. Both Scalia and Kennedy indicated that they agreed with O'Connor.

As senior justice in the majority, Brennan, who had by then served on the Court for thirty-three years, had the right to assign the opinion. On March 31, he wrote Rehnquist that he had decided to write it himself, and Rehnquist formally assigned *Johnson* to him on April 3. Brennan's decision to take the case was not surprising, given his well-known view that the Bill of Rights and the First Amendment, in particular, were at the heart of the American political system. Thus, Brennan told reporters in interviews in 1987 and 1991 that the Constitution's essential purpose was "the protection of the dignity of the human being and the recognition that every individual has fundamental rights which government cannot deny him," and that its heart was the First Amendment because "its enforcement gives us this society" and "the other provisions of the Constitution merely embellish it." In 1990, shortly before his retirement, in response to a reporter's query whether he was disappointed about the increasingly conservative direction of the Court, Brennan responded that he was "not discouraged to the point of giving up," partly because "after all, Kennedy and Scalia joined me on the flag-burning case, for God's sake." Although by 1989 Brennan had participated in over 250 Court decisions concerning free speech since his appointment to the Court in 1957, his *Johnson* opinion would become, in the words of former *New York Times* reporter Tom Wicker in a 1997 book, "probably what Americans remember most vividly of Brennan's long, distinguished service on the Court."

As was Brennan's habit—and that of most of his colleagues—he asked one of his clerks, Lisa Heinzerling, a former editor-in-chief of the *University of Chicago Law Review,* to write a draft opinion. One former Court clerk, in a 1990 interview with a journalist, described this experience by saying, "You go back to your office, you take a deep breath, you stare at your computer screen and you go, 'Holy shit, I'm going to write the law of the land.'" In a 1986 interview, Brennan told a journalist that he typically tries to get his clerks to write opinions that will directly appeal to other justices, attempting to answer such questions as, "Has John Stevens written any cases which may suggest how he is thinking and about which we should be aware? What does Sandra [Day O'Connor] think? You try to get, in advance of circulation, a sense of what will sell, what the others can accept." In a 1990 interview, Brennan told a reporter that he always asks all four of his clerks to agree on a common analysis of the case before submitting a draft to him and that "if we didn't have the benefit of their writing and research, we couldn't handle the workload here," but that he always makes final decisions about wording; according to one of his clerks, quoted in a 1990 interview, Brennan sometimes engaged in "dramatic rewriting."

On June 3, Brennan circulated his opinion—which subsequently became the Court's majority opinion in virtually unchanged form—to his colleagues. Kennedy and Marshall quickly signed on, but Rehnquist circulated a dissenting opinion on June 5, which

White joined two days later. Although Brennan's opinion clearly sought to attract Stevens's vote by declaring, "We reject the suggestion, urged at oral argument" by Kunstler, that the government lacked "any state interest whatsoever" in regulating the display of flags, on June 13 Stevens circulated a dissent, leaving the formal lineup at 3 to 3. However, on June 19, Scalia and Blackmun joined Brennan's opinion, with the latter noting in a letter to Brennan that he had "struggled with this difficult and distasteful little (big?) case but I join your opinion." O'Connor signed on to Rehnquist's vehement dissent the same day, making the final vote 5 to 4. With all the votes counted, on June 20 Rehnquist sent a letter to his colleagues that announced that *Texas v. Johnson* was "ready for [public] announcement Wednesday, June 21."

On June 21, 1989, the Supreme Court made headlines across the nation by ruling 5 to 4 that the Texas Court of Criminal Appeals had correctly held that the Texas venerated objects law had been unconstitutionally applied to deprive Johnson of his First Amendment rights. The very manner in which the Court released its decision provided a foretaste of the intense, bitter, and emotional debate that the ruling was about to touch off in American society. Although typically when the Court announces a ruling its full text is handed out by the Court's press office, while, in public session, the author of the majority opinion reads only a short summary of the Court's holding and dissenters remain silent, in announcing *Texas v. Johnson*, both Brennan, for the majority, and Stevens, in dissent, read lengthy portions (or, according to some accounts, the entire texts) of their opinions. As Edward Lazarus, a Court clerk at the time, noted in his 1998 book *Closed Chambers*, as Stevens read his dissent, an action taken by those in the minority only "a few times each term" on those "rare occasions" when a justice cares "so deeply about a case" and feels "so strongly that the Court has reached the wrong result," his voice was "raw emotion" and as he concluded "his face was flush, his eyes just shy of tears." According to Lazarus, "I doubt anyone who was there has forgotten the moment." The unusual manner of the announcement itself encouraged the news media to massively publicize the ruling: in 1990 interviews, *Washington Post* Supreme Court reporter Ruth Marcus declared that the "extremely emotional" nature of the opinions, especially that Stevens felt "strongly enough to dissent from the bench," was a "pretty good barometer for us, for our news judgment," considering the importance of the case, and CBS News Supreme Court reporter Rita Braver said she concluded that *Johnson* would be a "big story" because of the "soaring quality of the language" of the opinions and "because the justices so passionately cared."

Brennan's opinion resembled that of the Texas court, although it was more elaborate, somewhat more legally rigorous, and more explicitly tied to Supreme Court precedents. Legally, the critical— and only truly new—finding of the Court was buried deep inside the opinion in the statement that, because the 1984 Dallas flag burning had been purely "expressive," any distinction between "written or spoken words and non-verbal conduct" was "of no moment," and therefore the Court's 1969 *Street* ruling invalidating laws that penalized verbal criticism of the flag applied equally to physical flag desecration. After ducking this very issue for twenty years, in *Johnson* the Court not only faced it squarely but avoided an easy out suggested by Johnson's lawyers, who had argued that under the Texas law of parties the jury might have convicted Johnson solely for his speech activities in violation of *Street*. In a little-remarked footnote, the Court brushed aside this possibility, because it was "too unlikely" that Johnson had been convicted "for his words alone" to "consider reversing his conviction" on that basis.

Having concluded that Johnson had been convicted for "burning the flag rather than for uttering insulting words," Brennan next held, using the *Spence* guidelines to determine whether Johnson's flag burning constituted "expressive conduct," that the "expressive, overtly political nature" of Johnson's act was "both intentional and overwhelmingly apparent," given its context in Dallas on the day that the Republican Party was meeting to renominate Ronald Reagan. Having thus held that the Dallas flag burning potentially qualified for First Amendment protection, the Court declared that one of the two interests advanced by Texas to justify overriding any presumptive First Amendment rights, "the state's interest in maintaining order" was simply "not implicated," because "no disturbance of the peace actually occurred or threatened to occur because of Johnson's burning of the flag." Citing its own holdings in *Chaplinsky* and *Brandenburg*, which effectively declared that political speech could only be punished if it threatened to immediately incite disorder, the Court held that to sanction punishing Johnson's flag burning on such grounds would "eviscerate" the high value placed on free expression by Court precedents. Although the Texas law effectively claimed that all flag burnings "necessarily" posed a threat to the peace, Brennan declared, "We have not permitted the government to assume that every expression of a provocative idea will incite a riot, but have instead required a careful consideration of the actual circumstances surrounding such expression."

Turning to the second interest that Texas argued justified overriding Johnson's rights, "preserving the flag as a symbol of nationhood and national unity," Brennan declared that "such concerns blossom only when a person's treatment of the flag communicates some message" and therefore Texas's purpose in passing its law was related "to the suppression of free expression" and "the likely communicative aspect" of Johnson's "expressive conduct." Since this meant that Johnson's expression had been "restricted because of the content of the message he conveyed," Brennan continued, the Texas law was "content based" and therefore the "relatively lenient" 1968 *O'Brien* test—which applied only if the state had no suppressive goal in mind and required only that the government demonstrate an "important or substantial" reason for regulating "expressive conduct"—was completely inapplicable.

Instead, the Court held, the Texas law must be subject to "the most exacting scrutiny" and Texas must demonstrate a "compelling state interest" to justify abridging Johnson's rights, a standard that the Court had recently invoked in *Boos v. Barry* (1988), another case in which it held that "content based" laws that restricted expression were at issue. Brennan declared, however, in what became the most quoted statement from the opinion, the Texas law could not meet this standard, because in seeking to prevent citizens from conveying messages that were perceived as "harmful," it violated the "bedrock principle underlying the First Amendment," namely "that the Government may not prohibit expression of an idea simply because society finds the idea itself offensive or disagreeable." Citing the *Street* holding that "a State may not criminally punish a person for uttering words critical of the flag," Brennan declared that any attempt to distinguish between "written or spoken words and nonverbal conduct" was "of no moment where the nonverbal conduct is expressive, as it is here, and where the regulation of that conduct is related to expression, as it is here."

Responding in part to the dissenting opinions, Brennan rejected the argument that Johnson could express his viewpoint through some other means, holding that "the enduring lesson" of Court precedents, namely that "the Government may not prohibit expression simply because it disagrees with its message" was "not dependent on the particular mode in which one chooses to express an idea" and therefore the state could not "criminally punish a person for burning a flag as a means of political protest." Invoking its 1970 *Schacht* decision striking down a government ban on the unauthorized use of military uniforms when their use tended to "discredit" the armed forces, the Court also rejected the contention that the state could constitutionally demand that a symbol "be used to express only one view of its referents" and thus allow the government to "foster its own view of the flag by prohibiting expressive conduct relating to it." Such a position, Brennan argued, would open up a legal "territory having no discernible or defensible boundaries" and thus could ultimately lead to banning protests involving other symbols such as copies of the Constitution or the presidential seal.

The Court also rejected Drew's suggestion that it create a "separate juridical category for the American flag alone" that would exempt the flag from the "joust of principles protected by the First Amendment," especially since previous Court rulings had held that other concepts "virtually sacred to our Nation as a whole," such as the principle that racial discrimination was "odious and destructive" were not protected from questioning "in the marketplace of ideas." Declaring that "we do not consecrate the flag by punishing its desecration, for in doing so we dilute the freedom that this cherished emblem represents," Brennan suggested that the proper means of preserving the flag's role was "not to punish those who feel differently" but to "persuade them that they are wrong," and that there was "no more appropriate response to burning a flag than waving one's own."

Although Justice Kennedy joined Brennan's opinion, he also wrote an extraordinary concurring opinion that declared his decision had taken a "painful" and "personal toll," but the "hard fact is that sometimes" the Constitution commanded that "we must make decisions we do not like," in this instance because Johnson's flag burning was "speech, in both the technical and fundamental meaning of the Constitution." Kennedy lamented, "It is poignant but fundamental that the flag protects those who hold it in contempt," and added, "so great is our commitment to the process that, except in the rare case, we do not pause to express distaste for the result, perhaps for fear of undermining a valued principle that dictates the decision. This is one of those rare cases."

In separate dissents filled with patriotic oratory but with relatively few references to legal precedents, Rehnquist (joined by White and O'Connor) and Stevens essentially argued that ordinary principles of law were simply inapplicable when the flag was involved. Stevens maintained that the flag was "unique" and not subject to legal doctrines that might apply "to a host of other symbols" because "this case has an intangible dimension that makes those rules inapplicable" (although he struck from his final opinion a draft statement that if "judges had the souls of computers" the case might be "less difficult"). Rehnquist also termed the flag "unique" and rejected the majority's suggestion that it could not be exempted from the "marketplace of ideas" because it was "not simply another 'idea' or 'point of view' competing for recognition," as "millions and millions of Americans regard it with an almost mystical reverence" and a "uniquely deep awe and respect." Both Rehnquist and Stevens wrote lengthy discourses on the flag's history, including, in Rehnquist's case, extended quotations from patriotic poetry as well as examples designed to prove the flag's unique importance, including that the flag had appeared "more times than any other symbol" on American stamps. Rehnquist's dissent was so bitter and impassioned that legal author Peter Irons declared in a 1994 book that it read "as if the Court were personally responsible for the deaths of the marines who died on Iwo Jima, 'fighting hand to hand against thousands of Japanese.' "

Rehnquist and Stevens both compared flag burning to defacing the Lincoln Memorial, and Rehnquist suggested that it was a "high purpose" of a democratic society for majorities to legislate against conduct that they regarded as "inherently evil and profoundly offensive," whether such conduct was "murder, embezzlement, pollution or flag burning." Both dissents completely rejected Brennan's argument that the right to free expression did not vary with "the particular mode in which one chooses to express an idea," maintaining that any limit imposed on Johnson by forbidding flag desecration was trivial because, in Rehnquist's words, Johnson could have conveyed his views "just as forcefully in a dozen" other ways, including verbal criticism of the flag or burning government leaders in effigy, proof, according to Stevens, that he was not prosecuted for "disagreeable ideas" but only "because of the method he chose to express his dissatisfaction." Aside from the argument that Johnson could still make his position known via other means, the only legally oriented contention in the dissents was Rehnquist's declaration that the Dallas flag burning should either not be considered expression at all because such acts were only "the equivalent of an inarticulate grunt or roar" that were "most likely" designed "not to express any particular idea, but to antagonize others" or, alternatively, that they amounted to "fighting words" that were exempted from First Amendment protection under the 1942 *Chaplinsky* doctrine. Rehnquist denounced the Court majority for advocating education as a response to flag burning, terming this a "regrettably patronizing civics lecture" that admonished American political leaders "as if they were school children." Stevens concluded that if "liberty and equality" were "worth fighting for," then it could not be true "that the flag that uniquely symbolizes their power is not itself worthy of protection from unnecessary desecration."

CHAPTER 5

The Post-*Johnson* Firestorm, Summer 1989

The Immediate Response to *Johnson*

News coverage of *Johnson* was so massive and prominent that it inevitably implied that the Court's ruling was some combination of the extremely important and extremely bizarre and, not surprisingly, it provoked extraordinary levels of public interest. Two of the three major television networks, the prime source of news for most Americans, led with the *Johnson* story in their June 21 evening newscasts, and major newspapers across the country headlined it the next morning. The June 21 ABC evening news devoted an extraordinary one-fifth of its broadcast to *Johnson*, and news anchor Peter Jennings practically told his audience that the Court had issued an odd decision that they should get upset about. He reported that it had come from a "supposedly conservative court," that the reaction to it (which had hardly begun) "deeply divides the country," and that "there are very few" Court decisions "which we can imaging evoking such a gut reaction as this one."

Altogether, the three major television networks evening newscasts featured an extraordinary thirty-seven stories, consuming about seventy minutes of airtime, about the flag desecration controversy during June and July, the vast majority of which were broadcast during the two weeks immediately following *Johnson*. According to Pew Research Center, an organization that studies public interest in the news, 51 percent of those surveyed reported that they had followed news about *Johnson* "very closely," a figure exceeding the level of public interest measured in 95 percent of about seven hundred other news events between 1986 and 1999—

slightly exceeding interest in the fall of the Berlin Wall in late 1989 and only slightly lower than interest in the death of Great Britain's Princess Diana in 1997.

Brennan's opinion had repeatedly made clear his distaste for flag burning, for example stating that "this one gesture of an unknown man" would not "change our nation's attitude towards its flag." However, much of the news coverage—which on TV was repeatedly accompanied by film of burning flags and thus implicitly but incorrectly suggested that such events were frequent occurrences— left the quite misleading impression that the Court majority had actively approved of flag desecration. For example, the June 22 editions of *Newsday* and the *San Jose Mercury News* respectively headlined, "Top Court OKs Flag-Burning" and "Flag Burning Ruled OK." Most such headlines no doubt simply reflected the difficulties of compressing a complicated legal decision into a few words— and many headlines gave a far more accurate summary, as in the *Newark Star-Ledger*'s banner, "Justices rule flag burning is a right of free speech"—but in some cases newspapers seemed deliberately to distort the Court's position, as in the headlines respectively run by the *Salt Lake City Tribune* and the *New York Post:* "Court Hands Match to Flag Burners" and "Supreme Court Gives Protesters OK to Burn this Flag" (accompanied with a photograph of Johnson holding a scorched flag under the headline "Revolting Communist Sneers at the Verdict"). Presumably, coverage such as this led Brennan, in a 1991 interview granted after his mid-1990 retirement, to complain to a journalist that "most of your colleagues in the press simply don't do a good job."

The superficial impression conveyed by much of the media was compounded by similar misleading summaries of the ruling from politicians who criticized it. For example, Attorney General Richard Thornburgh told a July 2 national television audience that the ruling amounted to saying "it's all right" to burn the flag. Republican Congressional Campaign Committee chairman Ed Rollins said that if Democrats were "stupid enough to argue for the flag burners" and vote against a constitutional amendment to overturn *Johnson* because "they think it's OK to desecrate the flag, we're going to win on that issue," and Admiral William Crowe, former chairman of the Joint Chiefs of Staff, declared that American military bases would continue to fly the flag, "legal or not."

Although some of the most important newspapers such as the *New York Times* and the *Washington Post* printed extensive texts of the Court's opinions, most printed and broadcast accounts were too sketchy to convey the legal context of Brennan's ruling. No doubt as a result, as Marcia Coyle, Supreme Court reporter for the *National Law Journal*, noted in a 1990 interview, most coverage failed to convey "the rationale for the decision as clearly as it could have and didn't fully put it into the perspective of the First Amendment. Brennan's reasoning got a little lost in the political reaction to the decision." Coyle added that mainstream news media flocked to the story because "everybody relates to the flag," because "the flag and patriotism had played such a major part in the 1988 presidential campaign," and because "it was an easy legal story to write, you didn't have to worry about boring the public trying to explain exactly what happened."

Baltimore Sun Supreme Court reporter Lyle Denniston was quoted in a 1994 book as similarly noting that he "couldn't give enough" stories about the flag desecration controversy to his editors, at least partly because "it was kind of a residual carryover" from the 1988 campaign and additionally provided a "wonderful mix of personality and patriotism." ABC congressional correspondent Cokie Roberts suggested in a 1990 interview that the "inflammatory" nature of the repeated film of flag burnings shown on TV played a major role in provoking political and public outrage because "the pictures are so much more powerful than the words that the television spots on this subject are propaganda" and were "literally incendiary," and CBS Supreme Court reporter Rita Braver, in a 1991 interview, similarly noted that in making news judgments "outrageousness seems to take precedence and sometimes the pictures tell you more of the story than is really maybe right for them to tell you." Several members of Congress and congressional staff similarly viewed the press as responsible for inflaming the flag desecration controversy: in 1991 interviews, Representative John Porter (R-IL) lamented that the press "is always looking to stir emotions" and "sometimes it's not very responsible," and a key Senate Democratic staffer declared that the flag controversy became "a big deal because the press made it a such a big deal" and "really poured fuel on the fires," especially because "it was coverable by the news with video tape and it was easy to explain."

No doubt propelled at least in part by such massive, emotional, and sometimes misleading press coverage, the reaction to *Johnson* was probably greater, more immediate, and more negative than to any other Supreme Court ruling in American history, touching off what *Newsday* characterized as a "firestorm of indignation." According to a 1997 article by former *New York Times* reporter Tom Wicker, "so vociferous was the criticism of Brennan and the Court ruling that it might have been thought that flag burning was the most threatening problem faced by the republic, and that the Court had rendered the nation incapable of defending itself against a rampant epidemic of torched flags." Senator Strom Thurmond (R-SC) declared that the ruling "opened an emotional hydrant across our country demanding immediate action to overturn it," and Senator John Warner (R-VA) declared that the decision reached the "core of every individual's mind, heart and soul." Representative Douglas Applegate (D-OH), one of scores of congressmen from both parties who immediately denounced *Johnson*, declared on the floor of the House of Representatives:

> I am mad as heck. We have witnessed the greatest travesty in the annals of jurisprudence. . . . What in God's name is going on? . . . The flag right here in this Chamber that we pledge to, we can take it down, throw it on the floor, step on it, defecate on it, do anything we want, burn it, as long as we have a message, and the Court is going to say it is all right. . . . Are there any limitations? Are they going to allow fornication in Times Square at high noon?

Much of the rhetorical criticism of the Court during the immediate post-*Johnson* period was couched in similarly highly vitriolic terms. Representative Ron Marlenee termed the decision "treasonous" and, referring to the six marines depicted in the Iwo Jima memorial, declared, "These six brave soldiers were symbolically shot in the back by five men in black robes." Conservative columnist Pat Buchanan—who would later repeatedly run for president stressing the theme of a need for a "cultural war" to reverse what he characterized as a massive collapse in American values—termed the decision an "atrocity" and labeled the Supreme Court a "renegade tribunal" to which the American people should respond by putting "a fist in their face." Mayor Robert Price of Sharon, Pennsylvania, said that the ruling "shows just how stupid the Supreme Court is" because "our forefathers never meant free speech to mean having Commies burning the flag." Flag burners came in for even more bitter criticism than did the five majority justices: thus, Miami Beach mayor Alex Daoud said they "should be shot" and Senate Republican leader Robert Dole declared that "if they don't like our flag, they ought to go find one they do like." Among the terms used to characterize flag burners in remarks made by congressmen or reprinted by them in the *Congressional Record* were "pukeheads," "political jackasses," "contemptible maggots," "pathetic morons," and "insensitive cretins."

Similar sentiments were unquestionably widespread among the American public, with numerous polls indicating that overwhelming majorities opposed *Johnson* and favored a constitutional amendment to overturn it. National polls published in *USA Today* on June 23, in the *San Francisco Examiner* on June 30 and in *Newsweek* on July 3 indicated that 69 percent supported a constitutional amendment. Supreme Court spokeswoman Toni House told reporters on June 22 that the Court was receiving calls from a "surprising number of rude callers," some of whom were "outraged to the point of profanity." According to a published report that was later confirmed by Justice Scalia, Scalia told a friend that on the morning after *Johnson*, "I came down to breakfast to find my wife marching around the kitchen table singing, 'It's a Grand Old Flag.'" A Tampa, Florida, disk jockey reported that after he mentioned *Johnson* the day after it was announced, "people were just going nuts" and responded with over one thousand calls although "it wasn't even a talk show," and a *New York Daily News* columnist sarcastically reported on June 27, after listening to weekend radio talk shows, that among those calling in to protest

Johnson, "a lot of wimps seemed willing to settle for a constitutional amendment or impeachment" of the Court majority, but "an encouraging number held out for execution."

According to two Supreme Court sources interviewed in 1991, the justices expected the decision to be controversial but were shocked by the volume and virulence of the reaction. They reported that Brennan was "deluged with American flags [mailed in by opponents of his opinion], they were all over the place," and that, at least in retrospect, the justices had been "unbelievably blasé" about *Johnson* and were not prepared for "all the flag waving that went on" and were shocked by "seeing people shouting and screaming about it." A third Court source, interviewed in 1999, recalled that when *Johnson* was under consideration there was not "all that much tension about it," partly because the Court was simultaneously considering important cases involving abortion, civil rights, and the death penalty "and in the scheme of that *Texas v. Johnson* was viewed as very important, very big, but not up there with the absolutely biggest cases." (One measure of general interest in a case is the number of "amicus curiae" or friend of the court briefs that are filed by parties not directly involved in a case: five amicus briefs were filed in *Johnson*, slightly higher than the average of four such briefs filed in the 85 percent of Court cases heard between 1986 and 1991 in which any amicus briefs were filed, but well below the record number of seventy-eight amicus briefs filed in a 1989 abortion case, *Webster v. Reproductive Health Services*). According to the source, it became apparent fairly early during the Court's consideration that Scalia and Kennedy (as well as two of their most conservative and influential clerks) favored upholding the Texas Court of Criminal Appeals, thus creating a consensus "about flag burning that just didn't exist on most other issues" which frequently bitterly divided the justices and clerks along conservative-liberal lines during the 1988–1989 term. He added that after word circulated that six justices had indicated that they intended to vote against Texas at the Court's March 24 conference, the case "never seemed ultimately that suspenseful." The source said that O'Connor's decision to reverse her tentative conference vote and join Rehnquist's dissent on June 19, after four

justices had joined Brennan's opinion, led to considerable speculation that she had acted out "of political cowardice" because "she
wanted to make sure the case came out the way she wanted it to
legally, but she didn't want to be a party to it," especially since the
majority justices also didn't "like the idea of what Johnson was up
to but they felt compelled by law" to vote as they did. (Such vote
switches are not rare: between 1969 and 1986, 7.5 percent of all
justices' votes reflected a switch, and at least one vote changed in
37 percent of the cases.)

According to a 1999 interview with Brennan's son, New Jersey
lawyer William Brennan III, his father was not "terribly upset" by
the post-*Johnson* uproar, which included a short-lived effort to
remove his father's name from a Hudson County, New Jersey,
courthouse that had been named in his honor. Although Brennan's
son said, "I was probably more upset that he was being attacked
than he was," his father's contemporary correspondence gives the
impression of someone who felt under siege and welcomed any
encouragement he could get. For example, when Senator Edward
Kennedy sent him a letter of support on June 22, Brennan replied,
"I hope your view is the prevailing one, because it's so very right."
Brennan responded to a similar letter on June 30, "It was not an
easy case for any of us here," but "I saw no way to escape either
the responsibility or the result," and in reply to a letter from a former Supreme Court clerk praising him for his "courageous" and
"eloquent and persuasive explanation of the essence of our system
of liberty and free speech," Brennan wrote on July 24, "I'm most
appreciative and deeply touched. It's most welcome in this time of
surprising reaction. Thanks so very, very much."

Like the Court, Congress was also swamped with angry phone
calls and mail. Thus, the HJC reported on June 22 that the committee had been swamped with calls from "outraged citizens."
Congress began to react almost immediately: within a week, 172
representatives and 43 senators sponsored thirty-nine separate resolutions calling for an amendment to outlaw flag desecration. In
the first official congressional response, the Senate voted 97 to 3
on June 22 to express its "profound disappointment" with *Johnson*
in a resolution cosponsored by Dole, Democratic majority leader

George Mitchell, and over sixty other senators. The Senate resolution compared flag desecration to "desecrating a public monument such as the Lincoln Memorial," which would "never be tolerated as speech," and termed flag burning an "affront" to the American people, especially those who had "fought valiantly" and "died, to protect this sacred symbol of nationhood." On June 23, after only ten minutes of debate, the Senate passed (again by 97 to 3) a proposal by Senate Judiciary Committee (SJC) chairman Joseph Biden that was designed to head off demands for a constitutional amendment by supposedly legislatively overturning *Johnson:* it claimed to outlaw flag desecration in a "content neutral" manner that would supposedly pass Supreme Court muster by banning all forms of flag desecration, regardless of whether, in Biden's words, they "intended to offend others or cast contempt" on the flag. The Biden bill proposed to amend the 1968 federal flag desecration law so that it would punish anyone, regardless of motive, who "knowingly and publicly mutilates, burns, displays on the floor or ground or tramples upon any flag."

The Biden proposal proved to be the forerunner of a successful effort in both houses that culminated in passage of the similar Flag Protection Act (FPA) in October to legislatively short-circuit demands for a constitutional amendment, which greatly intensified after President Bush endorsed an amendment on June 27. Even on June 23, however, this threat loomed large: according to a Senate source interviewed in 1990, "If you were on the Senate floor that Friday night as I was, you would know the speed that train had. The Constitution was about to be amended on the floor of the U.S. Senate with no hearings, no nothing." Another congressional source added, "There was a tremendous, tremendous, tremendous push on the floor of the U.S. Senate for an immediate push for a constitutional amendment."

On June 27, the House of Representatives voted 411 to 15 to express "profound concern" over *Johnson* in a resolution that termed flag desecration "so offensive to individuals in the United States that it may be considered an incitement to violence." The House continued to promote flag patriotism for the next two days: a virtually unprecedented all-night session on June 28/29 was devoted to speeches denouncing *Johnson*, and on June 29 the House designated July 4 "Take Pride in the Flag Day."

Local governments and state legislatures also quickly responded to *Johnson*. By September, at least two dozen cities or counties across the country, including governing bodies in Detroit, Miami, and Dallas, passed resolutions urging Congress to pass a constitutional amendment to overturn *Johnson*. For example, the governing authorities of Lasalle County, Illinois, declared that *Johnson* had "horrified the vast majority" of Americans, who "do not consider our nation's flag to be just a piece of cloth that various revolutionaries and subversive activists can destroy," and demanded a constitutional amendment to "guarantee that our nation remain free." By mid-July one or both of the legislative chambers of almost all the approximately twenty state legislatures still in session passed resolutions denouncing the ruling, demanding constitutional or legislative action to overturn it, or both, usually with extraordinary speed and virtually no dissent. For example, both legislative houses in South Carolina approved resolutions calling for a constitutional amendment within twenty-four hours of *Johnson*, and both the Massachusetts Senate and the California Assembly acted likewise on June 26 by respective votes of 32 to 1 and 58 to 2. Most state legislators predicted that if Congress endorsed a flag desecration constitutional amendment it would be quickly ratified by the states: thus Kansas Senate president Paul Burke forecast that an amendment would whip through the legislature there "like a thunderstorm through Kansas."

In Texas, the legislature approved a resolution that declared:

Whereas the United States flag belongs to all Americans and ought not be desecrated by any one individual, even under principles of free expression, any more than we would allow desecration of the Declaration of Independence, Statue of Liberty, Lincoln Memorial, Yellowstone National Park, or any other common inheritance that the people of the land hold dear; . . .

[T]he incineration or other mutilation of the flag . . . is repugnant to all those who have saluted it, paraded beneath in on the Fourth of July, been saluted by its halfmast configuration, or raised it inspirationally in remote corners of the globe where they have defended the ideals of which it is representative; . . .

Whereas this legislature concurs with the [Supreme] court minority that the Stars and Stripes is deserving of a unique sanctity, free to wave in perpetuity over the spacious skies where our bald eagles fly, the fruited plain above which our mountain majesties soar, and the venerable heights to which our melting pot of peoples and their posterity aspire; now, therefore, be it Resolved, That the 71st Legislature of the State of Texas . . . petitions the Congress . . . to propose to the states an amendment to the United States Constitution, protecting the American flag . . . from willful desecration.

Eventually, during 1989 and 1990 at least eight state legislatures (including Texas) also enacted new flag desecration laws in attempts to salvage existing statutes that had been apparently rendered unconstitutional. The new laws essentially adopted the argument advanced by Biden in the Senate on June 23 and later endorsed by both houses of Congress in the FPA. For example, Arkansas passed a supposedly "content neutral" flag desecration law in November 1989 that had been proposed on July 14 by Democratic governor William Jefferson Clinton. Clinton termed his approach "a lot quicker [than a constitutional amendment] and there's no direct infringement of the First Amendment," supposedly because the law banned all flag desecration, regardless of motive (with an exemption for burning worn flags) and therefore allegedly did not specifically target dissenters. The Clinton proposal passed the state legislature by 33 to 1 in the Senate and 91 to 0 in the House.

Many Americans complemented the negative responses to *Johnson* by Congress and state and local governments with their own forms of often-symbolic rejections of a ruling that had upheld the right to peaceful symbolic protest. Conservative protesters burned judges' robes on the Supreme Court steps on June 22, scores of people flew flags upside down or at half-mast to protest the ruling (in violation of a voluntary 1942 congressional flag code), and thousands of Americans purchased and flew flags to express their views. In Manchester, Massachusetts, the American Legion branch announced that their previously planned July 4 burning of worn-out flags would be dedicated to protesting *Johnson*, thus burning flags to symbolically protest a Supreme Court decision that guaranteed their right to burn flags to symbolically protest. Greg Wald, president of the National Independent Flag Dealers Association, reported in early July that *Johnson* had spurred enormous enthusiasm for flag sales and that "dealers across the country are reporting sell-outs," and the manager of a Virginia K-Mart declared, "It's great for business." The primary public response to the *Johnson* decision was such a general upsurge of flag patriotism that *Houston Post* columnist Larry Ashby suggested that perhaps Gregory Lee Johnson was secretly a "deep and devoted patriot" who had set out on a one-man crusade to "rejuvenate" America's "flabby" spirit.

There were also some scattered symbolic statements from apparent supporters of *Johnson:* during the summer of 1989, perhaps a dozen or so flag burnings occurred around the nation, mostly without incident and almost totally unreported by the national news media, which had treated a ruling theoretically legalizing flag desecration as of enormous significance, but which apparently viewed flag burning in practice as not even newsworthy. No doubt the most bizarre "flag burning incident" in the aftermath of *Johnson*—and the only one widely reported—occurred on the Supreme Court steps on July 20 in response to a rumor that Johnson himself was planning to burn a flag there. After alerting members of the news media to their plans, about a dozen Republican congressmen who favored a constitutional amendment gathered, equipped with fire extinguishers and buckets of water. Arizona Representative Bob Stump told reporters, "We're going to kick some ass today," but when Johnson failed to appear, the congressmen doused an effigy of him, leading one reporter to note that the incident may have been "the first time someone was doused in effigy." The congressmen also recited the Pledge of Allegiance and sang patriotic songs, but had to give up on "It's a Grand Old Flag" when it turned out that they didn't know the words.

Johnson turned out to be a block away, where he was expressing his opposition to the proposed "fascist flag amendment" at a "people's flag hearing," held to protest the HJC's refusal to let him testify at their ongoing hearings on proposals to overturn the decision that bore his name. At a news conference, Johnson denied ever planning to burn a flag that day, adding, "People should stop baiting and daring me about when I am going to burn the flag. It's not high noon at the OK corral." As Johnson spoke, his supporters handed reporters press releases that included small paper flags wirh cigarette burn holes, whereas hostile congressional staffers hissed and displayed signs reading, "Flag Burning Burns My Butt" and "America, Love It or Leave It."

The Bush Administration and the Proposed Constitutional Amendment

Despite the massive immediate adverse reaction to *Johnson*, the controversy began to fade from the front pages by the weekend of June 24–25 and by June 26 it had completely disappeared from the network news programs after five days of slowly diminishing coverage. In the opinions of many observers, especially those who opposed a constitutional amendment, the entire firestorm might have slowly died out if President Bush had not announced at a hastily called June 27 press conference that he would sponsor a constitutional amendment to overturn *Johnson*. ACLU Washington office director Morton Halperin expressed the consensus view in a 1990 interview: asked why the 1989 flag desecration controversy became so massive, he responded, "The answer is just two words—George Bush. If he had said the right thing and opposed an amendment, or if he had even said nothing, the issue would have gone away."

White House officials had carefully monitored congressional reaction to the *Johnson* ruling before Bush's June 27 announcement. A June 26 memorandum to a top Bush administration official from White House congressional lobbyist Jack Howard reported on the Senate's June 22 passage of the Biden bill, noted that Republican House leader Robert Michel was planning to introduce a constitutional amendment and included a six-page, single-spaced summary of over thirty measures already introduced to condemn the Court or overturn *Johnson* by law or amendment. Howard reported that he had heard "a rumor" that 247 proposals to overturn *Johnson* would be introduced when the House reconvened after a weekend recess on June 27, but that the appropriate House official told him there was "no evidence of any mass drafting" although "they are drafting six or seven more bills."

Bush declared at his June 27 press conference that although he would "uphold our precious right to dissent," burning "the unique symbol of America" went "too far" and that his legal advisers had indicated that ordinary legislation could not "correct" the *Johnson* decision, which he maintained had legalized an "egregious offense" about which he felt "viscerally." On June 30, at a media extravaganza at the Iwo Jima World War II memorial at Arlington National Cemetery in Virginia, Bush unveiled the text of his proposed amendment in the presence of masses of flags, the Marine Corps Band, numerous dignitaries, and a crowd of 4,500, who sang the "Star Spangled Banner." Bush declared that the flag must be protected because it has "guaranteed and nurtured" the "precious rights" of the nation such as freedom of speech. He added, "What that flag embodies is too sacred to be abused" and that "like all powerful ideas, if it is not defended, it is defamed." Dole also addressed the rally, declaring that they had gathered to warn flag burners to "keep your hands off Old Glory" and threateningly invited opponents of the amendment to "voice your opposition" as "part of the wonderful process we call democracy."

Bush's June 27 announcement and his Iwo Jima speech three days later propelled the flag desecration controversy back into prominence with a vengeance: it led eight of the twelve evening network news programs broadcast between June 27 and June 30 (with NBC and CBS both devoting an extraordinary one-third of their June 27 program to the issue). When Senator Arlen Spector (R-PA) addressed a veterans' convention on June 29, he unquestionably reflected the consensus of the news media when he declared that flag desecration was "the number one topic in the country today."

Ironically, Bush's June 27 endorsement of a constitutional amendment, which was followed the next morning by a White

House statement (later reversed) that he was planning to present the proposed text later that day, angered both Republican and Democratic congressional leaders—Republicans because they felt Bush was stealing their thunder, and Democrats because they were convinced that Bush was trying to repeat what they viewed as his totally cynical, partisan—and above all effective—use of the "flag patriotism" issue from the 1988 campaign. The dispute with Republican leaders was quickly patched up and had little long-term significance, but the panicky immediate reaction of Democrats and many of their liberal supporters to the Bush announcement essentially guaranteed that Congress would take *some* form of action to attempt to overturn *Johnson*.

According to congressional and White House sources interviewed in 1990, when the White House announced on June 28 that Bush would soon reveal the text of an amendment (that had been drafted by White House counsel C. Boyden Gray), Senate Republican leader Dole and House Republican leader Michel immediately protested privately that they had been drafting their own language for an amendment and demanded to be credited for authoring any text endorsed by Bush. According to a White House source, Dole and Michel "made clear they wanted their own language" and "wanted to be able to say they wrote the damn thing," with the result that Bush issued orders to "let the Hill do what it wanted" because he "just wanted it taken care of and didn't care about authorship," partly in hopes that this approach would help defuse allegations that he was acting out of partisan motives. According to a key House Republican congressional source, "there was some tension between wanting the president's help, because everybody understood that unless Bush was extremely involved in this it wasn't going to happen, and not wanting him to come in at the last minute and take what Michel or Dole" had been working on "for a day or two before the White House became involved" and "suddenly turn that into the president's amendment."

These behind-the-scenes developments were only hinted at by a White House announcement later on June 28 that the earlier statement had been "mistaken" and the text would "not be ready today" after all, because Bush hoped to "join with members of

Congress in supporting a proposal that will receive swift consideration" and was "working with members of Congress" who "wanted to be a part of it" to develop "appropriate language." This announcement was followed by several days of frantic meetings, variously described by sources as a "real tussle" and "hard negotiations," in which Gray's assistant, Brent Hatch, met with Dole's counsel, Dennis Shea; Michel's counsel, Charlene Vanlier; Assistant Attorney General J. Michael Luttig; and Thad Strom, an aide to ranking Republican SJC member Strom Thurmond (who had introduced a constitutional amendment to ban flag desecration on June 22). According to multiple sources, Dole, still "upset about the display in Chicago, where people walked on the flag" was determined to specifically ban putting flags on the floor and "really wanted to specifically say you can't do that," and, with Thurmond's support, wanted a "laundry list of [specific] things he wanted to prohibit being done to the flag." Michel reportedly maintained, however, that such specificity was inconsistent with other constitutional provisions, which generally authorized broad grants of government authority, especially since unforeseen forms of flag desecration might necessitate further constitutional amendments if they were not specifically listed. According to a congressional source, Dole and Michel were both "adamant," but in the end a compromise of sorts suggested by Hatch was reached by "getting people to sit on their egos a bit" yet "still allowing each to claim they wrote it. They wanted it to be known as the Dole-Michel amendment, and the President said, 'Fine, I'll be happy to endorse your amendment.'"

The operative text of the amendment, formally unveiled by Bush on June 30, reflected Michel's view, stating only, "The Congress and the States shall have power to prohibit the physical desecration of the flag of the United States." The preamble was closer to Dole's position, stating that "physical desecration" included but was "not limited to, such acts as burning, mutilating, defacing, defiling or trampling on the flag, or displaying the flag in a contemptuous manner." According to the sources, Dole and Thurmond gave the most ground because the preamble was in practice "meaningless," but "after reflection they decided you weren't going to be able to list every method of defaming the flag through a physical act." With the amendment text solidified, White House officials drafted letters for President Bush to be sent in response to what they termed a "growing volume of mail" about flag desecration from the general public. The response said that although Bush had the "highest respect" for the Supreme Court and for "an individual's right to protest government action," he was "deeply disturbed" by *Johnson* because flag burning was "simply wrong" and amounted to turning "our backs" on "our history," "the ideals of honor, freedom and liberty," and "all those who fought and died to protect the ideals we cherish." He added that the "surest way to preserve these ideals is to protect the spirit that sustains it" and because the "flag sustains these ideals and if it not defended, it is defamed," he had determined to support a constitutional amendment "to protect the flag," yet preserving "the widest possible conceivable range of options for free speech expression."

The outraged response of Democrats to Bush's endorsement of an amendment had profound and long-lasting consequences for the subsequent development of the flag desecration controversy. Democrats' memories of Bush's perceived cynical manipulation of the "Pledge of Allegiance issue" during the 1988 presidential campaign made them inherently inclined to deeply distrust further pronouncements by Bush concerning the flag, but their basic predisposition was greatly intensified by the context of unfolding events. In his first response to *Johnson* on June 22, Bush had never hinted at any intention to seek to overturn it in any way: voicing what he termed his "personal, emotional response" that the flag was "very, very special" and that burning it was "dead wrong," he added, "I understand the legal basis for that decision, and I respect the Supreme Court" and "as President of the United States, I will see that the law of the land is fully supported." Intervening between this response and his June 27 endorsement of an amendment came not only the general public and congressional post-*Johnson* uproar, but also a June 26 lunch with Republican National Committee (RNC) chairman Lee Atwater, whom Democrats viewed as the evil genius behind Bush's 1988 election strategy. Although both Bush and Atwater denied discussing the flag at the lunch, it quickly became an unshakable article of faith among Democrats that Bush decided to back the amendment purely to gain partisan benefits by again "outflagging" Democrats.

Bush and his backers vehemently denied any such motivation. Thus, a White House official involved in handling the amendment declared in a 1990 interview that although "there's no doubt Atwater and others probably saw strong political benefits to backing the amendment, and there probably was," Bush gave "clear marching orders not to make a partisan effort because he felt strongly about this as a moral issue and not something to play games with. I've heard him get really pissed off about charges that he wrapped himself in the flag. He felt very, very strongly about this, going back to his days in the military."

Democratic bitterness over their conviction that Bush and other Republicans were motivated by partisanship pushed the Democratic leadership toward opposing the amendment, but their panicky fear of being perceived as "antiflag" also led them to quickly endorse a statutory alternative that led directly to passage of the FPA. The outrage of Democrats over their perception that Bush was cynically manipulating the flag issue, especially by his massively publicized speech at the Iwo Jima memorial, became a constant theme. Democratic National Committee communications director Michael McCurry responded to the Iwo Jima speech by declaring, "The heroes of Iwo Jima didn't die so they could become a backdrop for some political photo opportunity," and Democratic senator Edward Kennedy maintained that Bush had failed a "critical test of leadership" by deciding to "launch a high-profile campaign" in support of the amendment "after lunch with Lee Atwater" in an attempt to repeat his "partisan political campaign around the flag." Similarly, Representative David Skaggs (D-CO), in a 1991 interview, lamented that he had been "impressed" with "the president's initial reaction" to *Johnson*, "in which his untutored instincts were to recognize that the Supreme Court has a tough job and to respect their judgment," but "after the political handlers got hold of him" and the president was "disabused of his better instincts he ended up at Iwo Jima." In a 1990 interview, HJC Civil Liberties Subcommittee chair Don Edwards (D-CA) referred to the Iwo Jima speech as "that outrageous thing" that Bush did "with bands and flags flying, he almost shot guns off into the air." California State Senate Democratic majority leader Barry Keane told the press that the "chief desecrators" of the flag were Bush and "his socio-pathic sidekick" Atwater, who were engaged in a "shameful, cynical, tawdry manipulative exploitation of the flag for political purposes." But, Keane added, he was voting for a proposal in the California legislature to urge Congress to pass an amendment, because to oppose the measure would create a "death-trap for Democrats," since "we can't take the risk of being thought unpatriotic."

Although the Democratic congressional leadership in Washington opposed the amendment, Keane's worry about their party being portrayed as "unpatriotic" became a dominant concern to them. As reporters for the *New York Times* and the *Washington Post* noted in late June, "many Democrats swore they would never be outflagged again" and they "kept up a fusillade of pro-flag rhetoric," matching "the Republicans word for word" and talking "barroom tough, essentially saying no Republican had better call them soft on the flag." Within hours after Bush endorsed the amendment on June 27 the Democratic congressional leadership in both houses announced hearings would be held on responses to *Johnson;* House Democrats sponsored what they termed a "Democratic resolution" attacking *Johnson* (the House resolution passed by 411 to 5 on June 27); and many Democrats, including HJC chairman Jack Brooks and Speaker Thomas Foley, declared their support for the constitutionally dubious proposition that the ruling could be overturned by a *statute*, which could supposedly both more quickly circumvent *Johnson* than an *amendment* and simultaneously avoid officially "tampering" with the Constitution.

HJC civil liberties subcommittee chair Edwards, who made clear during a 1990 interview that he felt he had lost thousands of votes for opposing the 1968 federal flag desecration law, told reporters shortly after *Johnson* that he had "never seen more panic among members" who feared being labeled antiflag. Similarly, according to *Washington Post* congressional reporter Don Phillips, interviewed in 1990:

I've worked on the Hill a long, long time, since 1973, and I don't think I've ever seen a time when people were so scared of their own shadows and where they paid so little attention to the consequences of their actions. . . . The Pledge of Allegiance issue was all very fresh [in the minds of Democrats] at that time, so naturally many of them had only one thing in mind, and that was to prevent political damage, so that's one reason they jumped into the fray so quickly.

Shortly before the Senate ultimately defeated the amendment on October 19, Senator Robert Kerrey, a Congressional Medal of Honor winner whose opposition played a key role in its defeat, complained that the Senate had been debating an "essentially non-existent" threat from flag desecrators for more than fifty hours, largely because of "panic" and "terror" induced by President Bush's "call for action" and the fear of "negative 30-second commercials." According to a Democratic SJC staffer who was asked in 1990 about the widely reported fears of such commercials in the immediate post-*Johnson* atmosphere:

Fear is a thing that, if you feel it, it is real. People felt it, so it was a real fear, and it was a widely-discussed topic in the cloakrooms. Politicians are always fighting the last battle and people had on their mind that Dukakis had lost because he was bad on the flag. That factor hung over the entire process up here. If this had been 1987 instead of 1989 it would have been entirely different.

On July 14, the day after the HJC began hearings, Senate Democratic leader Mitchell announced an agreement with Dole for votes on both a statute and the Bush amendment in October, following SJC hearings and reports on both proposals to be submitted to the Senate by September 22. This agreement assured Republicans that the Senate would vote on the amendment, but, even more important in the end, it also ensured that Democrats would have a full opportunity to argue for their alternative and that voting would not occur until (Democrats accurately hoped) public interest and pressure over the flag issue in general and for an amendment in particular had dissipated. Moreover, since Dole agreed to hold the vote on the statute first, Democrats hoped that if the FPA passed this would allow them to argue that there would be no need for an amendment. In short, the Democratic FPA strategy was an attempt both to delay and provide an alternative to a vote on the amendment until passions had died down and to simultaneously position themselves as "pro-flag."

With most Republicans committed to a constitutional amendment and Democratic leaders increasingly committed to a legislative attempt to overturn *Johnson* along the lines of the eventually passed 1989 FPA, the political possibility that Congress would take no action at all in response to *Johnson* effectively disappeared by late June. Yet, ironically, the general public uproar and massive media attention focused on flag desecration issue quickly died down after Bush's Iwo Jima speech. Nonetheless, the powerful veterans' lobby, led by the three-million-strong American Legion, focused enormous energy on backing the amendment, so strong pressure for congressional action continued. According to a 1992 interview with a Democratic congressional source who closely followed veterans' affairs and attended many closed-door meetings dealing with the 1989 flag uproar, many congressmen "fall down in a dead faint when veterans say anything" and "it is amazing how powerful veterans are on the Hill, it is astonishing." Therefore, he added, although typically one issue "dies fairly quickly as the next issue arises," the veterans' pressure operated to keep the flag controversy "on the front burner, to keep a continuance of the [early] outrage. It got to the point where congressional offices weren't counting their mail [from veterans demanding an amendment], they were weighing it."

CHAPTER 6

The Congressional Debate on Responding to *Johnson*, July–October 1989

By early July, leaders of both parties had virtually committed Congress to taking some action to ban flag desecration, and therefore discussion during the following months centered only on exactly how *Johnson* should be overturned, rather than on *whether* a response to *Johnson* was either required or wise. Thus, in announcing planned HJC hearings on June 27, Chairman Brooks announced that the focus would be only on whether *Johnson* should be circumvented via "a constitutional amendment or possible statutory remedies." The witness lists of the two judiciary committees reflected this preordained limitation: although SJC chairman Biden told the HJC on July 13 that "most leading constitutional experts in this country" to whom he had spoken did not want Congress to do "anything," of the over forty witnesses who testified, about 75 percent endorsed a statute, an amendment, or both; only 25 percent recommended that no action be taken.

Many members of Congress who privately believed that neither legislation nor an amendment were really desirable felt compelled for political reasons to support at least one of these approaches. When Harvard law professor and former Reagan administration solicitor general Charles Fried, a well-known conservative, advocated what became known as the "bravely do nothing" option before the HJC on July 19, Representative Pat Schroeder (D-CO) responded that since Bush "changed his position when Atwater went up and had lunch," a "political ball [began] rolling," and "We're not talking about a purist world. We're talking about a very political world." HJC subcommittee chairman Edwards told Fried that the only practical choice was between an amendment and a statute because "When you are faced with . . . either the much lesser of two evils [the FPA] or an absolute loser [the amendment], your point of view is the correct point of view, but it's such a [political] loser," as Congress's freedom to act had been "taken away from us by the President of the United States." Edwards subsequently told the HJC that he personally opposed the FPA but had decided to cosponsor it, since although the "wisest course of action, the one truest to the Constitution and to the values of the country is to do nothing," that was politically "not an option open to us" and the FPA was the alternative that "causes the least violence to the First Amendment."

According to a key House Democratic congressional aide who was interviewed in 1990, "in the minds of the vast majority of members" the "bravely do nothing" approach was simply "not feasible given the way the choices were structured" by July, although, he added, when public excitement died down far more quickly than many Democrats had expected "some people realized that they had been put into a stupid and unnecessary position and they could have withstood it. But when the choice was do nothing, amend the constitution, or pass the statute, passing the statute was the easy way out. You had the ability to say, 'I can defend the flag and I support the Constitution.'"

The statutory approach proved ultimately successful over the amendment in Congress in 1989, although the FPA was quickly struck down as unconstitutional by the Supreme Court in its 1990 *U.S. v. Eichman* ruling. As ultimately enacted in October 1989, the FPA decreed up to one year in jail and a $1,000 fine for anyone who "knowingly mutilates, defaces, physically defiles, burns, maintains on the floor or ground, or tramples upon any flag of the United States," with "flag" defined as "any flag of the United States, or any part thereof, made of any substance, of any size, in a form that is commonly displayed." In response to Republican complaints that litigation over the FPA would last for years, the law contained an extraordinary provision mandating expedited review by the Supreme Court following any constitutional ruling on it by a federal district court, thus bypassing the ordinary intermediate appeals process and also denying the Supreme Court its usual power to decide what cases to hear. In response to complaints from veterans that they might face criminal penalties for disposing of worn flags by burning them in patriotic retirement ceremonies (the recommended means of "retiring" old flags in a 1942 voluntary flag code), the law exempted "any conduct consisting of the disposal of a flag when it has become worn or soiled."

The FPA failed to provide any definition of what constituted a "worn or soiled flag" and also failed to define other key terms, such as "mutilate" or "deface," as well as what "any part" of a flag or what "commonly displayed" meant. Even cosponsor Edwards expressed bafflement as to what "any part" of a flag meant, asking "What are we talking about?" and wondering aloud if people might be jailed for "let's say, cutting up four stars that they might just happen be carrying around with them, or stripes." Moreover, by exempting ceremonial burnings to retire worn flags, the FPA seemed to directly contradict *Johnson*, as the Supreme Court had stated:

> If we were to hold that the State may forbid flag-burning where it is likely to endanger the flag's symbolic role, but allow it wherever burning a flag promotes that role—as where, for example, a person ceremoniously bums a dirty flag—we would be saying that when it comes to impairing the flag's physical integrity, the flag itself may be used as a symbol . . . only in one direction . . . that one may burn the flag to convey one's attitude toward it and its referents only if one does not endanger the flag's representation of nationhood and national unity. . . . To conclude that the Government may permit designated symbols to communicate only a limited set of messages would be to enter territory having no discernible or defensible boundaries.

The Argument for "Bravely Doing Nothing"

Only a handful of congressmen publicly advocated the "bravely do nothing" position and, aside from the American Bar Association (ABA) and the vast majority of newspapers editorials, they received very little organized support. As will be seen below, even bedrock civil liberties organizations like the American Civil Liberties

Union (ACLU) and People for the American Way (PAW) effectively supported the FPA as a means of blocking what they feared would be the otherwise certain passage of the amendment. Only six senators voted in 1989 against both the amendment and the FPA; the House did not vote on the amendment in 1989, but only about twenty House members voted against both the FPA in 1989 and the amendment in 1990.

The "bravely do nothing" approach endorsed *Johnson* as a legally and morally correct decision that the country should be proud of. For example, *The Progressive* magazine declared that the "First Amendment, not the American flag, is the sacred object at the foundation of our freedom" and that speech offensive to majority viewpoints was "exactly what the First Amendment is designed to protect." Senator Howard Metzenbaum, one of only eight members of Congress who voted against the condemnatory immediate post-*Johnson* resolutions, asked the SJC, "What example is more American, more faithful to American values? Jailing flag burners or tolerating them? Deep down, we know that tolerating even outrageous protests is truer to our tradition than jailing those who offend us." Many *Johnson* supporters favorably contrasted the ruling with the recent killings of Chinese dissidents in Beijing's Tiananmen Square and with the recent death sentence pronounced by Iranian leader Ayatollah Khomeini on the author Salmon Rushdie for his novel *Satanic Verses*. Thus, syndicated columnist Clarence Page maintained that if the United States punished people for offensive political expression it would be adopting the "reasoning of Ayatollah Khomeini or the justice of Beijing." According to a 1993 book by Kim Eisler, Justice Brennan made similar comparisons when discussing *Johnson* with his clerks, reportedly asking "how Americans would feel about Chinese protesters sentenced to a year in prison for burning the Chinese flag," and declaiming that "he couldn't see someone sentenced to a year in prison for making a political statement."

The House of Delegates of the ABA—an organization that had formally recommended the passage of flag desecration laws in 1918—overwhelmingly approved at its August 1989 convention a committee report opposing passage of either the FPA or the amendment. The report declared that *Johnson* had been properly decided because "the principle that expression of an idea may not be penalized simply because the idea is offensive or disagreeable" was at the "core" of freedom of speech and that the FPA would violate this principle just as much as an amendment would. The flag commanded "respect and love" because the country adhered to "its values and its promise of freedom, not because of fiat and criminal law," the report concluded, whereas throughout history, as in Nazi Germany, "tyrannies have tried to enforce obedience by prohibiting disrespect for the symbols of their power." Apparently fearing adverse public reaction, the delegates added to the committee report a condemnation of flag desecration and voted to begin all future meetings with the Pledge of Allegiance.

During his HJC testimony, Fried, whose family had fled Nazi and Communist tyranny, declared:

> I came here from Czechoslovakia, a country with a deep and humane tradition of democratic values, crushed first by the Nazis and then by the Soviets and their disgusting little puppets. To the Czechs, . . . America was a model and ideal. So America, its traditions and values and its flag are important to me. Foremost among those values is the principle that no one shall be punished for his political expressions—no matter how offensive or bizarre. . . .
>
> I beg you not to tamper with our tradition. [Others] have testified that a statute might be drawn that would pass constitutional muster. . . . I agree with the judgment that whatever the technicalities, the evident purpose of such a statute would still be to punish acts of expression, acts that do no harm except as they express political convictions—mistaken and sordid as those convictions are. . . .
>
> In short, I believe the *Johnson* case is right not just as a matter of present constitutional law. It is right in principle.

The basic argument for "bravely doing nothing" advanced by Fried, namely that the *Johnson* decision was right in both principle and law and that any attempt to override it would damage America's fundamental and historic commitment to freedom of dissent, was supplemented by many other arguments by the few congressmen and the many newspapers that supported it. For example, opponents of both the amendment and the FPA argued that many backers of these alternatives were primarily motivated by political opportunism, that the entire flag desecration controversy was a huge storm in a teacup that was diverting needed attention away from far more pressing and important matters, and that no law or constitutional provision would ever be able to satisfactorily define the key terms "flag" or "desecration," with the result that the courts would, as during the Vietnam War period, be plunged into an endless and tedious morass of litigation over a minor issue.

Those who supported *Johnson* criticized both Bush and his fellow Republicans and many Democrats for alleged political pandering. The interpretation of Bush's motivations as basically seeking to duplicate his successful 1988 manipulation of American patriotic attachment to the flag became almost universal in the press: Thus, in his June 27 report on Bush's endorsement of an amendment, ABC White House correspondent Brit Hume reported that the announcement was "not surprising for a man who made the flag a centerpiece of his campaign for president" and an editorial cartoon in the June 30 *Washington Post* depicted a flag reading "politics first" hoisted over the White House.

Democrats also came in for considerable criticism for political opportunism. For example, John Gomperts, legislative counsel for PAW in 1989–1990, declared during a 1990 interview that "many Democrats were incredibly intellectually dishonest and very disappointingly so" during the flag uproar, as they "poured into the issue all of their anxieties over issues of patriotism" in an "incredibly cynical" way, with the result that "a number of very serious minded, good politicians" said "things about the Supreme Court that were completely out of line and out of character." The July 2 *Philadelphia Inquirer* published a cartoon portraying a Republican elephant and a Democratic donkey tearing a flag to shreds amid a tug-of-war. Senator Metzenbaum testified during congressional hearings that both parties were engaged in a "crude form of political one-upmanship, a crass competition about who loves the flag more" that reduced "political debate to shameful and crass demagoguery," all "with a cold eye" aimed at avoiding "giving our opponents an issue in the next elections," especially out of "fears of negative 30-second TV spots."

Many critics of both the amendment and the FPA argued that the entire flag desecration controversy was diverting public attention away from real issues. For example, a humor column by Cactus Pryor in the July 13 *Austin-American Statesman* described an imaginary Texas legislator, who, when asked a detailed question about allegations of personal corruption, responded, "We've got to stop these traitors from burning the United States flag!" An October 14 *Seattle Times* editorial elaborated this idea:

> Into a nation plagued by inadequate housing, rampant drug abuse, a mammoth federal budget deficit and the growing specter of AIDS, those wonderful folks in Washington, D.C. have introduced a flag law [the FPA]. . . . No one will be fed or housed because of this law. Nothing will be done to clean the environment, force better government or address even one of the pressing national concerns that truly affect people's lives. . . . The real desecration of democracy occurs when people don't have places to live or work or adequate health insurance.

Another criticism frequently made of both the proposed amendment and the FPA was that their phraseology was hopelessly vague and, in particular, satisfactory definitions of "flag" and "desecration" would prove impossible. Harvard professor Laurence Tribe argued that "nobody knows" what the amendment meant and therefore it amounted to "little more than a blank check authorizing unspecified withdrawals from America's most precious heritage, the Bill of Rights." Senator Gordon Humphrey (R-NH), who along with John Chafee of Rhode Island was the only Republican senator to vote against both proposed alternatives, asked whether "flag desecration" would include "American flag patches we see on the fannies" of jeans and warned that Congress was headed for an "endless riddle" if "we are going to get into this kind of arcane minutia."

Many critics of the amendment especially targeted the preamble's definition of "physical desecration" for including "displaying the flag in a contemptuous manner," as well as the amendment's authorization of both Congress *and* the states to ban flag desecration. Thus, Representative Schroeder warned that "clothing or artistic symbols could be illegal" in one state but not another and "you may have to have a dress code as you go across" state boundaries. Many newspaper writers had satirical field days discussing similar topics, as in a *Washington Post* column that suggested that "desecration" be defined to include "subjecting the flag to damage, disrespect or funny business" and proposed that anyone who "misfolds, improperly launders, shreds" or "deep-fat-fries" a flag, or who "fails to get kinda misty" in the presence of one be jailed and condemned to make license plates with the motto, "Land of the Free, Home of the Symbolically Obedient."

The Argument for the Constitutional Amendment

The argument for passing a constitutional amendment to overturn *Johnson* combined a dominant emotional component with secondary legal elements. The emotional aspect of the argument essentially amounted to the position, not dissimilar to the *Johnson* dissents, that the American flag was a unique, special, and incomparable symbol and that whether *Johnson* was legally correct, a constitutional amendment was warranted to protect it against physical desecration. Senate Republican leader Dole captured the essence of this position when he maintained that "The need for this amendment will not be found in a textbook or a treatise on constitutional law. No, it will be found in the emotions of the heart, emotions deeply rooted in the real-life experiences of millions of American, and emotions that are crying out today to give the flag real and lasting protection." Similarly, House Veterans Affairs Committee chairman Sonny Montgomery (D-MS), one of the amendment's House cosponsors, declared that the flag had been "consecrated through 200 years of loyalty and love and sacrifice and reverence, of a special, almost sacred, kind," and "we seek only to protect it, just as you'd protect any loved one under attack." In response to the argument made by amendment critics that its passage would begin a "slippery slope" of endless subsequent limitations on the First Amendment, for example banning destroying copies of the Constitution or the presidential seal, Robert Bork, a prominent conservative legal scholar and failed Reagan nominee for the Supreme Court, told the SJC:

> No other object remotely resembles the flag as the symbol of our identity as a nation. . . . Forty-eight states have not enacted statutes prohibiting the burning of copies of our Constitution. Copies of the Constitution do not fly over our public buildings. . . . Nobody pledges allegiance to the presidential seal. Marines did not fight across Iwo Jima and up Mount Suribachi to raise the flag of Rhode Island, to raise a copy of the Constitution or of the presidential seal.

Amendment proponents repeatedly maintained that, although free speech was an important value, flag burning simply went "too far," because the flag was a "sacred" symbol of "freedom" that was especially treasured by American society and because too many sacrifices had been made on its behalf to tolerate its physical destruction. Thus, President Bush maintained that he would "uphold our precious right to dissent, but burning the flag goes too far" because the flag was "very, very special." Representative Henry Hyde (R-IL) compared the flag to "the sacrament in the Catholic Church" and the "holy book in other places or religions." Representative C. Thomas McMillen (D-MD) termed *Johnson* a "travesty of justice" that amounted to "a slap in the face to all Americans who have fought and died in defense of that symbol."

Most arguments for the amendment were more emotional than legal in nature, but its defenders also did mount legal arguments, especially after Democratic congressional leaders promoted the FPA as an alternative approach. One such argument was that the *Johnson* majority had erred because, as ninety-seven senators declared on June 22 in a Senate resolution criticizing the ruling, flag desecration "is clearly not 'speech' as protected by the First Amendment." Similarly, *Los Angeles Times* columnist Tom Bethell argued that by identifying flag burning with "speech," *Johnson* departed from "common sense," and since "millions of people" understand that "flames should not be confused with 'ideas,'" they "are likely to conclude that the law is an ass."

Alternatively, amendment backers maintained that even if flag desecration constituted expression, the courts had long held that some forms of expression, like "fighting words," obscenity, perjury, and libel served no significant social or political function and did not deserve constitutional protection. For example, Paul Kamenar, executive legal director of the conservative Washington Legal Foundation, told the HJC that the Court's reasoning was "inane" because

> The First Amendment is not an absolute and does not protect, for example, obscenity, libel, fighting words or even statements that rise to the level of treason, i.e. those which gave aid and comfort to the enemy. A civilized society must be able to say that there are certain things which are sacred and can be protected from desecration such as cemeteries and places of worship. Certainly, our nation's flag, as a revered and unique symbol, and one to which we all pledge our allegiance, should be protected as well.

Proponents of the amendment added that depriving citizens of the right to desecrate flags hardly oppressed them since they could still verbally abuse flags or engage in a wide variety of other forms of protest activity. Thus, Senator Orrin Hatch (R-UT) argued that the amendment would not prevent a "single idea or thought from being expressed," but only prevent "conduct" with respect to "one object only," still allowing a full panoply of expression through "speech, use of placards, leaflets, newspapers and even more." In response to those who supported the FPA but opposed the amendment, he asked how it could be that "a statute which prohibits flag desecration" was "not a threat to the First Amendment while a constitutional amendment achieving the same thing is such a threat?"

To those who argued that the FPA could constitutionally overturn *Johnson* by statutory means, thus avoiding the need for amending the Constitution, supporters of the amendment argued (correctly, as it turned out), that the Supreme Court would reject any such maneuver, with the result, as Bork put it, that "after several years of litigation, we would certainly be right where we are today." As will be discussed in greater detail below, the key legal argument by FPA backers was that *Johnson* did not strike down flag desecration laws in general, but only the Texas law, because its particular language, namely the "seriously offend" provision, targeted expressive content, whereas a supposedly "content neutral" law that banned all physical flag destruction regardless of the motive or "offensiveness" of such conduct would withstand legal scrutiny. Amendment supporters argued that this was simply a misreading of *Johnson*, however, because the Court had made clear that flag desecration laws were invalidated, not by their specific wording, but because their purpose was to suppress the message conveyed and therefore all such laws would violate the First Amendment.

This argument was made most forcefully by Assistant Attorney General William Barr, who told the HJC that the Bush administration had concluded that a statute "simply would not suffice" because no law that sought to outlaw flag desecration, even in a facially "content-neutral" manner, could withstand the *Johnson* analysis. Barr summarized his argument by declaring that *Johnson* had clearly established that

> whenever someone burns the Flag for expressive purposes, that conduct is protected by the First Amendment; that to prohibit such conduct, the Government must have a compelling reason that is unrelated to expression; that the Government's reason for protecting the flag (to preserve it as a symbol of national unity) is inherently and necessarily related to expression; and that the Government's interest in protecting the flag as a symbol of our national unity can never be sufficiently compelling to overcome an individual's First Amendment interest in burning the Flag for communicative purposes.

Barr rejected any comparisons of a "neutral" flag statute to laws that protected government monuments and animals from physical damage, regardless of what motivated such assaults, as "false analogies," because those objects were "inherently rare and irreplaceable" and therefore had value beyond and above any valued symbolism, whereas the flag was "inherently reproducible" and the only reason to seek to protect it "is because of its symbolic value," an interest "inherently related to expression." Thus, he continued, although the government could protect the actual Statue of Liberty because it is "both unique, one of a kind, and it is symbolic," without a constitutional amendment the government could not validly forbid people to "build an exact replica of the Statue of Liberty in their front yard and blow it up," because the only possible government interest in outlawing such conduct would be to suppress political dissent. The only truly "neutral" flag law, Barr added, would be one that "would either say everyone can use it [however they wished] or no one can." He termed arguments that "nonsuppressive" reasons could justify banning flag desecration "intellectually dishonest," "absurd," "chicanery," a "pretext," and a "weird contortion" that the Supreme Court "is not going to be fooled by."

Barr and other supporters of the amendment maintained that the falsity of the claims of FPA backers that their statute was "content neutral" and therefore would be upheld by the Supreme Court was clearly demonstrated by the FPA's exclusion of flag burnings conducted to retire soiled flags, which demonstrated that its true intent was to suppress only "unpatriotic" flag desecration rather than to protect all flags. In any case, backers of the amendment added, they were not interested in any "content-neutral" protection of the flag, but explicitly wanted to punish disloyal conduct with regard to flags while protecting patriotic conduct like ceremonial flag retirements, an objective that clearly required a constitutional amendment since otherwise such content discrimination would be illegal. Thus, Barr maintained that only an amendment could allow the government to single out for punishment "in a narrow and focused manner" those who "are really acting contemptuously toward the flag, who really want to harm the flag and harm the symbol," whereas the FPA would in an "intellectually dishonest" manner, punish "every form of conduct [physically damaging the flag], regardless of intent," such as a child "who innocently steps on a flag" or movie producers who sought to "honor the flag" by reproducing battle scenes from American history in which flags were damaged, in order to "get to" what "the American people are upset about." Similarly, former assistant attorney general Charles Cooper proclaimed that he did not "really want a neutral flag desecration statute" because he didn't want to punish conduct that damaged flags if such conduct was "dignified and respectful."

Although some amendment supporters unquestionably simply viewed *Johnson* as a terrible decision, had no legal qualms about amending the Constitution to overturn it, and had no ulterior political goals, some Republicans clearly were motivated, at least partly, by a quest to politically embarrass Democrats who might oppose the amendment and could be portrayed as unenthusiastic about defending the flag. In 1990 interviews, Assistant House Democratic whip David Bonior (D-MI), a leading opponent of the amendment, said, "There were people, Republicans and Democrats, who really believed in the need for an amendment" although "they were outnumbered by those who saw it in more political terms." Representative John Porter (R-IL), one of the few Republicans who voted against the amendment in 1990, reversed Bonior's emphasis, arguing that although some Republicans took a "certain degree of satisfaction in making the Democrats vote in a way they think they could take advantage of, I don't think that was a primary motivating factor of any significant percentage of people in my party."

That some Republicans had at least partly partisan motivations in backing the amendment was an open secret. Shortly after Bush endorsed the amendment, for example, House Republican leader Michel told reporters that White House chief of staff John Sununu had urged Republicans to push the amendment because it was a "wedge" issue that would divide Democrats. According to an anonymous White House source quoted in the press, Bush endorsed the amendment after Sununu had told him, "This train was pulling out of the station fast and the president might as well lead the parade," and another was quoted as declaring that Bush's "disgust with flag burning is genuine, but if he can get some political

mileage out of it, well, there's nothing unconstitutional about that."
In a 1990 interview, a key House Republican aide close to Michel
confirmed that Republican ranks in the House had been generally
split between those aligned with Michel, who preferred a low-key,
nonpartisan approach to dealing with the flag desecration issue,
and those aligned with Michel's lieutenant, Newt Gingrich (who
subsequently became Speaker of the House after Michel retired
and Republicans gained control of Congress in 1994), whose orientation was far more partisan. According to the aide, with regard
to the amendment, there was

> tension from the beginning between the Republican leader, who
> was going for the finish line, and people who were going for
> more immediate [political] enjoyment, and that tension never
> really ended. I spent a great deal of time with a number of our
> members, really trying to rein them in and have them be a lit-
> tle faithful to Bob Michel's long-term goal, rather than the
> short-term political gain. I spent a lot of time playing the cler-
> gyman on the political gain issue, and I was not a popular per-
> son for it.

In a 1998 interview, Michel revealed that, although he had been
a cosponsor of the amendment in 1989 and 1990, he had since
decided "now that I'm responsible only to myself and my family"
that "if the amendment was brought to a vote today, I would vote
against" it and "try to do whatever one could by statute," because
"I've always been one who said 'Be very, very careful of amending
the Constitution'" and "by gosh we're strong enough to withstand"
flag burning. Michel said there was "some validity" to the argument that "some" Republicans favored the amendment primarily
to politically embarrass Democrats. Michel attributed his support
for the amendment in 1989–1990 to the fact that "sometimes in
the heat of an issue you maybe let your better judgment run away
with you just for the expediency of satisfying an immediate need"
and because "those of us who are very patriotic guys" were
"incensed and ticked off and wanted to get back at those flag burners." Michel added that he thought Bush's support for the amendment "tipped the scale" among "Republicans who might have

thought we are a strong enough country to weather" flag burnings "without a constitutional amendment."

The Argument for the Flag Protection Act

The arguments and motivations of legislators who favored the FPA, or at least those who backed the FPA but opposed the amendment, were often extremely complicated. (Some congressmen supported *both* the amendment and the FPA, and their motives ranged from the completely genuine to completely politically fear-driven support for any and all measures that might overturn *Johnson*.) Such congressmen, overwhelmingly but not exclusively Democrats, held the balance of power in 1989, ensuring passage of the FPA but defeat of the amendment: in the Senate, which unlike the House voted for both alternatives in 1989, forty-three senators, including thirty-three Democrats, voted against the amendment but for the statute, with the result that the FPA passed 91 to 9, but the amendment fell far short of the required two-thirds majority. In the House, where only the FPA was voted on in 1989 and it passed 380 to 38, about 150 members who voted for the FPA opposed the amendment in 1990, with the result that the latter failed to receive the needed two-thirds, obtaining 254 positive votes to 177 negative votes (in the changed circumstances created by the intervening *Eichman* ruling, which left an amendment as the only possible means of outlawing flag desecration). Had all those who voted for the FPA in 1989 backed the amendment a year later, it would have obtained over 400 votes.

The legal argument for the constitutionality of the FPA, advanced most strongly by SJC chairman Biden, by Democratic majorities on the judiciary committees and by several prominent law professors with liberal reputations, most notably Harvard law professor Laurence Tribe, centered on the contention that *Johnson* had not banned *all* flag desecration laws, but only those that clearly targeted dissent and were not designed to "neutrally" protect the flag's "physical integrity" against all assaults, no matter what the motivation or intended message (or lack thereof, as in simple vandalism). The overwhelming thrust of *Johnson* seemed to contradict this theory: for example, it declared that the state could not "criminally punish a person for burning a flag as a means of political protest" and could not "foster its own view of the flag by prohibiting expressive conduct relating to it." Every news account interpreted the ruling as simply banning flag desecration laws outright, as in the *New York Times* June 22 story, which began by stating "the Supreme Court ruled today that no laws could prohibit political protesters from burning the American flag." This interpretation was also clearly that of Rehnquist's dissent, which complained that *Johnson* invalidated the 1968 federal flag desecration law as well as all state laws "which make criminal the public burning of the flag."

Nonetheless, FPA backers pointed to several phrases in *Johnson* they claimed bolstered their approach. Above all, they pointed to Brennan's statement that the Texas law at issue in *Johnson* unconstitutionally discriminated against expression on the basis of content because it was "not aimed at protecting the physical integrity" of flags "under all circumstances, but is designed instead to protect it only against impairments that would cause serious offense to others." They also stressed that this statement was accompanied by a footnote reference to Blackmun's 1974 *Goguen* dissent, in which he had maintained that a Massachusetts law the Court found unconstitutionally vague was constitutional because it outlawed all acts that "harmed the physical integrity of the flag" and therefore was not targeted at any "communicative element."

In the analysis and legal-political strategy of FPA backers, this footnote was intended to signal that Blackmun, at least, might support a so-called "content neutral" law that outlawed all conduct that impaired the flag's "physical integrity" without any reference to "offensive" impact on observers or the requirement that such action cast "contempt" upon the flag, as was the case with the 1968 federal law and many of the state flag desecration laws. This position was ultimately based on the argument that such a "content-neutral" law would be upheld by the Supreme Court because it would not seek to suppress expression and therefore would be legally subject only to the relatively lenient "important or substantial governmental interest" standard of the 1968 *O'Brien* ruling, rather than the virtually insurmountable "compelling" interest standard of *Johnson*, which the Court held applicable to statutes motivated by suppressive intent.

To an extraordinary extent, the drafting and legal argument for the FPA was shaped by the *Johnson* footnote reference to Blackmun. Thus, in an amicus brief urging the Supreme Court to uphold the FPA, House of Representatives legal counsel Steve Ross declared that Congress had paid "the most acute attention" to "Justice Blackmun's signal pronouncement," and in a 1990 interview PAW legislative counsel John Gomperts, who attended many Capitol Hill meetings in 1989 focusing on the flag desecration issue, declared that the FPA and the legislative reports explaining it amounted to a letter to Blackmun reading, "Dear Harry: We did what you said in *Goguen*. Now tell us it's OK." In a chapter entitled "The Supreme Court's Self-Inflicted Wounds" in a 1993 book published by Louis Lusky, the author accurately characterizes much of this stress by backers of the FPA as amounting to a "clear" warning to the Court that "if the new statute were held invalid, an overwhelming majority of both houses might favor an amendment" and therefore *Johnson*'s "life expectancy as a precedent might be short."

The legal argument for the FPA ultimately rested on the claim that the government could conceivably have any purpose in protecting the physical integrity of all existing American flags that was unrelated to seeking to suppress political dissent. Fried, the advocate of "bravely doing nothing," told Congress that any such claim was "so transparent that the [Supreme] Court is going to see right through them." According to Tribe and other promoters of the FPA, however, the government's interest in protecting flags had the nonsuppressive purpose of seeking to honor them as particularly valued objects against all physical threats, like laws that outlawed the killing of bald eagles or the defacing of gravesites or government buildings regardless of what might motivate such acts. Thus, according to the pro-FPA SJC majority report, the FPA would focus "solely and exclusively on the conduct [as opposed to any intended message] of the actor" and protect the "physical integrity of the flag in all circumstances," consistent with the alleged right of Congress to "protect symbols and landmarks," in recognition of the "diverse and powerfully held feelings of our citizens for the flag." The report maintained, "When it comes to the American flag—that one symbol of the spirit of our democracy—we care more about protecting its physical integrity than about determining why its integrity has been threatened"; it added that protecting the flag's physical integrity because "of what it expresses and represents" would pose no First Amendment problems because such protection was not intended to "censor or suppress the person who might attack it."

Because FPA proponents clearly suggested that flag desecration was an evil serious enough to warrant criminalizing it, their stance against a constitutional amendment with the same goal was inevitably largely eviscerated of any arguments on behalf of freedom of speech. Therefore, they were essentially reduced to the tactical position that flag desecration was too trivial a matter to warrant a constitutional amendment or that a constitutional amendment, especially one that for the first time would formally limit First Amendment rights, was such a grave step that a statutory approach should at least be tried first. For example, Geoffrey Stone, dean of the University of Chicago Law School, told the SJC that an amendment would "clutter, trivialize and indeed denigrate the Constitution and the broad principles for which it stands," because flag desecration was of "secondary importance to the overall scheme of American government."

Many leading FPA proponents, including SJC chairman Biden and HJC chairman Jack Brooks, pledged that they would back an amendment if the FPA was struck down, reducing their argument to the position that, as the SJC majority stressed, "the amendment process should be invoked as a last, not as a first resort." Tribe and others even argued that the FPA was preferable to an amendment because it could become effective much more quickly than an amendment and thus facilitate the speedier jailing of flag burners. Thus, Tribe told Congress that because a "simple statute" could be "easily and quickly enacted" it would be "folly" to "reach for the heavy artillery of the amendment process," which would take months and amount to using a "sledgehammer" when a "scalpel" could solve the problem. Such arguments completely removed any issues related to freedom of speech from the entire controversy, as Tribe, who first popularized the statutory approach in an op-ed article in the July 3 *New York Times*, made clear when he ended his article by stating that an amendment would be acceptable as a "last resort."

After the FPA was struck down by the Supreme Court in 1990, many of those who had voted for it but continued to oppose the Bush amendment were reduced to maintaining, as Biden did, that the wording of the amendment was flawed, or, as most did, that the symbolic importance of the First Amendment was so critical that although abridging freedom of speech by statute was acceptable, limiting exactly the same freedom by amendment was not. Thus, Representative Barbara Boxer (D-CA) explained her vote for the FPA in 1989 but against the amendment in 1990 by declaring, "There is a difference between voting for a law to ban flag burning and voting to change the Constitution" for the same purpose because the Bill of Rights was "sacred" and "the greatest document of freedom in the world."

The motivations of legislators who favored the FPA but opposed an amendment were at least as complex as their legal arguments. Some of them sincerely believed that flag desecration was an evil serious enough to warrant criminal penalties but not serious enough to warrant formally limiting the First Amendment for the first time in American history, especially because they feared such action might open up a "slippery slope" for further abridgments of fundamental freedoms. Many other members of Congress, mostly, but not all, Democrats, clearly primarily supported the FPA less because they wanted to jail flag burners than because they both opposed amending the Bill of Rights for the first time and above all feared the political consequences of appearing to support flag burners. As columnist Nat Hentoff wrote in early August, for many Democrats the FPA was designed to "both ward off a constitutional amendment and prove to the frenzied voter that Democrats too" loved the flag. They viewed the First Amendment—both in terms of its substance and its symbolism—as just as "sacred" as amendment supporters viewed the flag, and therefore felt that any measure that could help save it from erosion was justified. In short, a large percentage of Democrats who backed the FPA privately were either unenthusiastic about it or believed that *Johnson* was correctly decided, but were convinced that Bush and other Republicans were out to repeat their perceived successful 1988 manipulation of the flag and were determined to oppose such efforts, yet felt they had to support some alternative to give themselves political cover against charges that they were unpatriotic. As People for the American Way 1989–1990 legislative counsel John Gomperts noted in a 1990 interview, the "whole purpose" of the FPA for many was "not to have a constitutional amendment." The mixture of Democratic rage against Bush and fear about the perceived potential political consequences of seeming to support *Johnson* was perhaps best reflected by the comments of House Speaker Foley on June 27, the day Bush endorsed an amendment: "Anyone who suggests that there is a party difference in respect for the American flag is using the deep affection of Americans, twisting it, manipulating it, using it for the most base and crass political purposes."

In an 1990 interview, ABA president Stanley Chauvin, who lobbied on Capitol Hill for the "bravely do nothing" position, summed up the complex motives of FPA backers by declaring that some "thought there could be a statute and that it was a valid exercise of legislative authority," some were "outraged" at the prospects of a constitutional amendment and "thought that the statute might slow it down," and some "were just outright frauds in the deal and said, 'Hell, here's a good chance to make some 30-second [advertising] clips out of the deal.'" Chauvin added that in his view the overwhelming support for the FPA—fewer than 50 senators and representatives voted against it but over 470 backed it—"wasn't a sincere test" of what many congressmen felt and "if the vote had been in a dark room it would have been totally different." According to a 1990 interview with a key House Democratic leadership aide, Speaker Foley was convinced that by supporting the FPA,

if time was allowed to work, the pressure would decrease, the hysteria would decrease and the atmosphere would get more normal. But it wasn't just a delay strategy because lots of folks felt that [the FPA] would [be held constitutional] and clearly it warranted a try because there was a very good argument that you don't go to the Constitution if you can achieve the goal through other means, so on both of those counts independently the statute made a lot of sense.

That many proponents of the FPA primarily favored it as a means to block the amendment rather than as a desirable piece of legislation is especially evident from the fact that the two leading civil liberties organizations, PAW and the ACLU, and some of the most prominent constitutional law professors in the country who had long been associated with highly libertarian interpretations of the First Amendment, such as Tribe and Duke University's Walter Dellinger, either overtly or tacitly supported the FPA although they almost certainly did not really favor it. PAW hailed *Johnson* as a "victory for free speech" and condemned the amendment in testimony submitted to the SJC as a "frontal attack" on "freedom of expression," but the organization never took a stand on the FPA, even though it sought exactly the same end as the amendment. Behind the scenes, according to civil liberties and congressional sources, PAW effectively urged congressmen to back the FPA; as one civil liberties activist who attended many 1989 Capitol Hill meetings put it, the "whole point" of PAW lobbying was to get across the message, "Don't pass the constitutional amendment," with the "understood message" being "If you need to pass the statute for political reasons, go ahead and do that, make it least as bad as possible, but don't ever amend the Constitution."

PAW legislative counsel Gomperts lamented in 1990 that

More than anything it was a testament to the political hysteria of the moment that two organizations that are as absolutist [in behalf of civil liberties] as the ACLU and PAW did not speak out strongly against this statute. That ultimately had a large effect on the political dynamic, it helped to frame the debate. There was essentially no one who was standing up and saying, "Do nothing!" That's the position that is supposed to be occupied by the PAW and the ACLU, that "We deplore flag burning but it's protected speech and you have to abide this to have the freedoms that all of us cherish." We didn't do that.

Gomperts added that the civil liberties groups feared that if they strongly opposed both the amendment and the FPA their organizations would not "get to play ball at all, they're the nutballs, they're the chorus but not the inside players," because such a stance was viewed as "outside the bounds of what was acceptable." On the other hand, he added, if they took the position

> "All right, we understand what you've got to do, we don't like it but we understand it" then they felt they would get to be in all the meetings, to negotiate about the FPA, to make it as inoffensive as possible and to strategize how to defeat the amendment. But they felt "If we take the purist position, we're out in the street." Of course, this posture added to the dynamics which fostered the passage of the FPA. With liberal constitutionalists like Tribe and Dellinger saying a statute might work, and with the ACLU and PAW saying, "All right, if you've got to do a statute, do a statute" and with people screaming bloody murder that we have to do something to protect Old Glory, how many people would listen to someone who's going to stand up and say, "Let's do nothing"?

In retrospect, Gomperts added, he regretted that PAW had not opposed the FPA in 1989 because "the flag burning issue lost steam" and "it is not clear that had we opposed both the statute and the amendment that we would have interfered with our ability to be able to be a legitimate spokesperson against the amendment."

Although the ACLU, unlike PAW, formally opposed both the FPA and the amendment—in an April 1990 letter to ACLU members executive director Ira Glasser termed the two proposals "equally disgraceful" and accomplishing the "same thing"—during the fall of 1989 the ACLU, like PAW, effectively lobbied Congress to pass the FPA as the only means of blocking the amendment. The ACLU circulated a lengthy briefing book on Capitol Hill entitled *The Case Against a Constitutional Amendment on Flag Desecration* that contained hundreds of pages on that theme but precisely one paragraph on the FPA, which stated only that ACLU "opposes" it (without giving any reasons) but that since "a number of witnesses have testified that there is a reasonable chance that the Supreme Court will uphold" the FPA "it would be inappropriate to considering amending the Constitution until and unless the statute is declared unconstitutional." One key Democratic Senate staff source interviewed in 1990 characterized the ACLU's behind-the-scenes 1989 role as "the same as PAW, which was encouraging people to vote for the statute," and according to a civil liberties activist interviewed in 1990 who was present at numerous Capitol Hill meetings in 1989, the ACLU acted as "a cheerleader for the statute" and behaved in an "incredibly disingenuous" and "intellectually dishonest" way that was "truly eye-opening to me because I never thought that would be the case." According to a 1990 interview with a House Democratic staff member who played a key role in his party's successful legislative strategy in 1989 of pushing the FPA as a means of stopping the amendment, the ACLU's secret role was "one of the reasons we won," because "the ACLU understood that you had to have a statute" to block the amendment.

In a 1999 letter in response to queries about these reports about the ACLU's 1989 role, executive director Glasser implicitly confirmed them, but defended his organization's tactics as reflecting "sophistication" rather than "hypocrisy," since in the end the amendment was defeated and the FPA was struck down, reflecting a successful outcome to the ACLU's "strategic considerations" in "doing what we could to make sure that this nation did not end up with either a statute or a constitutional amendment." Glasser declared that "no serious participant" could have believed that the ACLU actually "favored any law that would have resulted in making it a crime to use the flag expressively," but since no FPA-type statute "could have survived Supreme Court" scrutiny in the absence of a constitutional amendment

> if voting for a statute (that was doomed under the Constitution as it exists) allowed some members of Congress the political cover to vote against the amendment, that was good. Passing a

statute would change nothing; passing an amendment would have changed everything. The ACLU would have justly come under criticism had we naively worked to defeat a doomed statute, which defeat led to an invulnerable amendment. The bottom line is our strategy worked.

In a 1990 interview, ACLU Washington office director Mort Halperin, who was the frontline implementer of the organization's strategy, similarly effectively conceded that the ACLU had, at the least, not vigorously opposed the FPA. He said, "We hoped we would get the best of both worlds—the statute passes and that holds off the constitutional amendment, the statute is held unconstitutional [by the Supreme Court] and then we have enough time to calm people down and we [subsequently again] defeat the amendment. I think it was the right strategy and I'd do it again exactly the same way." Halperin maintained that "we opposed the statute" and "thought the statute was unconstitutional," but he conceded that "we made it clear to people that we were far more concerned about a constitutional amendment" and "the focus of our energies was not on the statute" because "there was no way to block the statute and if somehow that happened by a miracle there would be no way to stop an amendment." Halperin added, "I told people that I don't want on my tombstone, 'While he was in charge of the ACLU Washington Office the First Amendment was amended.'"

PAW and the ACLU were joined during the fall of 1989 in their vocal opposition to the amendment by either silence or tacit support for the FPA by hundreds of prominent constitutional lawyers, law professors, college presidents, and others who undoubtedly understood that their stance, under the existing political circumstances, amounted to a coded urging that Congress defeat the amendment by supporting the FPA, even though the same vigorous free speech arguments that they used to argue against the former presumably applied equally to the latter. According to a well-informed civil liberties activist, PAW helped to publicize and coordinate perhaps the most important such expression, a petition to Congress by 511 constitutional law professors that strongly opposed the amendment but failed to mention the FPA, which was published on September 21, shortly after House passage of the FPA and several weeks before scheduled Senate consideration of both alternatives. The petition was formally organized by three prominent law school deans, including Lee Bollinger, then dean of the University of Michigan and subsequently president of that institution (who declined to respond to requests for interviews concerning his role). The petitioners, who called themselves Constitutional Law Professors Against a Constitutional Amendment, urged Congress to reject the amendment as "unwise and inconsistent" with the Bill of Right's "core purpose" of protecting "unpopular speech from suppression by the political majority."

Two similar petitions were given significant organizational assistance by the ACLU's Washington office: the Emergency Committee to Defend the First Amendment, consisting of two dozen prominent American college presidents (including those of Harvard, Chicago, Stanford, Yale, and Virginia) and leading lawyers (including three past presidents of the ABA), stated in a September 29 letter to Congress that it took "no position" on the FPA, but urged defeat of the amendment because it would "violate the "well-established principle that an unpopular speaker may not be silenced because of his views"; a similar petition from over one hundred law professors, organized by Harvard law professor Tribe and Duke law professor Dellinger and sent to Congress on October 12 after both houses had passed the FPA, urged rejection of the amendment as "inappropriate" because there was a "reasonable basis" for believing that the Supreme Court "will find" the FPA constitutional.

The latter petition, according to a participant in a 1989 meeting with ACLU Washington director Halperin, was pointed to by Halperin as "one of the things that the ACLU was going to do to make people comfortable in voting for the statute, by telling them that it might be constitutional." It offered no opinions about the substantive advisability of either the FPA or the amendment, stating only that the signers had "differing views" about *Johnson*, but agreed that since "at least five [Supreme Court] justices might well uphold" the FPA, "which will accomplish the only legitimate objectives" of an amendment, Congress should not "restrict the Bill of Rights" while awaiting Court action. According to Dellinger, interviewed in 1991, the petition was deliberately not released until both houses had passed the FPA to "make it clear that many of us were not in any way promoting or endorsing the statute," but he conceded that some law professors refused to sign it because "they believed that it gave some indirect aid and comfort to the statute. It was a very respectable position to take, 'That you shouldn't make arguments that appear to praise with faint damns' or 'That to say that the Court might sustain seems to give comfort to such an illiberal project.'"

Dellinger and Tribe, two of the most prominent constitutional lawyers in the country, who (like Bollinger) were well known for their staunch defense of First Amendment freedoms, both gave extremely influential and well-publicized testimony before the two judiciary committees in the summer of 1989 during which they vigorously attacked the amendment but predicted that the Supreme Court would likely uphold the FPA. Dellinger noted in the 1991 interview that he had communicated to Congress his personal opposition to the FPA (although this was relegated to a footnote in his HJC written testimony, not included in his oral remarks, which stated that the FPA "is insufficiently tolerant of dissenting views," a comment that was modified to read "may be insufficiently tolerant" in his later SJC submission). However, he agreed that it was a "fair assessment" that in the 1989 political climate that his overall presentation "might well be seen as encouragement to Congress to enact such a statute." He conceded that he wished he "had been more emphatic about my opposition to the statute," but said he had "understated" his opposition to it because its passage was "an absolutely foregone conclusion" and it "was going to be almost impossible" to stop the amendment in the Senate "if the judgment had been that any statute was going to have utterly ridiculous prospects before the Court." Since, Dellinger continued, he genuinely believed that although the argument for the FPA's constitutionality was "not very plausible, it's an argument that comes out of" *Johnson*, and "launching an all-out attack on the constitutionality of the statute was just going to weaken the case against an amendment," it "seemed to me that holding off an amendment was far more important than making a wholly futile argument against passage of a statute that was sure to pass."

The 1989 testimony and role of Tribe, probably the single most influential constitutional law professor in the United States, was especially important in leading to passage of the FPA, which he helped draft and for which he was widely viewed as the intellectual "godfather": he was largely responsible for publicizing the position that a flag statute could constitutionally achieve the same end as an amendment in his July 3 *New York Times* op-ed piece, and he vigorously maintained this position during his congressional testimony. Tribe's op-ed article largely established the legal and political position that FPA backers maintained for the following five months, and, as a key Senate Democratic leadership aide recalled in a 1990 interview, his position "played a major role" in the minds of congressmen with "an overriding desire not to amend the Constitution," because his views and the similar stance of other "reputable legal scholars" lent considerable credence to the posture that it was at least "arguably constitutional" to reverse *Johnson* with a statute.

In his *Times* article and subsequent testimony, Tribe maintained that *Johnson* did not invalidate all flag desecration laws, but only required that "Government protection of the flag be separated from Government suppression of detested views" and in particular that laws not single out instances in which flags "are destroyed publicly or in a manner that expresses contempt." Tribe told the HJC that it could not be "responsibly" doubted that "at least six" and "perhaps seven" Supreme Court justices would uphold a "neutrally-drawn physical-integrity-of-the-flag law" so long "as it's not used just to target dissenters in a politically motivated way." In both his *Times* article and HJC testimony Tribe clearly personally endorsed a flag desecration statute, for example telling the HJC that "it is hard to see what could be a better way of protecting the flag than to pass a simple statute making it a crime to destroy a flag or mutilate it in any way."

Throughout his testimony, Tribe maintained that flag desecration laws would be upheld by the Supreme Court so long as they only sought to "give force to the community's shared sense that the object is worthy of special protection," without regard to "the presence or absence of any message" or any intent to "censor the views" of desecrators, just as gravesites or historic buildings could be protected regardless of the motivation of those who might want to disturb them. "Such laws are justifiable," he maintained, "not because there is a scarcity of gravesites or of historic landmarks, but because the people, acting through democratic principles, have the right to designate particularly significant things or places as off-limits to physical assault." In contrast to the FPA's "neutral" protection of flags, Tribe and other supporters of the statute argued, the proposed amendment would violate the fundamental principle of American democracy by explicitly targeting the message of dissident flag desecrators: according to Tribe the amendment would "rip the heart out of the First Amendment, whose most central truth" was that "in this country we do not go after people just because we do not like their message." Tribe and other FPA backers maintained that excluding the ceremonial disposal of worn flags would pose no constitutional difficulties because such objects would no longer truly be "flags." Dellinger said they would be "maybe a flag emeritus or a former flag, but it's no longer a flag," and Tribe suggested that old flags could perhaps be retired through the establishment of a "Federal repository institution maybe run by veterans to which one would have to send worn-out flags."

Because, in the aftermath of *Johnson*, Tribe probably had greater importance than anyone other than President Bush in shaping the 1989 congressional flag desecration debate, and because his argument that the Supreme Court would likely find a statute constitutional seemed so at odds with his well-established persona as a staunch civil libertarian, he came under bitter attack from a wide variety of partisans and observers who suggested that he (along with other constitutional lawyers of similar repute) had abandoned his principles in an attempt to save the Democratic Party from political catastrophe. These attacks were partly based on the fact that Tribe had published a major book in 1988 that suggested that flag desecration statutes were inherently unconstitutional for singling out unpopular expression for governmental suppression.

Moreover, immediately following Bush's June 27 endorsement of an amendment, he told reporters that only an amendment could overturn *Johnson*, because any statute would have the unconstitutional purpose of seeking to suppress dissent. He added that a statute would be undesirable in any case since, he asked, "What does the flag stand for" if that did not include the right to "express derision?"

Tribe exposed himself to further criticism when, after enactment of the FPA substantially contributed to heading off the amendment in 1989 and its constitutionality was being weighed before the Supreme Court in May 1990, he declared that the Court should strike the FPA down because its "real purpose" was "censorship" and it was not "viewpoint neutral," although he had previously defended it as "content neutral" and had predicted that the Supreme Court would uphold it. Explaining this shift, Tribe said that the early October 1989 congressional addition of the term "physically defiles" to the list of actions with regard to flags that would violate the law had been a "constitutional poison pill," amounting to the "thirteenth chime of the clock that makes the first twelve ring hollow" with regard to the "content-neutral" argument (however, even after this addition he had organized the October 12 letter to Congress from one hundred law professors that urged opposition to the amendment on the grounds that there were "reasonable" grounds" to believe the Court would uphold the FPA). After the Supreme Court struck down the FPA in June 1990, Tribe characterized the decision as "an extremely hopeful sign for the future of free speech," termed the FPA an "abomination" for which he hoped to "get as little credit as possible" and said that his earlier role in backing the FPA had "probably" been unprincipled, although he had not thought so at the time.

Representative James Sensenbrenner, a strong amendment backer and the ranking Republican HJC member, clearly targeted Tribe when he caustically referred during a July 1989 hearing to professors whose views on constitutional law had to be placed "in a loose-leaf binder where old worn-out views get replaced with a new page when a position has to change." From the opposite perspective, Kunstler wrote in August 1989 that he had been profoundly "shocked" that "formerly unremitting defenders of the First Amendment" like Tribe, in attempts to "head off a dangerous constitutional amendment" had sought to make violations of the First Amendment "legally palatable" in ways that permitted "the same damage to free expression." Even New York University law professor and former ACLU legal director Burt Neuborne, who, in a 1991 interview termed Tribe's approach a "politically brilliant" and "very sophisticated" maneuver for the admirable purpose of seeking to block the amendment, added that it was also "intellectually dishonest" and a "political game."

In a lengthy 1999 interview, when asked about Neuborne's comments, Tribe responded:

> I hate to turn down an offer of praise, but I think I was being less sophisticated than Burt would give me credit for, but more intellectually honest. The game he describes is not one that I would ever feel comfortable playing. I see my central identity in the professional world as a teacher and scholar, and saying what I really believe is much more important to me than the outcome of some success that I politically favor. I never testified in Congress or said anything in public other than what I really believed. I suppose you could defend the morality of tilting one's expression to achieve some greater good, but that wasn't what I was doing.

Tribe added that he "wasn't naive" in realizing that his position "could be helpful" in giving political assistance to Democrats "who wanted to oppose the amendment but make clear that they loved the flag as much as anyone," but "that wasn't my motive." He said he had testified that in theory *Johnson* had not precluded the constitutionality of a "neutral" flag protection statute, but he had "never supported" the final version of the FPA, which "was not by any conceivable definition the kind of neutral statute I was describing." According to Tribe, the inclusion of the "physically defiles" provision during the final congressional consideration of the FPA was the "straw I felt broke the camel's back," but he conceded, "I probably didn't do enough to publicly distance myself" from the FPA when it was finally enacted.

Tribe added that he was not "clear where I drew the line between predicting" that a genuinely "content neutral" flag desecration law "would be upheld [by the Supreme Court] and actively supporting it." Although he said he was an "agnostic" concerning the wisdom of a law when he testified before Congress in the summer of 1989, he said he "had much more sympathy" for such an approach "than others, often viewed as liberals, would have had" because he felt that "it was not so unreasonable to care about something like this at an emotional level." Tribe maintained that in his congressional testimony his position was "not that in my view a neutrally drawn law *ought* to be upheld" but rather that, as "an expert on what the Supreme Court would do," precedents, including *Johnson*, "would not support the idea that as a predictive matter" a statute "would be struck down by the Supreme Court" and indeed the "most responsible prediction was to the contrary."

On the other hand, Tribe agreed that there had been a genuine "change inside my head" since his 1989 testimony: "I wouldn't then endorse the view I now hold that you can't have a statute that would constitutionally protect the flag as a distinct symbol," because any "statute, no matter how neutrally drawn in terms of equating all possible forms of destruction of images of American flags, but which prohibits destruction selectively of that image and not other images" is "deeply problematic under the First Amendment." The reason for this, he added, is because when government "singles out particular symbols freighted with ideological meaning it is violating the First Amendment whether the destruction prohibited is disrespectful or expresses a particular viewpoint or not. Creating a special national symbol and preventing people from destroying it is in of itself a violation of the First Amendment." He continued, "I don't regard it as all that strange to change one's mind about something and have quite often done so in print." In hindsight, Tribe added, he wished he had opposed the amendment not on the "modest" basis that it was not needed and that the Supreme Court would uphold a statute, but on the "more compelling" grounds that passing it would make it "much harder for other groups that want to defend their symbols from symbolic assault to be satisfied with the conventional answer that our society is dedicated to supporting a full range of expression."

In retrospect, Tribe said, "I wish I had been clear about how narrow and limited my support" for the statutory approach was, since "I certainly meant to say that I wasn't affirmatively in favor of it as a piece of legislation. I didn't think there was a real problem that it was responding to, though I certainly sympathized with the visceral outrage it was responding to. But I think we sacrifice a lot more than we preserve when we punish acts of this kind, no matter how narrow and precisely drawn a statute like this is."

In predicting that the Supreme Court would uphold a truly "neutral" statute, Tribe added, he was influenced by three different factors. The first was the conviction that those advocating an amendment were "playing fast and loose with Supreme Court precedents" and specifically reading *Johnson* "more broadly than the opinion itself justified for reasons of political convenience," since it was "easier to defend an Amendment if Supreme Court decisions in this area had as sweeping an effect as the amendment's proponents insisted they did." A second motivating factor, Tribe said, was that he "very much wanted to believe, due to my personal experiences and history, that there was some way to protect the flag," a feeling he especially attributed to "my own memories of my father and the flag which he had smuggled into a Japanese concentration camp, which I still have in my study, which left me with powerful attachments to that symbol, which I wanted to see protected in law even though I felt that the Texas law [at issue in *Johnson*] and the [final version of the] FPA were no good." Third, Tribe added, he felt it would be "disastrous to start amending the First Amendment in this kind of way" because "an amendment should only be done as a last resort" and its backers "hadn't exhausted all [other] possibilities," and the statutory approach was a "modest position in the middle which would, among other things, help to prevent the Constitution from being amended, which I felt was a terrible mistake."

The Braking of the Drive
for a Constitutional Amendment

In the immediate aftermath of *Johnson*, and especially after Bush endorsed a constitutional amendment on June 27, it was widely predicted that an amendment was inevitable, especially if Congress voted quickly. For example, HJC subcommittee chair Edwards told reporters on June 24 that only "ten or twenty" members of the House would then vote against an amendment. Shortly after the Bush endorsement CBS White House correspondent Leslie Stahl reported that the proposal was "a steamroller going down hill" that "nobody is going to stop," and *U.S. News & World Report* proclaimed that opposing it "seems suicidal." In fact, the "steamroller" quickly stalled: when Dole formally introduced the amendment in the Senate on July 18, fifty-two senators were listed as cosponsors, but on October 19 it received only fifty-one votes, far short of the needed two-thirds majority.

The primary explanations for the derailing of the amendment steamroller were: 1) the Democratic-sponsored alternative of the FPA, which passed both houses by the time of the Senate amendment vote and had the practical effect of providing "political cover" for those who opposed the amendment but feared being depicted as antiflag; 2) the related "cooling-off" period engineered by the Democratic congressional leadership, designed to prevent Congress from voting until the immediate post-*Johnson* hysteria had died down, which was justified with the impregnable public explanation that time was needed to study the two alternatives; 3) a rising tide of opposition to the amendment, not only from the "usual" civil libertarian suspects, but also from the overwhelming majority of newspapers around the country and from a number of veterans and well-credentialed conservatives who could not plausibly be attacked as unpatriotic; and 4) the failure of the Bush administration to strongly push for the amendment during the late summer and fall of 1989.

The intertwined Democratic strategy of support for the FPA and the associated "cooling-off" period reflected a barely concealed effort by their congressional leadership to plausibly force a delay in voting on the amendment and simultaneously provide nervous troops with a "pro-flag" alternative to vote for as "political cover" from the perceived threat of Republican attacks on their patriotism. Immediately after Bush endorsed the amendment, for example, Foley announced that hearings would be "calmly conducted" on both an amendment and a statute "in the spirit of deliberation and care," and declared that he could not "imagine why anyone" would "lightly and frivolously" rush to amend the Constitution "unnecessarily" if "a statute can accomplish all of the objectives." Similarly, when Senate Democratic leader Mitchell announced on July 14 that the Senate would not vote on the statute or the amendment until October, he said the purpose of a delay was to allow consideration of the proposals in a "serious, mature, deliberate way."

In a 1990 interview, HJC subcommittee chair Edwards termed the FPA "marginally constitutional," but added that without it the amendment "would be part of the Constitution very easily," as it succeeded in halting the "frenzy" and "hysteria" on Capitol Hill that ensued after Bush endorsed the amendment, because its backers convinced enough congressmen that by supporting it "they would look just as patriotic" as amendment supporters. Assistant House Democratic whip David Bonior, also interviewed in 1990, agreed that the FPA was above all "a strategy to block a constitutional amendment at all costs" and that it was a "fair characterization" that many of its supporters did not view it as good or even constitutional, but backed it because the perceived certain alternative of an amendment was "so awful." According to Bonior, "Those are hard decisions for people because you have to give more sometimes than you want to achieve your ultimate goal," but "the fact of the matter is [the FPA] undoubtedly saved amending the Constitution [in 1989]." Similarly, after the FPA passed the Senate by 91 to 9 on October 5 and the Senate was about to defeat the amendment, SJC chairman Biden, the leading Senate FPA proponent, asked a group of reporters if any of them "doubted if this statute had not been passed the Senate would have passed a constitutional amendment?"

The Democratic hope that delaying voting on the amendment to allow consideration of the FPA would provide a "cooling-off" period unquestionably worked. As the judiciary committees held hearings between mid-July and mid-September and Congress recessed for a month in August, news coverage of the flag controversy became increasingly sketchy and intermittent: after July 4, the three network evening newscasts never mentioned the issue again on the same day until the House passed the FPA on September 12. Declining media interest in the issue was accompanied by—and probably significantly contributed to—a similar decline in general public concern. By mid-July, Speaker Foley was telling reporters that the "country as a whole seems to be taking this in a calmer way" than Congress and that there was "no firestorm of fervor" for an amendment," sentiments that were reflected in a series of newspaper articles in late July. Probably the most influential such report appeared on the front page of the July 25 *Washington Post*, a newspaper universally read on Capitol Hill, under the headline "Support Lags for Amendment to Prohibit Flag Burning." The article reported a considerable decline in constituent mail to congressmen about the flag since the immediate post-*Johnson* reaction; according to a Democratic SJC source interviewed in 1991, the article was "very significant" because it helped many congressmen tell themselves, "Gee, it's not just my anecdotal experience, but others didn't hear anything [from their constituents] either."

By late July, SJC chairman Biden was reporting, "there is not a single senator who's come up to me in the last three weeks and said, 'Hey, how about the critical issue of the burning flag?'" Numerous other congressmen reported that during the August recess they heard little about the issue when visiting their districts. For example, Representative Beryl Anthony (D-AR) related after returning to Washington that he "did not have one single person bring it up," and Senator Robert Kerrey (D-NE) said that he had heard "almost nothing" from his constituents about his opposition to both the amendment and the FPA, and that the flag controversy "looks like a hot political issue, but it isn't." According to an aide to a leading Democratic Senate opponent of the amendment interviewed in

1990, although "a vote before the August recess would have been a disaster for us, a lot of senators talked to people back home [then] and got the impression that people were ambivalent and concerned about amending the Constitution." By mid-October, shortly before the Senate defeated the amendment, amendment supporter Senator Alan Simpson (R-WY) conceded that backing for it was "just not out there in the land."

Aside from the impact of the "cooling-off" period and the "political cover" provided by the FPA, another major factor that helped derail the amendment was growing and increasingly vocal opposition to it after late June, which, particularly when it came from veterans or conservatives, helped to provide additional "cover" for those who feared the political consequences of voting against the amendment. Thus, opposition to the amendment by two Vietnam War veterans, Senator Kerrey, a winner of the Congressional Medal of Honor who had lost part of a leg in Vietnam, and James Warner, a former Vietnam prisoner of war and Reagan administration official, was especially influential.

In a widely quoted and reprinted July 11 *Washington Post* column, Warner related that he had humiliated a North Vietnamese captor by pointing to antiwar flag burnings as a sign of the strength of American democracy (although such acts were then illegal!). According to Warner, when his captor showed him a picture of flag burnings and told him it proved that he was "wrong" because "people in your country are against your cause," and he responded that rather the picture proved he was right because "in my country we are not afraid of freedom, even if it means people disagree with us," his interrogator's face turned "purple with rage" and he "smashed his fist onto the table and screamed at me to shut up." Warner concluded, "I have never forgotten that look, nor have I forgotten the satisfaction I felt at using his tool, the picture of the burning flag, against him." He added, "After that experience, I cannot compromise with freedom," nor was there any need to, because freedom "is the best weapon we have." In a widely quoted mid-July Senate speech, Kerrey attacked Bush for choosing the "path of least resistance and greatest political gain" on the flag issue, praised *Johnson* as "reasonable, understandable and consistent with those values that

I believe make America so wonderful," and rejected the common argument that the flag had to be protected because so many soldiers had died for it, because in his war experience, "I don't remember giving the safety of our flag anywhere near the thought that I gave the safety of my men."

PAW legislative counsel Gomperts recalled in a 1990 interview that Kerrey's speech made a "big splash and changed the dynamic of the debate" and that the Warner column was "quoted a million times" and "Washington was buzzing" about it. *Washington Post* congressional reporter Don Phillips similarly recalled in another 1990 interview that Warner had a "big impact" because "all of a sudden there was another side to patriotism, so a patriot doesn't have to wrap himself in the flag, a patriot can also see the flag as a piece of cloth which isn't that important, it's what it stands for. I think that got picked up and repeated all over the place."

Opposition to the amendment was almost universal in the press, extending far beyond major liberal and centrist publications and spokesmen to encompass many small and medium-size newspapers and even very conservative outlets such as the *Detroit News* and the *Washington Times*. When reporters asked Speaker Foley on June 28 how members of his party could explain opposing a flag amendment, he responded, "They should read the *Washington Times* editorial this morning and they would have a very good explanation." Moreover, with the notable exception of Pat Buchanan, all of the most prominent conservative political columnists, including James Kilpatrick, George Will, and William Safire, also opposed the amendment. In a 1990 interview, ABC congressional correspondent Cokie Roberts recalled that the "conservative columnists made a big difference" in providing "a tremendous amount of political coverage" for opponents of the amendment who feared being attacked for such a vote.

Much of the press editorial commentary and news coverage, along with the comments of other political analysts, suggested that Bush was primarily motivated by partisan ends. Thus, prominent political commentator William Schneider declared that Republicans wanted to "turn every Democrat into a liberal flag-burner— like they did to Michael Dukakis," while CBS White House correspondent Leslie Stahl reported on the day that Bush endorsed an amendment that he had "learned in the [1988] campaign that this is an issue that works for him." Popular comedian Jay Leno's joke that Bush wanted to outlaw flag burning because "if you're going to wrap yourself in the flag you don't want to get burned" was repeatedly quoted. In a 1990 interview, a White House aide who played a major role in the administration's handling of the amendment bitterly complained that although, by its early massive coverage, the press had "kind of jumped on the bandwagon" and helped spur Bush to endorse an amendment, the media had subsequently "turned tail from the initial days and portrayed it exclusively as all politics, that no one really wanted to protect the flag. It was just day and night." Even Bush, in a little-noticed newspaper interview published in late July 1989, complained about "a lot of columnists piling on now," and he rejected allegations that he was "wrapping myself in the flag" and what he termed the argument of the "columnists" that "people have thought about [an amendment] now and they don't think it's a good idea."

Bush's July statements were among the very few public comments about the flag controversy that he made in 1989 following his June 30 Iwo Jima speech, and because none of them were particularly newsworthy or highlighted by the White House, they generally went completely unreported. As Senate debate on the amendment began in mid-October, the only public statement from the White House—which had been coordinated by numerous top administration officials and personally signed off on by Bush—consisted of one sentence urging "prompt enactment" of the amendment, "which is needed to ensure that the Nation's flag is protected in a constitutionally sound manner." Thus, probably another reason for the amendment's failure was that, perhaps in response to the widespread criticism that he was out only for partisan gain, Bush made no significant public attempts after his Iwo Jima speech to whip up support for it—and, by all accounts, he also did little or no personal lobbying for the amendment even as support for it stalled on Capitol Hill. During the period immediately preceding the Senate's October 19 vote, Senator Kennedy, a leading opponent of the amendment, proclaimed that the "silence from the White House over the past few days has been deafening," and even Dole publicly complained that the issue "wasn't the highest priority at the White House" and "there hasn't been much done in the last few days."

The Passage of the Flag Protection Act and the Defeat of the Constitutional Amendment

On July 27, 1989, the HJC favorably reported the FPA to the House by a 28 to 6 vote after concluding four days of hearings during which Chairman Brooks, over bitter Republican protests, repeatedly ruled out of order all attempts to bring up the amendment for discussion and consideration. Although all but one of the fourteen HJC Republicans and all but five of the twenty Democrats voted for the FPA, ten Republicans declared in a written report that they were doing so solely to "show support for protecting the flag" and that they viewed the FPA as an unconstitutional "charade," as the testimony of Assistant Attorney General Barr and other FPA critics had demonstrated that the only possible government justification for protecting the flag was "related to the suppression of expression" and therefore "if the desire is to overturn" *Johnson* it "must be altered" through a constitutional amendment.

The heart of the HJC-approved measure, which was sponsored by Brooks and Edwards, was essentially identical to the Biden proposal that had passed the Senate on June 22 and that Biden had subsequently submitted to the HJC. It amended the 1968 federal flag desecration law by stripping out references to "cast contempt," "publicly," and "defiling," still subjecting anyone who "knowingly mutilates, defaces, burns, or tramples upon any flag of the United States" to one year in jail and a $1,000 fine. Clearly reflecting Tribe's analysis, the HJC majority declared that these changes constitutionally conformed to *Johnson* by creating a "content-neutral" law that sought to carry out the "national interest" in protecting the "physical integrity of all American flags in all circumstances" in a manner "unrelated to the suppression of free expression," by focusing "exclusively on the conduct of the actor, irrespective of any expressive message he or she might be intending to convey," thus reflecting "the government's power to honor" the "diverse and deeply held feelings of the majority of citizens for the flag" in the "same manner that protection is afforded to gravesites or historical buildings." In response to Republican complaints that the FPA would be litigated in the courts for years, the Brooks-Edwards proposal added to Biden's original language an unprecedented provision for immediate, mandatory Supreme Court review of the FPA as soon as any prosecutions were initiated under it. Additionally, to appease veterans who voiced concerns that they might be prosecuted for ceremonial flag "retirement" burnings, an exemption was added for the "disposal of the flag when it has become worn or soiled," on the grounds that, according to the HJC majority, such flags were "no longer a fitting emblem for display" and that without such an exception the FPA would require "the maintenance of all flags in perpetuity." The Brooks-Edwards additions to the Biden bill also defined "flag" as encompassing any "flag of the United States, or any part thereof, made of any substance, of any size, in a form that is commonly displayed."

Following the August recess, the House Democratic leadership scheduled floor debate on the FPA for September 12 under a suspension of the rules procedure that made it impossible to consider any amendments, a strategy designed to prevent proposed changes that might be politically difficult to oppose but could also make the statute transparently unconstitutional under *Johnson*. This procedure required a two-thirds majority, rather than the usual simple majority, to pass the FPA. In return for the Republican votes this required, Speaker Foley promised to bring the constitutional amendment to a floor vote later in 1989, in response to Michel's expressed concern that otherwise Republicans, like himself, who opposed the FPA as constitutionally inadequate not be politically "stranded out there with [only] a negative vote." Foley's promise might have been unnecessary in any case, since as Edwards pointed out, "It's pretty hard for politicians to vote against protecting the flag." The FPA passed by 380 to 38, with 230 Democrats and 150 Republicans supporting it. Only 17 Democrats and 21 Republicans opposed the FPA, all of the former on free speech grounds, and most of the latter on the grounds that only a constitutional amendment could adequately protect the flag.

The debate preceding the vote was sometimes heated, but the atmosphere was clearly much calmer than that of several months earlier, reflecting a drastic decline in public, congressional, and media interest. Only a handful of members were on the floor during the debate, and on September 12 the three television evening network newscasts devoted a combined total of less than one minute to report the House action. In preparation for the House debate, the White House, which had been carefully monitoring congressional developments, issued a statement that had been coordinated with the Department of Justice, White House Chief of Staff Sununu, Vice President Dan Quayle, and many other top administration officials that reiterated its support for a flag desecration constitutional amendment, but opposed the FPA because it "would likely not survive constitutional scrutiny" under *Johnson* and would therefore be "merely a symbolic gesture and not a serious effort to provide real protection for the flag."

Ten days after the House action, on September 21 the SJC, meeting in a heated and partisan atmosphere, voted to endorse the original, intact Biden FPA by 9 to 5 and recommended against passage of the amendment by 8 to 6. The balance of power in the committee was held by four Democrats and one Republican who voted for the FPA but against the amendment. The SJC majority report endorsed the Tribe theory that, based on Justice Blackmun's *Goguen* dissent, Congress could constitutionally protect the flag by focusing "solely and exclusively on the conduct of the actor," without targeting the "message." The report also approvingly quoted Biden's statement that protecting the flag, even at the cost of jailing those with a different view of its symbolism, was needed to bring Americans "together" and to "generate a kind of tolerance that is required in such a diverse society." In a separate report, the SJC majority attacked the amendment as containing "entirely uncertain" language and undermining the "spirit and structure of the Constitution" by authorizing "for the first time in our history" the criminalization of conduct based on whether "that conduct contains an idea or a message of which the legislature does not approve."

On October 4, the Senate began debating the FPA after Biden decided to bring to the floor the House-approved version (with the flag disposal and expedited review provisions). The Senate approved it with several amendments after eight hours of debate by a 91 to 9 vote on October 5. Two of the network news broadcasts that evening failed to even mention the Senate action, and leading newspapers such as the *New York Times* and the *Washington Post*, which had front-page accounts of House passage of the FPA, buried their Senate stories on inside pages. Two Senate amendments were approved by voice vote with little controversy: the first, proposed by Dole in response to the Chicago "flag on the floor" controversy, added maintaining a "flag on the floor or ground" to the forbidden acts; the second replaced the House expedited review provision with a less drastic measure that still required expedited Supreme Court review, but only after the completion of federal district court proceedings instead of upon the initiation of a prosecution. Another amendment, to add "physically defiles" to the list of forbidden acts, was approved 76 to 24 after a long, bizarre debate that centered on such questions as how "physically defiles" differed from "defiles," "defaces," and "mutilates," and whether this addition would dilute the FPA's "content neutrality."

On October 12, the House approved the Senate amendments by 371 to 43 and sent the FPA to the White House. The only significant debate centered on the "physically defiles" amendment, featuring a repeat of the surrealistic debate in the Senate as to the precise meaning of this phrase. The House action, taken after an hour of debate before a largely empty chamber, was supported by 217 Democrats and 154 Republicans and was opposed by 25 Democrats and 18 Republicans. Most newspapers reported this news on inside pages, and although all three evening network broadcasts mentioned it, only one devoted more than thirty seconds to the story.

Since the Bush administration had repeatedly maintained that the FPA was constitutionally insufficient to overturn *Johnson* and that only an amendment could do so, Bush was now placed in a politically awkward position, which he resolved by announcing at an October 13 press conference that he would allow the FPA to become law without his signature (under an obscure constitutional provision under which any bill passed by both houses of Congress becomes law automatically if the president fails to either sign or veto it within ten working days after its official transmittal to him when Congress is in session). Bush rejected a reporter's suggestion that he was "politically afraid" to veto the FPA, maintaining rather that he would not veto it in appreciation of the "overwhelming" congressional desire to "do something about protection of the flag," but could not sign it because the FPA was not "enough," since a constitutional amendment was the "most lasting and legally correct" form of action. On October 26, Bush formalized his news conference announcement in a published statement coordinated by the Justice Department and top White House officials. It commended the "intentions" of those voting for the FPA, but said Bush would let it become law without his signature; although it sought "our mutual goal of protecting our Nation's greatest symbol," the Justice Department had concluded that "the only way to ensure protection of the flag is through a constitutional amendment" since *Johnson* had indicated that "the government's interest in preserving the flag as a symbol can never be compelling enough to justify prohibiting flag desecration that is intended to express a message," yet "that is precisely the target of this bill's prohibition."

In the meantime, after more than ten hours of debate the Senate defeated the constitutional amendment on October 19, with thirty-three Republicans and eighteen Democrats supporting it and eleven Republicans and thirty-seven Democrats opposed, thus obtaining fifty-one votes and falling fifteen votes short of the required two-thirds majority. The Senate vote was reported on front pages across the country, and, for only the third time since July 4, the flag desecration controversy was covered that evening by all three network newscasts (although CBS gave it only twenty seconds). The imminent defeat of the amendment was clearly foreshadowed on October 17 when two Republicans who had been among its original cosponsors, John Danforth and Warren Rudman, announced that they had changed their minds. Danforth delivered his announcement in a dramatic and eloquent manner that attracted enormous media attention. According to *U.S. News & World Report*, his declaration that he had been "just plain wrong" and had committed a "mistake of the heart" symbolized the "sudden downfall of a movement that seemed a sure winner a scant four months ago."

The Senate debate covered well-trodden rhetorical ground amid an unusually high and widespread level of overt partisan invective. For example, Senator Patrick Leahy (D-VT) denounced those who, in a "travesty of patriotism," identified "patriotic fervor" with "who has the best 30-second ad, who films themselves with the most flags or who has the greatest band playing," and Republican leader Dole denounced Democrats opponents of the amendment for "playing politics" and seeking to "bash Bush," and bitterly urged his colleagues to listen to "real Americans" who were "willing to fight and die for their country" even though they were not lawyers, "did not got to Harvard," and "do not read Supreme Court decisions." On a less emotional level, Democratic senator Brock Adams summarized the argument of amendment opponents by declaring that the FPA would "uphold the dignity of the flag without decimating the Bill of Rights" and that the First Amendment was "hallowed ground" that should not be "tampered" with in the absence of a "dire emergency." Senator Trent Lott (R-MS), who would become Senate majority leader in 1996, maintained that since the FPA was doomed, the only real question was, "Do we want the flag of the United States to be burned and mutilated, destroyed or not?"

CHAPTER 7

Testing the Flag Protection Act in the Courts, October 1989–May 1990

Defying the Flag Protection Act

The FPA formally became law at midnight October 27 and triggered a wave of flag burnings designed both to defy and to test it, in some cases within moments after it became effective. Altogether, about three dozen flag burnings were reported (although generally only in local media) between late October 1989 and the Supreme Court's June 1990 *Eichman* ruling striking down the FPA. Noting this phenomenon, *Time* magazine reported that until the FPA was enacted "flag burning had virtually gone out of style as a means of radical protest," but that Congress had "restored its cachet by making it a criminal offense" and "now desecrating the Stars and Stripes has become a bit of a fad." Perhaps the only flag burning prevented by the FPA was a ceremonial Veterans' Day flag disposal planned by firefighters in Plymouth, Connecticut, which was canceled because, a spokesman announced, "Since we planned this, the situation has changed so dramatically in terms of feeling about the flag that you don't even dare try to destroy them for fear it will be misinterpreted."

The Justice Department decided to bring FPA test cases only in response to two late October flag burnings that received extensive national media coverage: charges were brought against seven persons (including three never-located "John Does") for burning a post office flag (along with an estimated one thousand small paper flags) in Seattle during the early morning of October 28, and against three persons, including "Dread" Scott Tyler of "Chicago flag on the floor" fame, in connection with flag burnings on the

Capitol steps in Washington, D.C., on October 30, 1989. Attorney William Kunstler, who would represent both the Seattle and Capitol defendants during the subsequent seven months of litigation, told reporters, "Here you have it. Congress wanted a swift case. They're going to get it." He added that "the only thing I ever agreed upon with Bush on in my life" was that the FPA was "wholly unconstitutional."

According to a well-informed Justice Department source, "no serious consideration" was given to not prosecuting alleged FPA violators, because whatever doubts were harbored about its constitutionality, "The Department has an obligation to defend acts of Congress unless they are clearly and unequivocally unconstitutional and in that mission it accords the appropriate deference to Congress's judgment." In particular, he added, the Washington, D.C., burning could "hardly not be prosecuted, since it was on videotape and on national TV in front of the Capitol," although, because the FPA was so new, officials in the U.S. district attorney's office were "desperately searching" for a copy of the law because "nobody had it." Officially announcing the charges against the Capitol defendants on October 31, U.S. Attorney Jay Stevens said that despite the "substantial doubts" about the FPA's constitutionality "it is our responsibility to enforce the law" to "vindicate the deep offense that Americans feel at desecration of their national emblem" and to "seek resolution of the constitutional implications." In a 1991 interview, Assistant U.S. Attorney in Seattle Mark Bartlett explained that the October 28 Seattle post office demonstrators were prosecuted, but similar action was not taken against protesters who burned flags two days later at the University of Washington, because the former incident had involved destruction of government property, whereas the latter involved burning "their own flags," and because decisions have to be made "as to whether resources are going to be put in," officials concluded that "a single prosecution would answer the [constitutional] questions we had."

According to Justice Department and FBI sources interviewed in 1990 and 1991, other flag burning incidents, like the October 30 University of Washington demonstration, were ignored because many Justice Department officials viewed further prosecutions as a waste of scarce resources to prosecute what they viewed as a relatively minor offense, especially because the FPA was generally viewed as doomed to be struck down soon by the Supreme Court. For example, a Justice Department source said that some of his colleagues felt "the whole issue was idiotic and hoped it would go away," especially because "there are always so many things that seem more important." Similarly, according to a 1991 interview with San Francisco FBI special agent Kathleen Puckett, the local U.S. attorney decided not to prosecute several flag burnings there because with "so many serious violations of life or civil rights causing damage to something other than a symbol," they "were just not considered worth the effort" pending resolution of the Seattle and Washington, D.C., test prosecutions.

The four defendants eventually prosecuted in Seattle—for violating the FPA and for destruction of government property, in what became known as *U.S. v. Haggerty*—appear to have been passersby or curiosity seekers who acted spontaneously without any connection to an RCP-affiliated group that organized the event. Mark Haggerty, twenty-three, told a Seattle news conference on November 30 that he had taken part in the post office flag burning to demonstrate that the way to protest "attacks on democratic rights being carried out by the ruling capitalist class is not through some kind of legal action through the court system but to organize the masses" to "assert their democratic rights by taking them into their own hands," especially since the "flag represents the interests of the ultra-rich ruling class who exploit and oppress the workers." Another Seattle defendant, Darius Strong, twenty, a self-described "street youth with a mohawk" haircut and an Iron Cross tattoo on his left shoulder who regularly wore metal-studded leather jackets, told reporters in 1990 that he had been jailed and incarcerated in a mental hospital and described himself as "the kid no one loved." Strong said that he had grown up "eating garbage in back alleys because my hippie mother rebelled and I didn't have a father, not one that cared to let me know who he was." Strong said, "I am your future. I am what comes off the streets. I am what oppression makes."

{ *Flag Burning and Free Speech* }

In 1990 interviews conducted on the day that their case was heard before the Supreme Court, the two other Seattle defendants, Jennifer Campbell, a twenty-two-year-old college student, said she had burned the flag because "they were trying to protect a piece of cloth and were using it as a distraction from real issues" and because of "all the anger built up from growing up in this society as a woman;" and Carlos Garza, thirty-two, who described himself as a Hispanic former gang member and recovering heroin addict who had served over four years in jail for armed robbery, said he had burned the flag because he viewed it "as part of the system that had me living in a social hell-hole" and severely oppressed Hispanics. He said:

> I went and burned an American flag because my Mexican race has been oppressed too long. We've been fighting too long and we just haven't been heard. When I burned that American flag, and this is the honest truth, I felt a sense of relief. I took out all my frustrations on that flag when I lit that match.

In the Capitol steps case, which became known as *U.S. v. Eichman*, prosecutions were brought against Tyler, twenty-four; Shawn Eichman, twenty-four, a self-described "revolutionary artist"; and David Blalock, thirty-nine, a Vietnam veteran and member of the RCP-affiliated Vietnam Veterans Against the War (Anti-Imperialist), which had sponsored the Seattle protest. Gregory Lee Johnson, the namesake of the 1989 Supreme Court ruling, was also originally arrested in connection with the Capitol incident, but federal officials soon dropped the charges against him on the grounds that he had failed to actually ignite his flag. In a May 1990 interview, Johnson said this amounted to "selective nonprosecution" because "it weakens their case to try to distinguish this statute [the FPA] from *Texas v. Johnson* if the same defendant is involved," but he conceded that the flag he was trying to burn did not actually "get going" before he was arrested. In a 1999 interview, Kunstler's law partner Ron Kuby, recalling Johnson's contemporary reaction, declared, "I've never seen somebody so upset that he was not arrested."

During a 1990 interview conducted on the same day that the

Supreme Court heard oral argument in the prosecution resulting from the Capitol steps burning, Tyler, wearing a shirt emblazoned with a picture of former Chinese communist leader Mao Tse-tung, described himself as a supporter, although not a member, of the RCP. Tyler said that the FPA and the earlier condemnation of his Chicago art exhibit demonstrated that "the ruling class can't tolerate any questioning, any thought or any dissent on the question of patriotism," but voiced hope that "a lot of people, one day, can not only burn the flag but do in the whole empire the flag represents." According to Tyler, class inequalities are so ingrained in American society that

> if people are going to be free, it's going to take revolution; that's cold and it's hard but it's also true. Right now the dog eat dog system gets in the way of human advancement and creativity and even on the simple level of just housing and feeding the people. To say that American capitalism works ignores that 50 million blacks were killed during slavery, up to 800 million native Americans and south and central American Indians died [during colonization], ignores the fact that one of three women are raped, all of those would be reason enough to overthrow the system.

Blalock, who was also interviewed in 1990, said that he had been radicalized by his experiences in Vietnam, where he said American troops had engaged in "massive destruction" of a country they were told they were saving from "the Russians," when in fact the enemy Vietnamese Communists "had a lot of broad support from among the population." Blalock said he had subsequently been involved in labor organizing and was vice president of his union at a New Jersey oil company when he was fired for the flag burning after some fellow workers who were "hard-core reactionaries threatened to kill me if I came back to work and the company said they couldn't guarantee my safety." Blalock said that "the flag has always been a bone in my side since the Vietnam War" and "when they started the whole thing about ramming patriotism down people's throats" with the drive to overturn *Johnson*, "to me it was just another hammer coming down on people's heads. Unless people start speaking out, then we're going to be just like in Nazi Germany. By the point you realize you should have opened your mouth it's going to be too late."

In another 1990 interview, Eichman described herself as a "revolutionary communist" and a supporter, but not member, of the RCP. She said that those who challenged the American status quo were deprived of the freedom of expression enjoyed by "the racists, the sexists, the anti-gay, the white helmets in power," and that burning the flag reflected her decision that "some people need to be shocked, need to be insulted to wake us up to the reality that something is rotten in the United States. This Constitution doesn't guarantee us a damn thing because supposedly under it we're supposed to have civil rights, but that doesn't stop racist murders, that doesn't stop a women from being beaten every 10 seconds and raped every three minutes, that doesn't stop sex discrimination. For me the Constitution holds no water."

Testing the FPA in Federal District Court, October, 1989–March 1990

The flag desecration controversy disappeared from the newspapers for over three months following the October 30 Capitol steps burning. On November 16, with test prosecutions of the FPA under way and the Senate having already defeated the constitutional amendment, House Republican leader Michel agreed to postpone a House amendment vote until 1990. In the meantime, government and defense attorneys had already begun writing their briefs in preparation for parallel FPA prosecutions in federal district courts in Seattle and Washington, D.C.

According to several Justice Department sources interviewed in 1990 and 1991, the government's identical briefs, which were submitted in the two parallel cases, while primarily written by Craig Iscoe, assistant U.S. attorney for the District of Columbia, were approved by the Justice Department's Office of Legal Counsel and reviewed by the office of Solicitor General Kenneth Starr, who would represent the government in any subsequent Supreme

Court litigation, so that, as one source stated, nothing would be included that might "damage [Starr's] later arguments before the Supreme Court." This unusual high-level scrutiny of misdemeanor cases, which are normally prosecuted completely at the discretion of local U.S. attorneys, clearly reflected the intense public interest and political sensitivity involved in the cases, as well as their certain end destination in the Supreme Court. In a 1990 interview, Deputy Solicitor General John Roberts said that the Office of Legal Counsel "just sent a copy of the [Iscoe] brief out to the people in Seattle" so that, since "everything was going to be going immediately to the Supreme Court [following a district court ruling, under the FPA's expedited review provision], we didn't have any problem with different positions" taken by federal prosecutors in the two cases. Starr confirmed, in another 1990 interview, that although his office had not been involved in "drafting" the district court briefs, there had been "close consultation" on them with Justice Department officials.

By joint agreement between the defense and federal attorneys, the district court pretrial hearings, which were scheduled for February 1990, would focus solely on the FPA's constitutionality, rather than on the guilt or innocence of the accused, since a finding of unconstitutionality would render all other issues moot. Federal prosecutors found themselves in an awkward position in defending the FPA because Assistant Attorney General Barr had so vehemently testified before Congress that it could not survive the *Johnson* standards for legally regulating symbolic expression. This left them only with the alternatives of either challenging the official Justice Department view elaborated only a few months earlier and arguing that the alleged "content neutrality" of the FPA made it substantially different from the Texas law struck down in *Johnson*, or maintaining that *Johnson* had been wrongly decided, a hopeless argument before lower courts that lacked the authority to overturn Supreme Court rulings.

The department briefs essentially adopted the second tack, declaring that Barr's position that the FPA was unconstitutional under *Johnson* because it was not based on "an interest wholly unrelated to expression" continued "to represent the Department of Justice." The briefs rejected the congressional claim that the FPA qualified under *O'Brien* as a "content-neutral" statute because the government's "only conceivable interest" behind the FPA was to protect "the symbolic value of the flag." However, the briefs maintained that nonetheless the courts should uphold the FPA because *Johnson* had been "wrongly decided," as the government's interest "in protecting the symbolic value of the flag" was a "sufficiently compelling" interest to override the First Amendment rights of flag desecrators. While recognizing that federal district courts "cannot overrule" the Supreme Court, the Justice Department argued that they could nonetheless sustain the FPA in a "principled way" because the intervening decisions of the president to endorse a constitutional amendment and of Congress to pass the FPA demonstrated that there was a "compelling" government interest that met the *Johnson* standard, especially since it was "the President and Congress, not state legislatures" that were "most competent to determine the need for protecting our national symbol."

This position amounted to asking the district courts to overrule a six-month-old Supreme Court ruling that purely suppressive government interests in protecting the flag's symbolic value could *not* override the First Amendment. Those who closely followed the case from various political positions almost universally regarded it as an extraordinarily weak argument, and some observers felt it amounted to the Bush administration purposefully taking a legal "dive" so that the FPA would fail and then the amendment would return to center political stage. A well-informed Justice Department source interviewed in 1990 conceded that the briefs did not provide a "vigorous" defense of the FPA and that anyone reading them would conclude, "You can't expect to win with this" and that they "seemed to be saying, 'We [Justice] agree it's unconstitutional.'" However, he maintained that it would be "overstating the effect of the brief to argue that it was designed to lose in district court," as "it wouldn't make much difference" whatever the briefs said since it was "abundantly clear that the law would be struck down" because it was "so hard to distinguish from *Johnson*." According to the source, the department was motivated only by a desire to be "intellectually honest," because it's "obviously not true" that the FPA sought to defend the flag in a "content neutral way" and above all because it was "confined by Barr's testimony," which could not be abandoned without hurting the department's "congressional credibility." Faced with the dilemma of its legal obligation to defend any law not "absolutely, clearly unconstitutional," the source added, the department opted for reiterating Barr's position and ultimately effectively saying to the district courts, "We don't think it's constitutional, but the courts should defer to Congress."

The Senate and the House filed separate and extremely divergent amicus ("friend of the court") briefs, a step typically taken by Congress only with regard to especially controversial laws or when the congressional leadership feels that its interests are not being adequately represented by the Justice Department. The Senate brief argued that the FPA sought to protect the flag's "physical integrity," admittedly because of its symbolic value, against all assaults, regardless of motive, in a "content-neutral" manner that did not conflict with *Johnson* and that qualified under the "important and substantial" *O'Brien* test for nonsuppressive restrictions on symbolic expression. Although the House brief endorsed the Senate's "content neutrality" argument, its central thrust was quite different and had never been advanced before during congressional consideration of the FPA: the brief maintained that the FPA's purpose was to protect the flag as an "incident of sovereignty," for example by demarcating American borders and ships, a function the brief implicitly argued had an even more convincingly constitutional "nonsuppressive" purpose than that advanced by the Senate.

In a 1990 interview conducted after the district courts struck down the FPA, but before the Supreme Court did likewise, House Counsel Steve Ross conceded that his argument was a "novel or oddball theory," but he contended that representing the nation's sovereignty was a valid "supplemental non-expressive interest" reflected in the FPA. He said the argument sought to challenge Barr's position that the FPA's failure to meet the *O'Brien* requirement of serving a "nonsuppressive" purpose to qualify for constitutional consideration under a lesser standard than the "compelling" interest test of *Johnson* was the "600-pound gorilla" that could not be legally overcome. According to Ross, this argument was needed because the Justice Department, in its district court briefs, had "abdicated its role" of defending laws enacted by Congress.

Ross maintained that because the flag was originally designed as an emblem of sovereignty predating "American patriotic attachment and iconization," protecting its sovereignty function was "clearly not a suppressive interest," and "there's every bit as much an appropriate [nonsuppressive] interest in preventing burning of the flag as there was in preventing the burning of draft cards [as the Supreme Court found was constitutionally permissible in *O'Brien*]." Ross declared that the nonsuppressive government interest ultimately protected by the FPA and threatened by flag desecration is "an injury to the claim of the legitimacy of the government."

In their defense briefs, Kunstler and Cole (who represented both the *Haggerty* and the *Eichman* defendants and submitted fundamentally identical briefs to both district courts), argued that all three government briefs conceded that the FPA was designed to protect the flag's symbolic value and maintained that *Johnson* had established that the government's interest in protecting the flag against physical attacks that might "somehow dilute its 'symbolic' value" was "necessarily related to the suppression of expression." Therefore, they maintained, *O'Brien* was irrelevant, and, under *Johnson*, protecting the flag's symbolism could not constitute a "compelling" state interest that would override the First Amendment. The briefs maintained that there was no nonsuppressive government interest that could justify protecting flags, because unlike gravesites, historical buildings, and bald eagles, the flag was purely communicative in function and could be both "infinitely replicated and privately created or owned," and that "physical destruction of one of a symbol's infinite representations can do the symbol no harm except by virtue of the message it communicates."

Addressing the Justice Department argument that presidential endorsement of a constitutional amendment and congressional enactment of the FPA demonstrated a "compelling" government interest in forbidding flag desecration, the defense maintained that the very purpose of the Bill of Rights and the courts was to "provide legal protection from the political inclinations of the majority" if they violated minority rights. The briefs also rejected claims that the FPA was "content neutral," maintaining that it only outlawed uses such as burning, "mutilating," and "defacing" flags "that people commonly do to show disrespect" to the flag, but allowed other uses that damaged flags but were not viewed as "unpatriotic," such as flying flags in bad weather or ceremonially disposing of "worn or soiled" flags. Moreover, the defense argued, the very fact that the FPA singled out a "particular symbol for protection" was "inherently content-based," as would be evident if Congress outlawed defacing Democratic Party emblems while maintaining it merely sought to protect their "physical integrity." A "truly neutral" flag law, the briefs maintained, would not permit "flag waving, while barring flag burning," but, as Assistant Attorney General Barr (whom the defense extensively quoted) had told Congress, "would say either anyone can use it [as they wish] or no one can use it."

The defense ridiculed the House's "sovereignty" argument, noting it had never surfaced in the "voluminous legislative history" of the FPA and that in any event the House "never explains" how acts such as the 1984 Dallas flag burning created a situation in which the flag "no longer serves its function in demarcating geographical boundaries" or diminished "the function the flag serves on a ship in the Persian Gulf." The defense also argued that the FPA was unconstitutionally vague by failing to specify the meaning of terms such as "worn or soiled" flags, since "the distinction between a soiled and an unsoiled flag" was "wholly evanescent," especially since "any flag that has ever flown" in an urban area "is soiled to some extent."

In a 1999 interview, Cole said that he always felt that "there was nothing" to the argument that it was possible to protect the "physical integrity" of the flag in a content-neutral manner "because there is no such thing as the physical integrity of the flag, because the flag is not a physical object, it's a symbol. You can preserve the physical integrity of a specific flag like the flag over Fort Sumter, but the flag can be and is physically reproduced millions of times by cocktail napkin producers and the like, so I felt it was not a serious suggestion that Congress could pass a statute to protect the physical integrity of the flag." Cole added that his position was "obviously helped by the fact that the Bush administration had taken the position before it was enacted that the FPA was unconstitutional. We felt our best strategy was to rely upon *Texas v. Johnson* and urge the courts to stick to their guns."

In two parallel rulings issued in February and March 1990, both the Seattle and District of Columbia district courts held that the FPA was unconstitutional under *Johnson* insofar as it was used to prosecute symbolic political dissent involving the flag. Both courts found that *Johnson* was controlling because the defendants had engaged in expressive conduct requiring First Amendment scrutiny and both rejected the Justice Department's argument that the government had "compelling" reasons to override their First Amendment rights, because, as Judge June Green declared in *Eichman*, "However compelling the government may see its interests, they cannot justify restrictions on speech which shake the very cornerstone of the First Amendment." Similarly, Judge Barbara Rothstein maintained in *Haggerty* that "in order for the flag to endure as a symbol of freedom, we must protect with equal vigor the right to wave it and the right to destroy it." In clear reference to the collapse of communism in eastern Europe at the end of 1989, she added, "This is an inspiring time for those of us who treasure freedom" and declared that freedom of speech "is the crucial foundation without which other democratic values cannot flourish."

The two courts also rejected the key arguments of the congressional briefs. Thus, Judge Rothstein rejected the House and Senate contentions that the FPA should qualify for the relatively lenient *O'Brien* test on the grounds that its motivation was nonsuppressive; although the three government briefs were "curiously split" in their arguments, all of them ultimately agreed that the FPA's "underlying purpose" was to "preserve the flag's symbolic value" and thus the FPA was clearly "content-based and subject to strict scrutiny." She further rejected the Senate contention that the FPA was content neutral because it forbade only conduct "generally associated with disrespect for the flag," yet allowed conduct that threatened the flag's physical integrity but did not "communicate negative or disrespectful messages." She similarly rejected the House argument alleging a nonsuppressive governmental "sovereignty" interest in protecting the flag, on the triple grounds that this interest was intertwined with protecting the flag as a symbol, since it could be threatened only by expression that amounted to a "rejection of United States sovereignty"; because this position had never been advanced during legislative consideration of the FPA; and because the House never explained "how the governmental interest in preserving the flag as an incident of sovereignty would be harmed by defendants' act of flag burning." According to Judge Rothstein:

> Burning the flag as an expression of political dissent, while repellent to many Americans, does not jeopardize America freedoms which we hold dear. What would threaten our liberty is allowing the government to encroach on our right to political protest. It is with the firm belief that this decision strengthens what our flag stands for that this court finds the Flag Protection Act unconstitutional as applied to defendants' conduct in burning the flag.

The Aftermath to the District Court Rulings, Winter 1990

In the aftermath of the district court rulings, which returned the flag desecration controversy to prominent media attention for the first time since late October, opponents of the FPA from both left and right declared that their positions had been justified, but the Democratic congressional leadership urged calm until the Supreme Court issued a final constitutional determination. Defense attorney Cole termed the rulings "wonderful," because they "reaffirmed that the First Amendment means that people must be as free to burn the flag as to wave it" and that the "government can't compel people under penalty of imprisonment to be patriotic." Senate Republican leader Dole declared that the rulings proved that the "only sure-fire way to give Old Glory the protection it deserves" was an amendment and demanded that FPA backers ensure that the expedited Supreme Court review provision "works as advertised" so that if the high court upheld the district courts "we may move expeditiously to pass" the amendment. Among supporters of the FPA, Senate Democratic leader Mitchell said that the district court findings were "expected" and nothing to "get too worked up about," since "we all assumed all along it would go to the Supreme Court."

On February 23, two days after the Seattle district court ruling, the Justice Department announced that it would ask for expedited mandatory Supreme Court review of the decision, as provided for in the FPA, "as soon as possible." A similar announcement was issued shortly after the second district court ruling was announced on March 5. In a June 1990 interview, Solicitor General Starr, the official who represents the Justice Department before the Supreme Court and who normally makes independent decisions about whether to appeal lower court rulings adverse to the government's position, stated that he "literally signed off" on the decision, with "no automatic pen, I used my own pen," and without any consultation with higher-ups such as Attorney General Thornburgh. Starr added that he served "at the pleasure of the president" and had no "commission that entitles me to go off and pursue my vision of the good," but as a "practical matter" his office has "historically enjoyed considerable independence in coming to its judgments" and that "certainly was true in this particular instance."

Starr said that the 1989 congressional testimony of Assistant Attorney General Barr declaring that any flag desecration statute would be unconstitutional under *Johnson* had posed no problems for his decision. Starr explained that although he "chatted" with Barr before the latter's testimony and thus was "keenly personally aware of what Bill had testified to," his function did not include "approving" Barr's testimony and that in any case Barr's statements were "entirely irrelevant" to his own subsequent responsibilities. According to Starr, Barr's views had been offered as "part of the congressional deliberative process" in which the Justice Department had offered Congress "our views, our legal advice," but once

Congress "worked its will" and passed the FPA it became the duty of the president "to faithfully execute the laws" and "ultimately the responsibility of this office to defend the constitutionality of the statute." He added, "That we had views, institutionally, previously" was "interesting from the standpoint of a case study in political science," but as a "legal matter" and "in terms of my role, utterly irrelevant."

In a separate 1990 interview, Starr's deputy solicitor general, John Roberts, said, "There are situations where we have to refuse to defend an act of Congress because it's indefensible," but that in the FPA case Starr was "the ultimate decision maker" and determined "that there were credible, reasonable arguments that could be advanced and that we had the obligation to make them." According to Roberts, the solicitor general's office includes about twenty-five lawyers and takes a position before the Supreme Court in about seventy-five cases annually. Although Starr typically took a strong interest, such as personally appearing before the Supreme Court, in only about "six or seven cases a year," Starr was "heavily involved" personally in handling the FPA appeal from the very start, Roberts said, both because of the legal importance of the issues involved and the "heightened degree" of general interest. Roberts added that the FPA appeal was "clearly one [Starr would] be arguing [before the Supreme Court]. It was an important act of Congress that had been struck down as unconstitutional. Congress had provided for immediate, expedited [Supreme Court] review to highlight its importance. We needed the government's top litigator on it and that was Ken."

Starr formally requested the Supreme Court to hear a consolidated appeal from the two district court FPA cases in papers filed on March 13. As with the Justice Department's district court briefs, Starr's filing failed to support the congressional argument that, as a "content-neutral law," the FPA complied with *Johnson;* instead, his primary argument was that the "people's elected representatives"—Congress via the FPA and President Bush by endorsing an amendment—had expressed their "considered decision that the physical desecration of the flag is—uniquely—anathema to the nation's values." His argument essentially amounted to urging the

Court to confess error and jettison its *Johnson* decision of only nine months earlier. He conceded that his position was "in tension" with *Johnson*, but urged that to the extent the Court had accorded flag burning "full First Amendment protection," the appeal presented "an appropriate occasion" to "consider more fully that analysis." Starr advanced one new position to advance this request: he urged the Court to "reconsider" its *Johnson* holding that flag desecration was a form of political expression fully protected under the First Amendment because, he maintained, like obscenity, libel, and "fighting words" (personal insults designed to incite personal retaliation), its value to society was "outweighed" by "its demonstrable destructive effect," especially since "suitable alternative means" were available to put forth "whatever protected expression may be part of the intended message."

Since the FPA explicitly mandated the Court to hear and expedite an appeal from a district court ruling "to the greatest extent possible," only the *timing* of the Court's consideration was really in doubt. Normally the Court grants thirty days for an opposing party to respond to a request that it hear appeals, but Starr asked this period to be reduced to ten days, that the Court announce it would take the appeal at its scheduled March 30 conference, that the ordinary subsequent period of seventy-five days or more for the exchange of briefs be collapsed to only twenty-five days, and that oral argument be scheduled for April 25, before the Court's scheduled summer recess (whereas normally when the Court agrees to a request to hear a case that is made after early February it is held over until the next term beginning in October). Starr justified his request to the Court for such extraordinary speed by declaring that "any routine [scheduling] treatment" would be "plainly incompatible" with the FPA's mandate.

Starr's March 13 filing was sent within twenty-four hours to the flag burners' lawyers by fax, hand, and overnight delivery. In a preliminary March 14 response, Cole did not oppose the appeal, but asked that the defense be granted the "ordinary thirty days" to fully respond to Starr's filing and that the cases be set for argument on "the first Monday of the October term." Cole argued that this schedule would still be "expedited" because "the cases would be heard ahead of those cases already accepted" for the next term, yet still allowed "the full briefing and careful consideration that an issue of this constitutional significance deserves," especially since the Court's ruling "might spark the first-ever amendment to the Bill of Rights." Cole maintained that Starr's proposed "rash" schedule would "severely prejudice" and "gravely and unnecessarily restrict" the defense's "due process rights," precluding its ability to provide a "careful and considered analysis" of the legal issues.

On March 16, the Court gave Cole until March 26 to formally respond to Starr's March 13 filing. In his March 23 formal response, Cole essentially reiterated the successful defense position earlier advanced before the district courts, adding that given the Court's "clear pronouncement less than one year ago in *Johnson*, and the two well-reasoned decisions below," the district court rulings might be "suitable for summary affirmance" by the Court without further formal proceedings. He said, however, that in keeping with the "spirit of Congress's statutory directive, the constitutional implications of the case and the strong public interest in the issues," he supported Starr's request that the Court grant a full review, with oral argument and an exchange of briefs. He again maintained that Starr's proposed schedule "gravely infringes" on the "due process rights" of defendants, but he dropped any suggested alternative schedule, instead asking only that the Court allow "the matters to be briefed with the care and consideration that they deserve."

The timing of the Supreme Court's hearing of the FPA became the focus of highly contentious partisan controversy after the House Democratic leadership filed a brief on March 15 supporting Starr's request that the Court grant an appeal but opposing his proposed schedule and suggesting instead that the case be given "priority" when the Court "devises its argument schedule for October." The brief, filed by House legal counsel Ross, declared that Starr's schedule suggested a "degree of haste scarcely compatible with the serious presentation" of the issues involved, especially given the "importance of the legislation under review with the alternative of a constitutional amendment, and the Justice Department's position on the merits, which has been to ask this

Court to reconsider" *Johnson*. Ross added that this was particularly so because Starr's filing failed to advance either the congressional "content neutrality" position or the House view that the FPA protected the flag as an "incident of sovereignty" rather than as a "suppression of expression," and that fully developing the House position required additional time for extensive research in "difficult-to-obtain sources."

The question of *when* the Court would hear the appeal gained enormous importance because of the extremely politicized atmosphere that continued to surround the flag desecration controversy in the winter of 1990: if the case was scheduled for the next Court term beginning in October, no decision would likely be forthcoming until after the November congressional elections, but a hearing before the Court's scheduled summer recess would produce a decision well before the elections. Since the general Washington consensus was that the Court was certain to strike down the FPA, this translated into the prediction that a preelection ruling would probably revive the drive for a constitutional amendment and would lead to its rapid endorsement by Congress, thereby placing congressmen who opposed it and sought reelection under the enormous threat of "thirty-second negative ads" directed against them. Moreover, according to this "conventional wisdom analysis," the flag amendment would likely become a hot issue in 1990 state legislative elections because a congressionally endorsed amendment would require state ratification. These state elections were in turn widely viewed as unusually significant because the newly elected state legislatures would draw congressional and state legislative district boundaries in the wake of the 1990 census, decisions of crucial importance for subsequent congressional and state elections.

In short, Washington insiders viewed a preelection Supreme Court ruling as likely to be especially helpful to legislators who favored a constitutional amendment and to Republican electoral interests, whereas a postelection decision was seen as better for Democrats and amendment opponents. Thus, in a 1990 interview, *Baltimore Sun* Supreme Court reporter Lyle Denniston declared that Republicans hoped that the amendment issue would "allow them not only to win a majority in Congress but to get a majority in the state legislatures so they can control redistricting after the 1990 census. The flag amendment is all tied up with redistricting in the Republican mind. Anyone who tells you it is not is smoking something." In another 1990 interview, ACLU's Washington office director Morton Halperin declared that the ACLU had "frankly hoped" that flag bumers would "wait a few months" precisely so that the Supreme Court would not hear any appeal "before the elections" and any future proposed amendment would be considered by "Congress in a non-election year."

In this explosive political context, the House Democratic leadership brief urging the Court to wait until October to hear the appeal sparked an extraordinary political brawl in the House of Representatives, as Republicans protested that this schedule clearly violated the urgency reflected in the FPA's expedited review provision. House Republican leader Michel touched off a bitter March 22 House debate by presenting a motion that termed the brief's proposed schedule "wholly inconsistent" with a "plain reading" of the FPA and directed that it be withdrawn and referred to a "full and proper review" by the bipartisan House legal advisory panel. Michel was supported by about half a dozen Republicans, including ranking HJC Republican James Sensenbrenner, who declared that the brief sought to "delay and delay this matter until after the November election," when the plain intent of Congress was to know "before we break for the election" whether it was necessary "to pass a constitutional amendment and send that matter to the States for their hopeful speedy ratification."

Democratic leaders denied any intent to misrepresent the views of the House and denied any motivation in asking for the October hearing beyond seeking the time needed to make a strong case, especially because they viewed the Justice Department's legal position as feeble. Majority leader Richard Gephardt declared that Starr's filing amounted to little more than saying to the Court, "Change your mind," and Edwards said the timing problem had been caused by Starr's request for "this ridiculous superexpedited treatment" and because House lawyers needed more research time because Starr "in essence, is not in favor of the FPA." The House debate ended with the adoption of Michel's motion by 309 to 101. A few hours later the House's bipartisan legal advisory panel agreed to resubmit the brief intact save for the elimination of any reference to scheduling. The extraordinary vote amounted to a stunning repudiation of the Democratic leadership, not only by virtually all Republicans, but also by a majority of Democrats. Reporter Lyle Denniston declared in a 1990 interview that he concluded after talking to congressmen about the vote that:

> Everybody understood that this was the first test of [voting on] a constitutional amendment to protect the flag and that you better get on record right on this issue because somebody's going to sound-bite you. One staff guy told me, "These people can see vividly in their minds today the video of George Bush in the flag factory [during the 1988 campaign] and they know what happened to Dukakis on the flag issue. All you have to do is you have Gregory Johnson with his unkempt, disheveled look, his radical appearance, and you split screen him with your opponent's picture and say, 'Do you want people in the Congress or in the state legislature who supports guys like this burning the flag?' Ten seconds and the campaign is over."

In a lengthy 1990 interview, House counsel Ross vehemently denied that political considerations played any role in his scheduling request, declaring, "My view was that if the Court decided it before the 1990 election and struck down the statute there will be a political controversy in the 1990 election, and if they decide it after the 1990 election and strike it down, there will be a political controversy in the 1992 election. I don't see how one gets out of it being a political controversy." Ross said that he was particularly concerned that Starr was "simply going to march in [to the Supreme Court] and say, 'We think you made a mistake last year and you should change your mind.'" Although such a brief could be "written fairly quickly," Ross continued, the "sovereignty" argument that he wanted to develop required considerable research time and Starr's proposed schedule would give him only "two or three weeks" to file a brief. Since the Court planned to stop hearing cases in April and "I did not presume to suggest that they come back and have a special session" for the FPA appeal, Ross added, asking that the case be heard at the beginning of the next term in October was not "hatching a plot to get past the elections," but rather asking for the earliest possible date that would allow adequate time for his brief.

On March 30, the Supreme Court ended the suspense by announcing that it would consolidate the two district court cases for review under the rubric *U.S. v. Eichman*, docket numbers 89-1433 and 89-1434, and hear oral argument at a special session on May 14, thus clearly prefiguring a preelection decision. The Court's reasoning may have reflected that expressed in a March 16 memorandum to Justice Marshall from one of his clerks, which noted that Starr had argued that hearing the case in October "would be contrary to Congress's intent," but suggested that scheduling oral argument for May, rather than April 25, as Starr had requested, would create a "slightly less frantic, but nonetheless expedited, briefing schedule" that could alleviate the concerns expressed by the defense. According to the briefing schedule decided by the Court on March 30, the ordinary seventy-five-day period for an exchange of briefs, which Starr had asked be reduced to twenty-five days, was set at forty days.

The special post-April session marked only the fourth time in its recent history that the Court had so unusually accommodated a request for a rapid ruling (the other occasions included two truly monumental controversies, the 1971 Pentagon Papers case and the 1974 Nixon tapes case, which played a major role in Nixon's resignation). According to Court records revealed after the 1993 death of Justice Marshall, at the Court's March 30 conference all nine justices agreed to take the appeal; four (Brennan, Marshall, Blackmun, and Stevens) voted to summarily affirm the district court rulings without any further proceedings, and the other five (Rehnquist, White, O'Connor, Scalia, and Kennedy) voted to hear oral argument and request legal briefs. Marshall voted to summarily affirm after receiving a March 27 recommendation from one of his clerks that he vote thus because the case was "entirely controlled" by *Johnson* and "no argument by the government" could distinguish the FPA "from the statute condemned in *Johnson*."

Press coverage of the Court's March 30 announcement stressed its political implications: for example, the March 31 front-page *New York Times* report said that a decision striking down the FPA, "which many constitutional scholars consider likely, would renew political pressure for a constitutional amendment" and "inject the issue into the fall campaigns for Congress and state legislatures." Following the Court announcement, House Speaker Foley promised to schedule a vote on the amendment within thirty days of any decision declaring the FPA unconstitutional. Republican Senate leader Dole declared if the Court struck down the FPA by July, as he expected, there would be "plenty of time to act" on an amendment "before we adjourn" before the November elections. PAW president Arthur Kropp, whose organization would soon file, along with the ACLU and over forty other public interest groups, a joint amicus brief with the Supreme Court asking it to strike down the same FPA that the PAW and the ACLU had effectively supported six months earlier, lamented that if the Court upheld the lower court rulings, "we can expect that last year's favorite political football, a constitutional amendment, will be back to kick us a whole new generation of 30-second attack ads."

The FPA Before the Supreme Court, Spring 1990

The flag desecration controversy disappeared from the front pages again for six weeks following the Court's March 30 announcement, while the lawyers began writing and submitting a new round of briefs. In his April 17 submission, Starr, conceding that he was ask-ing the Court to "reconsider," "revisit," and "abandon" *Johnson*, largely followed the Justice Department's lower court briefs in es-sentially urging the Court to overturn its nine-month-old ruling, which he summarized as holding that flag burning merited "full First Amendment protection" as a form of expressive conduct. Starr rejected the "content neutrality" argument—instead endors-ing in a footnote the district courts' conclusion that the FPA was "based on a view that the flag stands for something valuable, and should be safeguarded because of that value"—but nonetheless urged the Court to uphold the FPA because protection of the flag's physical integrity was "necessary to the maintenance of a democratic political system" owing to "Congress's determination regarding the weight of the governmental interest at stake and because the proscribed conduct, even when undertaken for communicative purposes, should not fall within the protection of the First Amendment."

Elaborating on his "weight" of government interest argument, Starr urged the Court to now find, unlike in *Johnson*, a "compelling" government interest to override any First Amendment rights of flag desecrators because of the "representative consensus articulated by the Congress and the President in connection with the enactment" of the FPA, a consensus that he declared identified a "substantial potential harm posed by physical damage and mistreatment of the American flag," namely "the assault upon and injury to the shared values that bind our national community." He argued that passage of the FPA had created a situation different from that faced by the Court in *Johnson*, because the law reflected a "considered" congressional determination "as opposed to that of a single state legislature [that is, Texas]" that the flag is a "unique national symbol deserving special protection." Even if the Court disagreed, Starr maintained, it should "defer to the considered judgment of the elected branches."

Starr also maintained that the Court should find that because "physical destruction" of the flag was so uniquely "anathema to the Nation's values," such conduct should—in clear contradiction to *Johnson*—be exempted from First Amendment protection, just as the Court had previously excluded other marginal forms of expression such as obscenity, child pornography, defamation, and incitement to violence. According to Starr, flag burning imposed "an injury that society should not be called upon to bear," because, just as "concern for the moral sensibility of the community" justified excluding obscenity from First Amendment protection, similar concerns should allow the "unique" symbol of the community's "existence to stand above the fray of physical assault and destruction."

In amicus briefs, the House and Senate both presented lengthy analyses of the history of flag protection legislation that sought to demonstrate, although via different arguments, that the FPA was justified on nonsuppressive grounds, and therefore should be subject only to the relatively lenient *O'Brien* test of meeting an "important or substantial" government interest, rather than the far tougher "compelling" government interest standard applied by the Court in *Johnson* to the Texas law because it was found to be motivated by suppressive purposes. The House brief (which Republican House leaders refused to join) simply reiterated its earlier "sovereignty" argument. The Senate largely abandoned its previous stress on the "content neutrality" of the FPA's text in favor of a history of flag desecration legislation that argued that the original aim of such laws was to outlaw commercial and partisan political misuse of the flag solely to "preserve the flag's value as the nation's salient symbol." The Senate maintained these laws were "not directed at suppressing dissent," thereby suggesting that the FPA was similarly motivated by nonsuppressive purposes and met the *O'Brien* test. Apparently because none of the three government briefs focused on the textual "content neutrality" argument that had been the focus of congressional discussion of the FPA, SJC chairman Biden filed a personal amicus brief advancing that position and maintaining that the "deference" owed the Court to Congress was "at its zenith" when the legislature had determined that the government had "powerful" interests in protecting the flag.

In response to Starr and the amicus briefs, the flag burners' brief, largely written by Cole, essentially reiterated the successful arguments earlier advanced before the federal district courts. Cole maintained that the lower courts had correctly held that the FPA could not withstand the searching scrutiny required by *Johnson* because it was motivated by the suppressive purpose of seeking to protect the flag's symbolic value and because such an interest "did not justify criminally punishing respondents for their politically motivated flag burnings." To accept Starr's argument that protecting the flag should override First Amendment rights because government officials felt strongly about it, Cole argued, would "leave the Bill of Rights to the whims of legislators" and decimate the role of the Constitution and the courts in providing minorities "legal protection from the political inclinations of the majority" which violated fundamental rights. Cole further rejected Starr's attempt to compare flag desecration with forms of expression excluded from First Amendment expression, such as pornography, because his examples had "no serious political value" and his argument contradicted numerous Court rulings that held that "offensiveness" could not justify banning speech in a political context.

Cole also rejected the claim, stressed by Biden and inferentially supported by the House and Senate briefs, that the FPA was content neutral. He argued that the very act of singling out a particular symbol for special protection was itself "content based," and that, in any case, the FPA banned "virtually all conduct associated with dissent," even acts that would not harm the flag, such as maintaining a flag on the floor under a glass cover, but allowed "patriotic" conduct that imperiled the flag, such as burning it to "respectfully" retire worn flags. In response to the Senate brief, Cole declared that even if flag desecration laws had not originally targeted political protest, in practice they had "invariably been enforced" against dissidents, and even their original purpose was unconstitutional because it sought to suppress the "message of disrespect" conveyed by advertising and political uses of the flag. Cole also rejected the House "sovereignty" argument, maintaining that it was irrelevant because burning a flag could not threaten the flag's ability to identify American ships at sea and because the government's "interest in having a symbol to mark ships cannot justify jailing its citizens for burning reproductions of that symbol."

On April 30, two weeks before the scheduled May 14 oral argument, a technical decision by the Court provoked turmoil within the defense team by allowing only one attorney to appear before it. In 1989, Kunstler had been the unquestioned and obvious choice to speak before the Supreme Court, even though Cole had primarily researched and written the defense brief, if only because Kunstler had been originally approached by Johnson. The *Eichman* defendants, however, had approached both Cole and Kunstler through the Center for Constitutional Rights (CCR). Cole and Kunstler had both appeared before the district courts to argue their case, but when the Supreme Court rejected their request that they be allowed to share the defense presentation, each maintained that he should be the defense spokesman and the subsequent dead-lock could only be resolved, according to interviews with both at-torneys, when they finally agreed to submit the decision to a vote of the seven defendants shortly before oral argument. Kunstler won the vote by 4 to 3, in what he told a reporter was "a test for me."

In interviews in 1991 and 1999, Cole said that he argued that it was only fair that he be the defense spokesman because Kunstler had argued the previous year and "I had done all the work," and by tradition, "at CCR the attorney who does the work on the case is generally presumed to be the one who should do the argument." Cole recalled that "many people at CCR urged Bill to step aside, but in the end neither of us was willing to back down," with Kunst-ler arguing that "I was a young lawyer, up and coming and would maybe get an opportunity to argue before the Supreme Court again [as he did in three cases by 1999], while he was an old lawyer and it might be his last opportunity, which turned out to be true [Kunster died in 1995]."

In a 1991 interview, Kunster agreed that Cole "certainly had good claim" to argue the case, because he had done the "lion's share" of the work, and that "he was probably very hurt by [the vote] and I probably would have been too, because everybody likes to argue before the [Supreme] Court." Kunstler added, however, that he "probably felt that as the older guy and maybe whose career was ending that some sort of internal equity would say I should do it," and "candidly I like arguing and probably felt I had a right to do it, and felt people—the outside world—sort of ex-pected me to do it. There were a lot of factors, it was probably egocentric." In his 1994 autobiography, Kunstler said he had "des-perately wanted" to make the presentation, but that although he originally felt "exhilarated" by what he termed the "surprising" results of the defendants' vote, he subsequently came to feel that "I should have done the generous thing and backed down. But the truth is that, psychologically, I couldn't do it. The public associ-ated me with the case and I couldn't accept being second seat to a much younger man who had been out of law school only a few years. . . . This was a clear case of my good angel fighting my bad one. The bad angel won out."

In a 1999 interview, Kunstler's law partner, Ron Kuby, recalled that he "could understand how David [Cole] felt," because after having "worked for Bill for 13 years, I saw him argue a lot of my stuff and felt I could do it better," but "Bill was the best known civil rights lawyers on earth at the time, a living statesman of the left" and "he had a vast reservoir of personal historical experience he brought to the case that no one his junior had, which was no reflection on David, a brilliant guy." Kuby recalled that Kunstler was "incredibly nervous" as he prepared for the May 14 oral argument:

> Bill was always nervous before appearing in court which was one of things that people didn't realize because he was so powerful and poised. When he was nervous, he had one tick: he would put his hand in his pocket and jingle his keys and change. We used to basically take away his keys and change before any major argument so he wouldn't jingle because he would jingle loudly. We walked to the Court from the hotel. It was a beautiful sunny day. Bill really felt at the very top of everything. This was one of the most important issues in American jurisprudence. He was arguing it before the Supreme Court and was completely prepared. It was an incredibly golden moment to be with him.

Kuby recalled that when the defense team met Solicitor General Kenneth Starr at the Supreme Court, "We found Ken to be a thorough gentleman in every respect. Bill introduced me, we shook hands and chatted. Bill tried to introduce the defendants to Ken and they refused to shake his hand. I sort of shook my head because Bill was always personally friendly to everyone and Ken Starr was articulating a position on behalf of the government, he wasn't the architect of Nazis."

Starr introduced two major new arguments when oral argument began before the Supreme Court at 10:29 A.M. on May 14, but the justices' responses suggested that he did not succeed in changing any minds from the *Johnson* lineup. Although earlier Starr had argued that flag desecration involved "expressive conduct," but like obscenity or defamation was not entitled to "full First Amendment protection," at oral argument he suggested that it was not "expression" at all because it failed to meet the Court's 1974 *Spence* test, which required the delivering of a "particularized message" to thus qualify. Instead, he argued, flag desecration left a "major message gap" and resembled "shouting or screaming or using a loudspeaker at full blast," or even the "mindless nihilism" that *Spence* indicated was totally undeserving of First Amendment protection. However, in response, Justice Kennedy termed such acts an "internationally recognized form of protest," and Justice Scalia said the message clearly was, "I am in opposition to this country" and added that, even with verbal expression, "You don't have to be precise to be protected, do you?"

Previously, Starr had consistently dismissed the "content neutrality" argument, but at oral argument he made it the central point of his presentation, maintaining that in the FPA Congress had paid close attention to *Johnson* and had "very carefully, very respectfully" crafted a law free of "content-laden language" that protected the physical integrity of the flag without "singling out certain viewpoints for disfavored treatment." Thus, he maintained, Congress had successfully fashioned a law that admittedly protected the flag "because of its symbolic value," but "not from criticism but from physical destruction or mutilation," much as governments could protect "houses of worship" or "the bald eagle" against destruction, regardless of what motivated such action. For example, Starr argued, the FPA was so "content neutral" that people could be prosecuted under it for "patriotically" desecrating the flag, such as emblazoning it with the message, "I love the Supreme Court." Scalia, however, referring to the FPA's text, ridiculed this argument by declaring, "If I get a spot on my tie, I don't say, gee I've defiled my tie . . . or if I tear my jacket I don't say, my, I've mutilated my jacket. These are words of—cast contempt upon."

Kunstler, who had vouched for his daughter Karin's admission to the Supreme Court bar shortly before Starr began his argument, responded to Starr in his sixth and last appearance before the Court by reiterating the main points in the defense brief and by rejecting what he termed Starr's "dramatically" new arguments about lack of a particularized message and "content neutrality." He argued that stripping vague forms of expression of First Amendment protection would relegate all "non-verbal expression to the scrap heap" and that the FPA was clearly not "content neutral" because it "singles out one particular political symbol" for protection and bans only acts that would "hurt" the flag "or cast it in a bad light." Responding to Starr's argument that flag desecration could be analogized with pornography or defamation and thus did not warrant full constitutional protection, Kunstler declared that with regard to "political speech, the government cannot make judgments of what is overly offensive or unimportant" and maintained that the courts had the responsibility to block the government's "inclination to suppress" what it deemed "offensive at any one time or another." Kunstler concluded by declaring that the government was seeking to turn the flag into a "golden image" that must be worshiped, but "once people are compelled to respect a political symbol, then they are no longer free and their respect for the flag is quite meaningless. To criminalize flag burning is to deny what the First Amendment stands for."

Press accounts of the oral argument overwhelmingly predicted that the Court was likely to strike down the FPA, largely because Scalia and Kennedy had indicated no sympathy for Starr's position (although Blackmun, the focus of most speculation about a possible change in votes, had remained silent). *Newsday*'s May 15 headline summarized the conventional wisdom in declaring, "Flag Burning Law May Not Fly." In a 1990 interview and published article, reporter Lyle Denniston termed Starr's position "desperate" and "nearly hopeless," especially his appeal that the Court find flag desecration not protected expression less than a year after that position had been "lost."

In an interview conducted in the Supreme Court's basement press room, Denniston, in response to a question whether the Court might be affected by concern that striking down the FPA would lead Congress to pass a constitutional amendment overturning its rulings, replied that he felt the justices would be completely unaffected by any external nonlegal considerations. He declared:

Most judges that I know, and I think the ones upstairs, who I know fairly well, don't think politically much of the time. It's astounding to me at times how apolitical they are. I think most of them have, at least in my conversations with them, a kind of ninth grade civics appreciation of the American polity. If you told them that members of Congress were going to vote on this issue primarily and maybe exclusively because of the threat of a thirty-second soundbite by an opponent who could say, "You're not in favor of the flag," they would think you were describing another political order, not this one. They expect that senators are going to vote as attentive, careful, considerate members of the nation's legislature and you can't disabuse them of that.

Very little media coverage of the oral argument noted how drastically the government's FPA defense had changed over time, from a complete rejection of the "content neutrality" argument by Barr, to an eventual complete embrace of this position by Starr. In a 1990 interview, House legal counsel Steven Ross termed this "incredible evolution of the Justice Department's position" the "biggest story" of the FPA's defense and "truly strange," but one that "nobody has picked up yet."

In an interview conducted in June 1990, shortly after the Supreme Court struck down the FPA, Starr agreed that his position on the FPA had changed considerably. Starr said that although at first he was not convinced that the statute was truly "content-neutral," over time he concluded that it was a "sincere," "respectful," and constitutionally adequate congressional response to various "caveats and disclaimers" in *Johnson* that "didn't need" to be there if the justices had intended to invalidate all flag desecration laws. Starr said that he had ultimately concluded:

When one reads the legislative record, one cannot but be taken by the fact that there was very thoughtful scholarly comment, and scholarly debate within Congress itself, that "We really are not doing violence at all to our system of free expression. It is completely consistent with that system of free expression to protect the physical integrity of the flag." That was the judgment made by the Congress, and the Court, I think, would be wise to give great respect to that judgment.

Starr added, "I viewed my role in defending the constitutionality of the statute—consistent with my own conscience, obviously, not willing to parrot something in which I do not believe, I did not do that and would not do that—to embody as best I could the collective wisdom of those who had rallied around the statute." Starr added that "if I were a legislator" he personally would be "inclined to protect the integrity of the flag, even though believing fervently in the First Amendment," because flag desecration was different from protected expression, above all because it was "conduct," which did not deserve the same protection as "speech," and also because it does not provide the "particularized" message the *Spence* ruling suggested was required for full constitutional protection as "expression."

Starr termed the flag "that one symbol of unity in a fractured society with so many points of friction" and therefore it was "understandable" that the community would view flag desecration as "morally offensive." Essentially echoing the constitutional theory originated by Tribe to defend the FPA, he added, "Congress should have the power to protect the physical integrity of things that are special to us, not to protect them from criticism," but because flags, like churches, gravesites, and bald eagles, are

> special to us and Congress doesn't need a health and public safety reason to justify protecting the moral sensibilities of the community against conduct, against action. I can embrace the proposition that Congress can neutrally protect things that are important to us, as long as they don't care what the thinking [of the "desecrator"] is, whether it is mindless spitting on the Tomb of the Unknown Soldier, whether you do it as an act of protest or just as an act of extraordinary insensitivity or just mindlessness. All that Congress is saying is, "Please, say anything you want, be as vile as you want, but don't burn the flag."

Supreme Court records indicate that the Court met in private conference to vote on *Eichman* on May 17, three days after the oral argument (after postponing its original plan to vote immediately after oral argument because Justice Blackmun had to travel to New York City to meet a long-standing commitment). The May 17 preliminary vote suggested the same split as in *Johnson;* five justices (Brennan, Marshall, Blackmun, Scalia, and Kennedy) voted to uphold the district court rulings, three (Rehnquist, White, and O'Connor) voted to reverse and uphold the FPA, and Stevens passed (as he had originally in *Johnson,* although in both cases he voted to uphold the flag desecration laws). The only conference remark recorded in Marshall's notes was Rehnquist's declaration that "*Johnson* was bad." Presumably Brennan's conference comments corresponded to the views expressed in a May 14 memo to him from one of his clerks, which rejected Starr's position that the FPA should be upheld as "content-neutral" and that the clerk characterized as declaring that "now Congress has spoken and we should defer to its judgment." The clerk declared that "this Court, not Congress decides what constitutes protected speech" and discarded the "content neutrality" argument because, as the FPA excluded burning worn flags "precisely" because such acts were "thought to express a message of respect for the flag," but banned similar conduct that was used to "express an anti-patriotic message," the statute was "aimed at the expressive content of flag-burning, and therefore must be subject to the same rigorous review we applied in *Johnson.*" However, he concluded, because Starr "professed no new compelling state interests for our consideration" beyond the "preservation of the flag as a symbol of nationhood and patriotism" that the Court had found not sufficiently "compelling" to override the constitutional rights of flag burners, "we must affirm on the basis of *Johnson.*"

As senior judge in the majority, Brennan assigned himself to write the Court's opinion (in a memo to Rehnquist dated May 14, the day of oral argument, even before the Court's May 17 conference, suggesting that the justices' views were firmly fixed and well known before the conference). Brennan circulated his first draft on May 18, which was joined by Marshall on May 21, by Blackmun on May 31, and by both Kennedy and Scalia on June 6. Brennan's first draft was substantially identical to his final opinion, with only minor adjustments made in response to a May 31 letter from Kennedy stating that the latter would join Brennan's "good opinion" if he would "make two changes of the footnote variety." Brennan incorporated Kennedy's suggestions that the ruling explicitly state that it did not impair "the extent to which the Government's interest in protecting publicly owned flags might justify special measures on their behalf" or affect laws designed to regulate the "commercial or like appropriation" of the flag's image.

Kennedy's delay in joining Brennan's opinion earlier led one of Brennan's clerk to write his "boss" (as Brennan's clerks called him) a May 26 memo expressing concern that Kennedy was "working on this case" with "one of the two most conservative clerks in this building," who in the past had kept "information from his boss in an effort to influence his vote" and might be "intentionally keeping [Kennedy] in the dark" concerning informal discussions between the clerks designed to let Kennedy know that Brennan was receptive to making the kinds of changes that ultimately occurred. On a lighter note, the same clerk forwarded to Brennan a poem, which read, in part:

> In *Texas v. Johnson*, we held five to four
> (Over impassioned dissents about history and war)
> That our nation's freedoms would not be erased
> So that symbols of freedom could stand in their place. . . .
> So once again we're obliged to affirm
> What we said so eloquently only last Term
> Any ban on flag-burning, however it's worded
> is unconstitutional: *It is so ordered.*

Among the minority justices, Rehnquist informed his brethren on May 23 that he would write a "brief dissent" that he circulated on May 31 and that White joined the same day. Rehnquist's draft was remarkably shorter and less angry than his *Johnson* dissent, simply declaring in two paragraphs that he remained convinced that the "Texas statute at issue in *Johnson* was constitutional" and that as a result he had no difficulty finding that the FPA was "consistent with the First Amendment" also. After Stevens circulated a dissent on May 31, however, Rehnquist withdrew his and joined with Stevens on June 4. O'Connor also joined Stevens's dissent (on May 31), as did White (on June 4). On June 7, Rehnquist sent a memo to his colleagues informing them that *Eichman* was among the decisions that were "ready" to be announced on June 11.

CHAPTER 8

The *Eichman* Ruling and Its Aftermath, June 1990

The Supreme Court Ruling in *U.S. v. Eichman*

On June 11, 1990, the Supreme Court announced its 5 to 4 ruling in *U.S. v. Eichman*, upholding the twin district court rulings that the FPA could not constitutionally be used to prosecute people seeking to express symbolic political dissent via flag burning. Justice Brennan read portions of his majority opinion aloud for six minutes before a crowded, hushed courtroom, but, unlike 1989, Justice Stevens did not read any part of his dissent. The ruling was announced less than a month after the May 14 oral argument, far more quickly than is typical, leading Deputy Solicitor General John Reports, in a 1990 interview, to quip that "the Court took seriously" the congressional directive "to expedite things, because they certainly did." According to a Court clerk who was interviewed in 1991, the Court's speed resulted simply from handing down an opinion "when the case was ready" and reflected the "normal course" of seeking to adjourn as scheduled by the end of June since the legal question was "the second time around" and only required "repeating what had been clear doctrine all along." According to the clerk, the justices fully expected their ruling to lead to passage of a flag desecration constitutional amendment, but "I don't think there was any justice for which that kind of consideration would affect the way they would vote" or that "there was anything unique or particularly political about how this case was determined."

Brennan's ruling followed the outlines of the *Johnson* and district court opinions. He declared that the "compelling" government interest standard, rather than the lower *O'Brien* guidelines, applied to the FPA because the government's reason for protecting the flag's "status as a symbol of our Nation" was related "to the suppression of free expression," and concluded that this purpose could not justify "infringement on First Amendment rights." The Court specifically declined to "reconsider our rejection in *Johnson* of the claim that flag burning as a mode of expression, like obscenity or 'fighting words' does not enjoy the full protection of the First Amendment." Brennan also refused Starr's "invitation" to reconsider *Johnson*'s holding that the government's interest in upholding the symbolic value of the flag could not override First Amendment rights in view of "Congress' recent recognition of a purported national consensus favoring a prohibition against flag burning." Rejecting the latter argument, Brennan bluntly declared that "any suggestion that the Government's interest in suppressing speech becomes more weighty as popular opposition to that speech grows is foreign to the First Amendment."

Although conceding that the FPA, unlike the Texas statute in *Johnson*, "contains no explicit content-based limitation on the scope of prohibited conduct," the Court nonetheless clearly rejected the "content neutrality" argument, holding that the FPA suffered from "the same fundamental flaw" as the Texas law because it "suppresses expression out of concern for its likely communicative impact" and could not be "justified without reference to the content of the regulated speech." The Court held that this was evident not only from the government's avowed interest in protecting the flag's symbolism, but also from the FPA's "precise language," since it punished anyone who "knowingly mutilates, defaces" or "physically defiles" the flag, terms that "suggest a focus on those acts likely to damage the flag's symbolic value," but exempted the disposal of worn flags in a manner "traditionally associated with patriotic respect," as well as allowing the flying of flags in storms and "other conduct that threatens the physical integrity of the flag, albeit in an indirect manner unlikely to communicate disrespect." The Court also rejected the House's "sovereignty" argument because, although the government had a "legitimate interest in preserving" the flag's symbolic representation of "the Nation as a sovereign entity," flag burning "does not threaten to interfere with this association in any way; indeed the flag burner's message depends in part of the viewer's ability to make this very association." Brennan concluded by proclaiming, "Punishing desecration of the flag dilutes the very freedom that makes this emblem so revered, and worth revering."

Stevens's dissent was far more temperate than his or Rehnquist's *Johnson* dissents but he maintained that the flag's unique importance, such as its representation of "the ideas of liberty, equality and tolerance," justified infringing upon political expression to protect its "symbolic value," especially when dissidents could still express their ideas "by other means." Stevens conceded that the case involved "a question of judgment" about which "reasonable judges may differ," and, whereas a year earlier he had compared flag desecration to placing "graffiti on the Washington Monument" and Rehnquist had lumped flag burning together with murder and embezzlement, Stevens repudiated such analogies by declaring that burning a privately owned flag "is not, of course, equivalent to burning a public building," as it "causes no physical harm to other persons or to their property," and its impact is "purely symbolic." In what was widely interpreted as a slap at the Bush administration, Stevens added that the flag's value had been damaged not only by what he characterized as "this Court's [*Johnson*] decision to place its stamp of approval" on flag burning, but also by "those leaders who seem to advocate compulsory worship of the flag even by individuals whom it offends or who seem to manipulate the symbol of national purpose into a pretext for partisan disputes about meaner ends."

The Aftermath of *Eichman:* The Second Defeat of the Constitutional Amendment, June 1990

Eichman sparked an immediate renewal of calls by President Bush and others for a constitutional amendment. The overwhelming consensus of early press reports suggested that congressional endorsement of an amendment was, in the words of conservative political analyst and amendment opponent Bruce Fein, "inevitable," and that the issue would take a central role during the forthcoming elections; thus the June 12 *Chicago Tribune* headline read, "Burning Issue for '90 Elections Is Ignited by Court's Flag Ruling." The general tone of the massive press coverage was typified by a June 16 *Congressional Quarterly* article, which reported that opposition to the amendment would be "political suicide" under the headline, "Congress Snaps to Attention over New Flag Proposal: Proposed Constitutional Amendment on Fast Track, Could Get Through Both Chambers by July 4."

Within an hour of the Court's announcement, Bush reiterated his backing for an amendment, although, according to Bush presidential library documents, White House officials prepared contingency statements in case the Court handed down an unexpected ruling: if the Court upheld the FPA by distinguishing it from the Texas law at issue in *Johnson*, they recommended he express pleasure that "the Court agreed with the government's argument" that the FPA was "constitutionally permissible" and announce he had asked the Justice Department to "determine whether a constitutional amendment is still needed to protect the flag"; if the Court both upheld the FPA and explicitly overruled *Johnson*, Bush was advised to say that the Court had made "clear that protection of the physical integrity of the flag poses no threat to the free political debate that makes American democracy possible."

On June 12, the day after *Eichman*, Bush told reporters, in remarks cleared with Chief of Staff Sununu and White House Counsel Boyden Gray, that *Eichman* had been predicted by his administration, and that although he was "all for free speech," flag burning "endangers the fabric of our country" and that "flag desecration is unacceptable and must carry a price" because what the flag "encapsules is too sacred to be abused." He called on Congress to pass the amendment "by July 4, this nation's birthday," since although "honest and patriotic Americans may differ on this issue, I am absolutely convinced this is the proper course for our country."

Many observers predicted that the amendment would quickly and easily be endorsed by Congress, since, as Republican House leader Michel put it, "Who wants to be against the flag, mother and apple pie?" Democratic political consultant Brian Lunde urged his party not to "get on the wrong side of a powerful symbol like the flag" because they "could not possibly explain [opposition to the amendment] in 30 seconds." Two national polls published immediately after *Eichman* indicated almost 70 percent favored an amendment, and, according to an Associated Press (AP) survey of Congress, by June 18 255 of the 290 votes needed for a two-thirds House majority in the House and 54 of the needed 67 Senate votes were pledged to the amendment.

Early reports from states legislatures also indicated strong support: for example, Kentucky Senate Republican caucus leader Jack Trevey and Pennsylvania House Republican minority leader Robert Mellow predicted easy passage in their states for a vote that both compared to "motherhood and apple pie." In Louisiana, a state Senate committee responded to *Eichman* by endorsing a proposal to lower the fine for "simple battery" from six months in jail and a $500 fine to only a $25 fine if flag desecrators were assaulted; the proposal, already passed by the state House in May by 54 to 39, was authored by Democratic representative James Cain, who proclaimed, "I'm tired of marijuana-puffing hippies desecrating our flag."

Numerous reports from around the country suggested that many politicians were too terrified of the potential political repercussions to seriously consider voting against the amendment even if they privately opposed it. Pennsylvania House Democratic majority leader H. William DeWeese said he would reluctantly cast a "political vote" lacking in "political integrity" for the amendment, and that it would be ratified in Pennsylvania because the "politics of the issue are such that very few individuals would be inclined to self-immolate." Representative Paul Henry (R-MI) declared that "no one likes or cherishes the prospect of a 30-second television commercial being aired which has a collection of American flags waving against the blue skies saying your member of Congress doesn't honor the flag." Democratic HJC civil liberties chairman Edwards lamented that "there's a mindless stampede out there" and although "hardly any" of his colleagues backed the amendment, "they are just afraid." Democratic pollster Harrison Hickman lamented that the fear of negative TV ads among his party was so great that the amendment should be known as the "30-second video amendment."

Supporters of the amendment essentially repeated their earlier arguments that the flag was so unique and important that it required special protection, that flag desecration went "too far" and amounted to conduct rather than expression, and, especially, that since, as Senator Dole put it, the FPA had "been tossed into the legal junkyard heap by the Supreme Court," an amendment was the only available remedy. According to House Republican leader Michel, the only question was, "Does Congress really want to protect the flag from desecration?"

Dole and other amendment backers asked why, if banning flag desecration seriously injured constitutional rights, overwhelming majorities of both parties had supported the FPA in 1989, and how anyone could consistently vote for the FPA but oppose the amendment. "Where was the first amendment in October [1989]?" Dole asked. "Did the first amendment go on vacation back then?" Assistant Attorney General J. Michael Luttig, William Barr's replacement as chief Bush administration spokesman for the amendment, told a June 21 SJC hearing that its passage would have no "measurable impact on free speech" because to the "average American" flag desecration had as "little to do with free speech" as "obscenity or pornography," and because the amendment was "almost laser-like" in solely overturning *Johnson* and *Eichman*, affecting no other constitutional rights. Luttig added that failure to pass the amendment could "break" and "cripple" the nation's "spirit" and thus threaten America's "social and political fabric."

Despite the overwhelming tide of early predictions that the amendment would easily pass, when the House voted on June 21, 1990—the exact anniversary of *Johnson*—it fell far short of the needed two-thirds, obtaining only 254 out of 431 votes (59 percent) after eight hours of dramatic debate in which almost two hundred representatives—an extraordinarily high number—participated. On June 26, the already-slain amendment also fell short in the Senate, winning fifty-eight out of one hundred votes after ten hours of a debate so anticlimactic that SJC chairman Biden apologized "to my mother for—if she is watching—wasting the taxpayers' money." The defeat of the amendment removed it from the political scene for five years, but even if the vote felt like an enormous moral victory to its opponents, it was hardly a massive triumph for civil liberties: as assistant House Democratic whip Bonior noted in a 1990 interview, in both 1989 and 1990 "there was still a majority" for the amendment, so "in essence it was the Constitution itself which saved the Bill of Rights, the fact that you needed a two-thirds vote."

A number of factors derailed what seemed in the immediate aftermath of *Eichman* an irreversible political steamroller. Perhaps the most important was that the general public had largely lost interest by June 1990 in a year-old issue that had effectively become a "summer rerun," a TV formula notorious for producing boredom. Thus, PAW chairman John Buchanon compared the 1990 flag dispute to a "tired sequel to a movie not worth seeing in the first place." In a 1991 interview Democratic representative David Skaggs, who helped lead the fight against the amendment, concluded that it lost in 1990 because the "half-life [the time it takes to diminish by 50 percent] of political passion over any given issue in this country is a couple of months" and the cooling-off period provided by the FPA "provided the opportunity for an awful lot of people" to "reflect and to have their intellect evaluate the whole thing differently than they did in the immediate aftermath of *Johnson*." According to a summer 1990 survey of 118 Democratic House members, 70 percent reported that support for the amendment among their constituencies had decreased compared to 1989. In short, although superficially the *Eichman* ruling was a defeat for the FPA's proponents, the deeper strategy of many of its less enthusiastic backers, namely to use it to postpone consideration of the amendment in hope that passions would cool, succeeded remarkably well.

Although two national polls conducted immediately after *Eichman* indicated almost 70 percent favored the amendment, two polls conducted about a month later indicated support had dropped to just 57 percent. Press accounts quoted Representative Dan Glickman (D-KS) as reporting, "We're hearing very little from con-stituents," and Representative Richard Durbin (D-OH) as declaring, "The phone isn't ringing, the mail isn't coming in. The intensity of this is much lower than a year ago." Shortly before the June 21 House vote, *New York Times* editorial writer John MacKenzie sum-marized the "conventional wisdom" by concluding that "the news so far is the lack of groundswell" for the amendment. In 1991 inter-views, Democratic representative Sonny Montgomery, an amend-ment cosponsor, conceded his cause lost in 1990 because "people lost interest in it" and another amendment backer, Representative Charles Douglas, agreed that in 1990 "there was definitely a cool-ing off of intensity of support."

Even veterans' groups, the strongest backers of the amendment in 1989, were far less visible in 1990. Although veterans continued to back the amendment, their physical presence in Washington was so diminished that one civil liberties lobbyist who was active in opposing the amendment in both 1989 and 1990 remarked in a 1990 interview that whereas in 1989 Congress had been "mobbed by 'hat people'" (a reference to the distinctive military-style head-gear worn by veterans), in 1990 amendment opponents found themselves asking, "Where are the 'hat people'? Where in the hell are they? It's astonishing." Similarly, in a 1991 interview, Repre-sentative Douglas lamented that the veterans' organizations "didn't have the ability to get warm bodies to the Capitol" in 1990.

No doubt at least partly as a result of the perceived lack of in-tense public demand for the amendment, 80 percent of congress-men who told the AP that they were undecided as of June 18—almost all Democrats—ended up voting against it (and more than fifteen congressmen who told the AP they were leaning toward the amendment ended up voting against it; hardly any switched in the opposite direction). According to a key House Democratic leadership aide interviewed in 1990, perhaps thirty House members decided to oppose the amendment between *Eich-man* and the vote, and "in the last four days all of a sudden the gates opened." Similarly, PAW legislative counsel John Gomperts reported, in an interview conducted the day after the House vote, that "you could palpably feel the mood shift yesterday," especially after "it was clear" the amendment would lose. According to Gomperts, after many representatives announced, in effect, "Look this is not easy, I love the flag, but it's the Constitution," others "thought, 'Jesus, if so and so can do that and if we're going to win, I'm against it too.'"

The lack of strong public support for the amendment and this "contagion" effect probably helped fortify several congressmen who declared that they had searched their souls in the days leading up to the final vote and decided that their consciences demanded that they oppose it. Five House members announced during the June 21 debate that they were withdrawing their earlier sponsorship of the amendment, including Representative Tim Valentine (D-NC), who told his colleague that "over the rhetoric of the past few days I have finally heard the voice of my own conscience." In a 1990 interview, he related that although he first "did not fully comprehend the significance" of "amending the Bill of Rights for the first time in 200 years, what the consequences of that might be down the road," his position gradually evolved and

> I found myself at one point thinking I would still support the amendment but hoping it would fail, and I finally reached the conclusion to vote against it without regard to the political consequences. I felt that I didn't want to be part of a Congress that had opened a floodgate [to further erosions of the First Amendment]. I just decided this was something I didn't want to be any part of.

Many late-deciders who voted against the amendment still feared the political consequences of their decision. Representative Robert Wise told a reporter, "People have to be wondering if this is a political AIDS virus that you will always carry and won't know when it will be activated [by a future political opponent]." Representative John Porter (R-IL) admitted in a 1991 interview, "Sure, I'm worried in a sense about how this could be used against me in the future," but added, "if I'm going to let those worries be paramount in my mind there's no purpose to my being here."

Along with the perceived decline in the intensity of public support for the amendment, perhaps the other most important factor in its 1990 failure was that Democratic opponents and their supporters were far more organized and effective than Republican backers and their allies. The superior Democratic tactics and strategy were especially reflected in their extremely effective "framing" of the flag desecration issue in 1990 in terms of "substantive" versus only "symbolic" freedom, aided by recent developments in eastern Europe in which anticommunists had been applauded for "desecrating" flags with communist symbols; on the other side, Republicans were weakened by internal divisions, ineffective support from the White House and their own frequent public statements suggesting that they were heavily focused on the political benefits of the issue.

One of the long-term consequences of the March 1990 eruption over the House Supreme Court brief was that House Democratic opponents of the amendment began organizing their troops immediately afterward in anticipation of its expected revival in the aftermath of an *Eichman* ruling adverse to the FPA. Although House Republicans also created a "flag task force" at about the same time, by all accounts the six-member Republican House effort was divided and ineffective, whereas the Democratic task force, with a floating membership of about a dozen members, proved united and effective. For example, Republican House Task Force cochair Douglas declared in a 1991 interview that "had we the united approach on the Republican side, it would have made a difference," but instead Republicans went "down two roads" because of long-standing existing tactical divisions between the party wing aligned with Republican House leader Michel, which favored attempting to work with the Democratic congressional majority whenever possible, and the wing allied with assistant House Republican leader Gingrich, which favored more confrontational tactics. According to Douglas, a member of the Gingrich faction, Michel's supporters took the "hands clasped and knees on the ground approach" of trying to "get any crumbs that should be thrown them" by the Democrats and "never made" the amendment a "priority," and task force members "were never met with and talked with about how we get this thing moving and get a game plan." From the other perspective, a key Republican staffer affiliated with Michel characterized the Gingrich element as "bombthrowers, who viewed this as the greatest political issue in the world," whereas Michel was dedicated to truly seeking to protect the flag.

One small indication of the chaos among Republican backers of the amendment centered around Speaker Foley's scheduling of the House vote for June 21, which both reflected his earlier promise to schedule a vote within thirty days of any Supreme Court ruling striking down the FPA and seemingly responded to Republican demands in the immediate aftermath of *Eichman* for a vote before the weeklong July 4 congressional recess. When Republicans discovered that they were short of votes, partly because, as Representative Douglas stated in his 1991 interview, the Republican task force "never did a good body count on the Democratic side," some of them demanded that the vote be postponed to allow veterans time to mobilize. Representative Gerald Solomon (R-NY) even maintained that the scheduled vote amounted to "kowtowing" to the "Communist Youth Brigade," and Gingrich threatened to make a refusal to postpone the vote the "first twelve seconds of the thirty-second commercials." Yet virtually simultaneously, Michel said the vote would be "fine" as planned and the White House issued a statement calling for a "prompt" vote.

In the 1991 interview, Douglas bitterly complained that disarray in Republican ranks was compounded by the Bush administration's failure to make the amendment a "priority" in 1990, so "we weren't getting any help or support from the White House." According to Douglas, "there never was any White House commitment" to the amendment and "had they really felt strongly" about it "rather than just political posturing, I think they would have done something" to foster support on Capitol Hill. According to press accounts, although Bush telephoned some congressmen to lobby for the amendment, his efforts were tardy and limited; *Congressional Quarterly* reported that by the time he contacted some originally undecided Democrats shortly before the House vote, they had already been repeatedly talked to by members of the Democratic task force and "it was too late." Perhaps not surprisingly, Bush administration lobbyists who were interviewed shortly after the amendment's defeat denied any lack of enthusiasm for it. For example, a Justice Department official maintained that about six department employees, including Attorney General Thornburgh, worked to round up votes, and that "I'm not sure the administration could have done more than it did," because "everybody already had a solidified position," and because "Congress really got a sense from outside the beltway" that "it's just something that doesn't warrant the extraordinary amount of time being consumed by it."

Whatever occurred behind the scenes, Bush's public support for the amendment was clearly far more limited than the previous year: compared to a full-fledged press conference and the Iwo Jima speech exclusively devoted to the issue in 1989, the only substantial public remarks he made about it in 1990 were delivered on June 12 in connection with a previously scheduled acceptance of a small model of the Iwo Jima monument from its architect, which was presented to him at the White House in the presence of a single flag attached to his lectern with a small pole. The June 13 *Los Angles Times* report on this event captured the seemingly diminished White House enthusiasm with the headline, "Bush Urges Flag Amendment, But Does It with Less Fanfare." Bush failed to mention the amendment at all during a June 13 press conference or at a Flag Day ceremony at the Vietnam War Memorial, and his only public references after June 12 were a couple of brief endorsements of the amendment buried in lengthy speeches delivered on June 20.

Another factor that significantly weakened Republican amendment efforts was that some of its leading supporters repeatedly and openly threatened political consequences against those on the "wrong" side of the issue and left the general impression that politics was more important to them than policy. For example, on June 14 Gingrich told a reporter that the flag question would be a "definitional issue" during the 1990 elections and opined that if he were the "mythical Republican strategist, I would want the amendment to lose by one vote," because then all Republican congressional candidates could argue that their election could determine a future vote. In the immediate aftermath of *Eichman,* Dole twice told reporters that a vote against the amendment "would make a pretty good 30-second spot" during the forthcoming elections, and the Republican National Congressional Campaign Committee circulated to Republicans an "issue alert" that termed the amendment a "great campaign issue" because it was "clear and simple," required "no elaborate explanations and it is understood by everyone," and was "easy to use this time of year" as Flag Day and July 4 approached.

Republican threats of political retaliation may have influenced some Democrats to support the amendment. Among House Democrats who had been elected by 55 percent or more in 1988, 66 percent voted against it, but among those elected by thinner margins, 71 percent backed it; and a 1990 study of House Democrats indicated that those whose constituencies were perceived to favor the amendment were 27 percent less likely to oppose it than those who viewed their constituents as against the amendment. But the overt Republican politicization of the amendment in 1990 probably backfired more than it succeeded: Representative Valentine, one of the early amendment cosponsors who abandoned it at the last moment, no doubt spoke for other colleagues when he declared in a 1990 interview that "after awhile you kind of get your back up" in the face of perceived naked political threats.

The partisan Republican comments significantly affected news coverage of the controversy and general public perceptions in a manner severely adverse to the amendment. In 1990 interviews subsequent to the amendment's defeat, assistant House Democratic whip David Bonior declared, "Dole and Gingrich exposed themselves [as out for political gain] at a very favorable time to us" and helped shape press coverage suggesting that the amendment was "a political ploy," and Representative Charles Stenholm (D-TX), who abandoned his earlier cosponsorship of the amendment, declared that overtly political comments of leading Republicans "cut the heart out of the argument" for it. Even Republican House task force leader Douglas termed the Dole-Gingrich comments "counterproductive" in a 1991 interview, adding, "If they want to make them in closed-door meetings as strategists, fine, but not out in public." During the House debate, even Michel, red-faced and clearly angry, bitterly denounced Republicans whom he said were seeking to politicize the issue, terming them "campaign operatives out there saying things they had no right to say" who were not "official leaders" of the party.

Attacks on Republican politicization of the amendment issue were numerous and unrelenting in mid-June. For example, a June 14 *Miami Herald* cartoon suggested general public disgust with Republican tactics by portraying Bush and a Republican elephant wrapping themselves in a flag, while one bystander asked another, "Got a match?" *Chicago Tribune* columnist Stephen Chapman wrote that Republicans were "bravely prepared to protect the flag, even if it means the loss of Democratic seats in Congress," adding that most Republicans, "if asked to sell their immortal souls for short-term political advantage, would reply: 'What's the catch?'" Representative Ben Jones (D-GA) declared that "if there's one thing people dislike more than flag burners it's politicians who wrap themselves in the flag," and warned that diminishing the country's "very principles" would only reward "pond scum" who burned flags. The partisan split over the amendment was clearly reflected in the voting: in the House, 159 Republicans and 95 Democrats backed the amendment, while 160 Democrats and 17 Republicans opposed it; in the Senate 38 Republicans and 20 Democrats voted "aye," and 35 Democrats and 7 Republicans voted "nay."

Although supporters of the amendment were divided in tactics and their cause was weakened by their open politicization of the issue, opposition legislators (especially in the House) and their external supporters in the press and civil liberties community exhibited impressive unity and organization. House Speaker Foley vigorously lobbied against the amendment with at least thirty wavering Democrats in a campaign that the *National Journal*, a well-informed political monthly, declared had "stunning impact" and was "his most aggressive stance" on any issue during his first year as Speaker. Foley's lobbying complemented the activities of the House Democratic task force. According to 1990 interviews with members David Bonior and David Skaggs, the task force met up to two or three times a week in May and June developing strategies that included working with civil liberties groups such as PAW, spurring newspaper editorial writers, and working to identify and persuade "swing vote" Democratic congressmen. Skaggs reported that the group was "successful in many cases" in convincing undecided congressmen to vote against the amendment because it "got started early and was persistent with a lot of people," particularly targeting congressmen who were veterans. Bonior recalled five months after the House vote that, "We got 62 vets who voted against the amendment."

One clear indication of the extraordinary effectiveness of the task force was that although the amendment won a 254 to 177 majority, its opponents circulated far more "dear colleague" letters, a common form of lobbying fellow members of Congress. One key House Republican aide lamented in a 1990 interview, "They must have out 'dear colleagued' us 40–3," so that "everybody's [mail]boxes have been flooded them." Another small, but telling, indication of the organizational impact of antiamendment forces was that, as PAW legislative counsel John Gomperts noted in a 1990 interview, in stark contrast with the post-*Johnson* congressional orgy of verbal assaults on the Supreme Court, in 1990 amendment opponents "were ready with speakers to go to the floor, instead of staying up all night condemning the Supreme Court decision, people were ready to make speeches in favor of the Bill of Rights" and "every time somebody stood up [on Flag Day, June 14] on their side, somebody stood up on our side."

Complementing the Democratic Capitol Hill lobbying, in 1990 the civil liberties community, now united in strong opposition to the amendment without the distraction of the FPA, was far more effective and fast-moving in both grassroots and congressional lobbying than the countervailing efforts of veterans' groups. When the HJC met on June 19 to discuss the amendment, the meeting room was dotted with people wearing PAW- and ACLU-supplied buttons with slogans against the amendment such as "Don't Burn the Bill of Rights," but veterans' groups had no visible presence.

According to PAW legislative counsel Gomperts, his organization sent four mailings to Congress within eight days of *Eichman* and extensively lobbied thirty wavering congressmen, almost all of whom ultimately opposed the amendment, by supplying them with arguments against it, poll data suggesting the political risks of opposing it had been exaggerated, and even draft texts of possible "30-second ads" defending an antiamendment vote. PAW field director Joseph Sternlieb added, in another 1990 interview, that these efforts were supplemented with a massive grassroots campaign that included over one thousand phone calls and over fifteen thousand postcards urging citizens to tell their congressmen to oppose the amendment. Sternlieb reported:

> We know that we turned around or helped turn around certain individuals who were leaning the wrong way two days before the vote. We flooded them with their old law professors or professors at their old law schools, local attorneys, constituents, if we could find family members who we knew agreed with us, we called them. Congressional staff members would volunteer that their boss was asking them to count letters and postcards. Some of the offices were telling me their mail was running 5-1, 10-1 against the amendment, even from conservative Republican districts.

The organizational efforts of the civil liberties community and Democratic leaders in 1990 was further bolstered by massive and almost unanimous press opposition to the amendment. In 1990 interviews, House Democratic task force member Skaggs recalled that "no heavy sell" was required to convince his home state newspapers in Colorado because their "immediate response was, 'As precious as the flag was, it was not as precious as the First Amendment'"; his task force colleague David Bonior reported that one "secret of our success" was "contacting all the editorial writers, the 'op-ed' people to get things written," and that in the end, "The press was very much on our side" and "very active and visible." Amendment cosponsor Sonny Montgomery lamented in a 1991 interview, "The newspaper editors just killed us."

To a even greater degree than in 1989, press hostility to the amendment often clearly colored news stories and analyses, particularly in portraying Republican support for it as crassly political.

For example, a June 13 NBC news account described the controversy as a conflict between the "conscience" and "principle" of
amendment opponents versus the "politics" of amendment backers, and the June 14 *Washington Post* reported that Republicans were
"salivating" over their anticipated political gains. All three major
American news magazines published June 25 "news stories" that
were extraordinarily opinionated and hostile to the amendment:
thus, *Newsweek* reported that "if naked cynicism were a crime, a
number of Republicans would be arrested."

Amendment opponents benefited considerably in 1990 not only
from their superior organization and fading public support for the
amendment, but also by "framing" their argument for public and
congressional consumption far differently than in 1989, in a manner that made the case for "bravely doing nothing" to override the
Supreme Court far more intellectually and political appealing. In
1989, the issue had been "framed" so that the only realistic congressional options became defined as overturning *Johnson* by
statute or by amendment. With the divisions and distractions created by the FPA eliminated by *Eichman*, however, in 1990 amendment opponents, including many who had previously shown no
compunction about legislatively diminishing freedom of expression, got "constitutional religion" in a united manner and "re-
framed" the issue as a battle of competing sacred icons: the *symbolic*
representation of liberty (the flag) versus the *substance* of liberty
(the First Amendment). This reflected what *Congressional Quarterly* termed the Democrats' "principal strategy" of shifting the
focus from the flag to the "sanctity of the Bill of Rights" as a
counter to the attempts of amendment backers to "frame" the issue
as "flag burners vs. flag protectors." Thus, in 1990 interviews,
PAW legislative counsel John Gomperts noted that in 1989 amendment opponents "lacked an effective counter-symbol" to those who
championed the flag, but in 1990 they found a "magical quality"
in the words "the Bill of Rights," and HJC subcommittee chair
Edwards declared that, "The magical slogan this time was one I
thought up, which was 'Leave the Bill of Rights alone.'"

In short, in 1989 the issue was framed by both sides as *how*, not
whether to "protect" the flag, but in 1990 it was framed by amend-

ment opponents as "Which is *more* important, the flag or the Constitution?" a formulation far more favorable to a civil liberties victory. This "framing" was constantly reiterated in the media, as in a June 12 *Atlanta Constitution* report on the House defeat of the amendment headlined, "It's Old Glory vs. First Amendment," and a June 23 *Washington Post* cartoon that portrayed President Bush as a rap singer, declaiming, "The Bill of Rights is just a rag / compared to burning our nation's flag!" The media portrayal of the flag desecration controversy along these lines in 1990, coupled with its heavily hostile and political interpretation of the motivations of amendment backers, was so pervasive that Republican representative Frank Horton complained on the House floor that the debate was being unfairly "framed as one dividing political opportunists seeking to wave the flag in an election year against those acting as courageous guardians of the Constitution" and that the media had "contributed largely to the simple framing of this issue."

During the 1990 debate, many congressional opponents of the amendment "framed" the issue in extreme iconic terms that depicted the Constitution and the Bill of Rights as virtually unexaminable and sacred texts, thereby avoiding any focus on the substance of the controversy involved or even on the contents of the very First Amendment they were now defending, but which many had been quite willing to undercut with the FPA. Several congressmen who had voted for the FPA a year earlier but opposed the amendment in 1990 compared the Bill of Rights to the Bible or the Ten Commandments; Representative John Dingell (D-MI) termed the Bill of Rights "perhaps the most sacred and perfect document which has ever been set forth in the entire history of mankind." Senate Democratic majority leader George Mitchell, an outspoken critic of *Johnson* and an FPA supporter, termed *Eichman* "wrong" and denounced flag burning as "offensive and obnoxious," but simultaneously fervently opposed an amendment that sought the same purpose as the FPA because, he maintained, the Bill of Rights was the best, clearest, most concise, and most "eloquent statement of the rights of citizens to be free of the dictates of government" in the "whole sweep of human history." Mitchell added, "I do not believe we should ever, under any circumstances, for any reason, amend the Bill of Rights."

Not all opponents of the amendment downplayed the substantive content of the document that they were seeking to preserve unaltered. For example, Representative John Lewis (D-GA) declared that he had not risked his life in combat for a "piece of red, white and blue cloth" but "for the freedoms" it represented. Representative Peter Kostmayer declared that the "choice is whether to plunger a dagger into the heart of America, for that is what the First Amendment is," and Senator Howard Metzenbaum declared that the amendment would result in "jailing people for expressing themselves" and warned that "when the government dictates which forms of protest are acceptable—and which are not—the right to dissent is all but meaningless." Most of the press criticism of the amendment also focused on the substantive issues involved, as did the testimony of opponents during an SJC hearing that was conducted even as the House was killing the amendment. Thus, Duke law professor Dellinger harshly criticized the amendment on free speech grounds at the hearing and sent a copy of his testimony to Justice Brennan, who replied, "It is right on target. If the Senate takes a vote notwithstanding the vote in the House, your remarks are all the support they need."

The reframing of the flag desecration controversy in 1990 was considerably enhanced in its appeal by the eastern European anticommunist democratic revolutions of late 1989, which so prominently featured widespread desecration of national flags to support demands for greater freedom that one book about the Rumanian revolution was entitled *The Hole in the Flag*, in reference to the frequent ripping of Communist symbols from that nation's flag. That "flag desecration" had been widely used in eastern Europe to express clearly understandable political views that were enthusiastically applauded by the American public easily lent itself to the argument that banning flag desecration would diminish American liberties just as freedom was being expanded in the former Communist totalitarian states. Even Justice Kennedy, during the *Eichman* oral argument, clearly referred to these developments when he asked Solicitor General Starr, "Would you be concerned if in

Eastern Europe or some foreign county a government punished demonstrators for marching with a defaced flag in support of the demonstrators' cause for freedom?" During the 1990 congressional debate, Senator Tom Harkin (D-IA) noted that Americans had not denounced protesters in eastern Europe for "cutting the Soviet hammer and sickle out of the center of their flags," and Senator Gordon Humphrey (R-NH) termed it "preposterous" that the Bush administration wanted to outlaw "the very same thing that we exulted in when it took place in Eastern Europe."

CHAPTER 9

From *Eichman* to the New Millennium, June 1990–Spring 2000

The Revival of the Constitutional Amendment, 1995–2000

Although, as will be seen below, flag desecration controversies, sometimes accompanied by seemingly illegal prosecutions, periodically erupted at the *local* level after the June 1990 defeat of the amendment, the issue disappeared thereafter from the *national* political scene with a stunning quickness and completeness for almost five years. In April 1991, PAW legislative counsel John Gomperts noted in an interview that the controversy appeared to be a "thing of the past," and termed it remarkable that "we almost passed a constitutional amendment over something that apparently no one cares about just a few months later." As humorist P. J. O'Rourke noted in a 1991 book, flag burning seemed to have been "vitally important to everybody right up until the moment we forgot all about it."

Although *Johnson* and *Eichman* had been decided by 5 to 4 margins, with both decisions written by Justice Brennan, after Brennan retired in mid-1990, David Souter, his successor nominated by President Bush, was never even asked his views about flag desecration during his successful Senate confirmation hearings. When the four Seattle defendants who had been prosecuted in the FPA test case were each fined, and two were given three-day jail terms in November 1990 for destruction of federal property in connection with their burning of the Seattle post office flag (a separate charge from the flag burning allegation dismissed by *Eichman*), the national news media did not even report it. Although the flag desecration issue was mentioned during the 1990 elections in perhaps two dozen congressional races, it virtually never became important and never seems to have significantly hurt Democrats: for example, all six House Democrats who had received less than 55 percent of the vote in the 1988 election and voted against the amendment won reelection. *Congressional Quarterly* characterized the issue after the election as "strictly flash-in-the-pan," a development that was especially surprising because for months Republican and veterans' spokesmen and news accounts had pronounced that any incumbent who voted against the amendment would pay dearly at the polls. For example, a June 29 *Christian Science Monitor* front-page story was headlined "GOP Strategists See the Flag Issue as a Sure-Fire Winner."

President Bush never mentioned the amendment again during the rest of his term, and only once referred to flag desecration during his unsuccessful 1992 reelection campaign against Democratic candidate Bill Clinton; Bush praised Clinton for telling the American Legion that he had sponsored legislation modeled on the FPA when he was governor of Arkansas in 1989. Even the Supreme Court *Johnson* and *Eichman* dissenters apparently had no interest in revisiting the issue: although the four minority justices remained on the Court in October 1992, fewer than the minimum four votes needed were obtained that month to hear an appeal from a Texas court that had struck down, on the basis of Supreme Court rulings, a 1989 Texas law modeled on the FPA. In a 1992 case unrelated to flag desecration, the Court, now lacking two of the *Johnson-Eichman* majority with the recent resignation of Marshall, reiterated that it was not constitutionally permissible to punish people who burned a flag "in violation of an ordinance against dishonoring the flag" (although it added that it was permissible to punish flag burning in violation of a general ordinance "against outdoor fires").

Although Supreme Court justices rarely comment on recent decisions, in August 1990 two of the *Johnson/Eichman* dissenters made clear that they had no interest in revisiting the flag desecration issue: Justice Stevens told an ABA meeting that the Court "should never have" heard the *Johnson* case, because if it had simply allowed the Texas ruling overturning his conviction to stand, the result would have been "a lot of ink and a lot of heartache saved," and Chief Justice Rehnquist told a legal conference, "There are not many people in this country who have burned flags, but now that it has finally been established as legal, there will be far fewer." Justice Scalia, a member of the *Johnson/Eichman* majorities, has repeatedly publicly reaffirmed his view that the Constitution protects flag burners because "the First Amendment protects your right to show contempt," although adding that he personally "can't stand scruffy, bearded people who go around burning the American flag."

The flag desecration amendment returned again to the national political stage only in 1995: in that year, and subsequently in 1997 and 1999, a modified form of the 1989 Bush amendment was endorsed by the needed two-thirds majority in the House, but it failed in the Senate in 1995 and again in 2000. The most important reasons for the revival of the amendment were that congressional elections in 1994 and thereafter gave Republicans control of both houses of Congress for the first time in more than forty years and that the American Legion, the nation's largest veterans' group, sponsored an extremely well-organized and well-funded campaign to resurrect it. Immediately after the amendment's defeat in 1990, the Legion began quietly organizing a drive to obtain from state legislatures so-called "memorializing" resolutions urging Congress to endorse the amendment and send it to them for ratification. Although the Legion's original goal of obtaining resolutions from thirty-eight state legislatures (the number needed to ratify a congressionally approved constitutional amendment) by May 1991 fell short by seventeen legislatures, by April 1995 forty-nine state legislatures (all save Vermont) had favorably responded.

In August 1994, the Legion publicly formalized its renewed amendment drive by creating the Citizens Flag Alliance (CFA), a coalition of (by 2000) about 140 civic, ethnic, and veterans' organizations with a claimed joint membership of over twenty million people. Although the CFA was technically independent of the Legion, it was completely dominated by it: for example, the Legion supplied the CFA with office space, staff, salaries, supplies, telephone lines, an Internet site and, most important, with about $15 million of the more than $17 million expended by the CFA by mid-1999. In an interview conducted in 1995 after the amendment won in the House, but barely lost in the Senate, CFA president Dan Wheeler declared that over a period of twenty-one months his organization had taken the "issue from not being on the radar screen whatsoever—when I talked to Congress at first they looked at me as though I'd just beamed down from the mother ship."

One clear indication of the CFA's impact was that, in sharp contrast to 1990, a survey of Senate offices in 1995 uniformly reported that an overwhelming percentage of constituent mail and phone calls favored the amendment—and that the vast majority of such communications clearly reflected the CFA's campaign. Thus, Senator Bill Bradley's office reported receiving 8,800 letters on the flag desecration controversy, with over 90 percent favoring the amendment, and Senator Christopher Dodd's office reported that communications were about 5 to 1 for the amendment, although those opposed to it were "usually a more thought out personal letter whereas the others are more form letters." In a 1995 interview, Kathryn Hazeem, Republican chief counsel of the HJC subcommittee on the Constitution, attributed the 1995 outcome to the CFA's "organization at the grassroots in terms of contacting members," and in a 1997 interview, Bill Teator, press secretary to House amendment cosponsor Representative Gerald Solomon (R-NY) similarly recalled that in 1995 the CFA "did a hell of a job" and as a result congressmen "came out of the woodwork" to support the amendment owing to "Legionnaires writing and pouring through their office doors."

Although the fundamental arguments for the flag amendment remained similar to those advanced earlier, such as the contentions that the flag was so unique that it deserved special protection, that flag desecration was "conduct" and not expression, and that the overwhelmingly majority of Americans supported such views, after 1994 the CFA/Legion and their congressional backers also advanced arguments that increasingly made clear that many amendment supporters largely backed it as a symbolic weapon in the post-1960s "culture wars." Just as the flag was the primary symbol of American identity, the perceived need to outlaw flag desecration reflected their apparent perception that the country was undergoing a national identity crisis, or at least a general collapse in moral standards, that passage of the amendment would help remedy. Thus, SJC chairman Hatch, the leading Senate sponsor of the amendment, began the 1995 Senate debate by declaring that the nation was being "increasingly bombarded by coarse and graphic speech and by angry and vulgar discourse," and complained that

> Drugs, crime and pornography debase our society to an extent that no one would have predicted just two generations ago. . . . There are no limits. Anything goes. . . . We are fighting for the very values that the vast majority of the American people fear we are losing in this country. . . . The Senate must decide whether enough is enough. . . . Have we gotten so bad in this country that no values count?

Hatch told the SJC in 1998 that the amendment was "about respect for our system, our way of life," and that therefore enacting it was a "perfect way of sending a message throughout our society that we are tired of this stuff," that "we have allowed some of this gibberish to go on far too long," and that "it is time to really start setting this country on its right course again." According to Hatch, "I think it is time to say in this country that we are tired of the way things are going. I don't know of any other issue that will allow you to do it as well as this issue."

The post-1994 congressional debates were filled with similar rhetoric by amendment proponents. For example, in 1995 Representative James Traficant (D-OH) said that the entire controversy was not "about the flag" but rather "about pride, it's about respect, it's about values"; Senator Charles Grassley (R-IA) maintained that the amendment represented a "rediscovery of core American values, like respect for authority" and a rejection of the 1960s "counterculture" values, including "anti-authoritarian" and "anti-Americanism" attitudes; and HJC chairman Henry Hyde (R-IL) termed the amendment "an effort by mainstream Americans to reassert community standards" and declared that the debate was less about "the flag itself" than about "a popular protest against the vulgarization of our society." During the 1997 House consideration of the amendment, leading sponsor Representative Solomon declared that the amendment would "put a stop to the erosion of decency and mutual respect facing our nation," and Representative Bob Barr (R-GA) declared that "maybe we can't stop the glorification of homosexuality, maybe we can't stop the deteriorating of families," but the amendment would at least give citizens "the opportunity to simply stand up for America" and to express "a tremendous frustration with what they've seen happen to this country over the last couple of generations." During 1998 SJC testimony, Los Angeles Dodgers general manager Tommy Lasorda said enacting the amendment would proclaim that "respect for God and country are basic to what our nation stands for," and Harvard law professor Richard Parker (who appeared on behalf of the amendment during four congressional hearings between 1995 and 1999) declared that the amendment was needed because "respect for the flag and the value of national community that it embodies is now, in fact, in jeopardy."

Similarly, during repeated appearances at congressional hearings, Northwestern University law professor Stephen Presser maintained that the country had come "disturbingly close" to "the fatal point of anarchy" and that the amendment would establish a "baseline of decency, civility, responsibility and order." According to Presser, it would "reconstruct a dangerously fractured sense of community," which had been fostered by Supreme Court decisions such as *Johnson*, which encouraged the kind of "moral chaos and irresponsibility in society" that had been evidenced by such events as "the recent explosion in the birth of children born out of wedlock, the increase in mindless and random acts of violence particularly in our schools, the [1995] Oklahoma city bombing" and the "recent widespread failure of many governmental officials, including even the President [in the Monica Lewinsky affair] to abide by the simplist moral principles." In 1998, amendment cosponsor Senator Max Cleland (D-GA) supported the amendment as "a necessary first step to rebuilding our faith in this country" at a time when the country was divided by the Clinton-Lewinsky scandal, and Senator Chuck Hagel (R-NE) told the SJC in 1999 that "some of the cultural problems today," including the April 1999 massacre at Columbine High School in Colorado, resulted from a "lack of respect for things bigger than ourselves," including the flag. During the 2000 Senate debate, Senator Bob Smith (R-NH) maintained that without the amendment "the country may not survive" the "kind of disrespect" evidenced by a "culture that suffers profoundly from a lack of common values, ideals, morals and patriotism," and marked by "moral decay and a lack of standards all around," so that "the bottom line is, if you are going out for the weekend and you want to leave your 14-year old daughter home, most of you say: 'I don't know if I want to leave her with the President of the United States.'"

Similar themes were repeatedly sounded by CFA and American Legion officials. In 1995 testimony, American Legion national commander William Detweiler declared that the Legion regarded flag burning as "a problem even if no one ever burns another flag." In 1998, CFA president Wheeler declared that the "greatest tragedy in flag mutilation" was the "disrespect" for "the values that it embodies," which "provokes the dissolution of our unity." CFA chairman Patrick Brady, who appeared four times before congressional committees on behalf of the amendment between 1997 and 1999, repeatedly termed "the legalized desecration of Old Glory" a "major domino in the devaluing of America," which he associated with the "incredible social cost of sexual license, crimes against our neighbors, the things we do to our land, our failure to vote and the level of disrespect" exhibited toward elected officials. Brady added that enactment of the amendment would reflect the will of the majority and thus "demonstrate who is in charge here." In 1999 issues of the CFA's newsletter, Brady lamented that the "threat to our Constitution today is domestic" and that "those who assault our Constitution were trained on the playing fields of the elite, and most have never seen a battlefield." He added, "Today's enemies of the Constitution are not armed with guns and tanks. They wear black robes and expensive suits. Their bunkers are courtrooms, classrooms, [congressional] cloakrooms and news rooms. Their missiles are law suits, legal dictates and media misinformation." According to Brady, the ACLU "stands out" in its "alien" values, using "millions of dollars and packs of lawyers to bully and sue . . . praying athletes and people of faith while defending atheists, pornographers and flag-burners." Given the threat that Brady claimed that flag desecration posed, his proposed penalty if the amendment passed struck many observers as a bit odd; he told Congress that violations should be treated "like a [traffic] ticket with a requirement that they take a class to teach them about the flag" and "how vital respect is in a society as diverse as we are" (although Paul McNulty, chief counsel for Republican House majority leader Dick Armey, told a national television audience in 1999 that he thought that if the amendment were enacted Congress would eventually pass a law providing for a penalty of "something like . . . up to ten" years of imprisonment for flag burning).

Far more than in 1989–1990, most amendment opponents attacked it during the 1995–2000 debates as a frontal assault on free speech, with far less emphasis on the totemic, or sacred character (as opposed to the content) of the Constitution as a counter-icon to the sacred flag. For example, five Democrats dissenters from the 1995 SJC majority report maintained that the amendment would do "unprecedented damage to the Constitution and the very principles the flag symbolizes," because "if our system of government and our society is to continue to define freedom and democracy throughout the world, it must, as a threshold, be a system open to free and diverse debate—that is what separates us from oppressive nations across the world."

In 1998, West Virginia ACLU director Hilary Chiz declared that because the flag only symbolized the Constitution, passing the amendment was "as if you go into a burning building to rescue a picture of your wife but leave your wife burning inside the building"; in SJC testimony former American Legion national commander Keith Kruel termed the amendment "akin to atomic-bombing a city because there may be a felon in the area." Kruel also attacked the CFA for using "high-tech lobbying" techniques and spending "millions" to pressure lawmakers to submit to a "false patriotism" that would "stain the image" of the flag by substituting the worship of a "golden calf" for the "principles, beliefs and ideals expressed in the Constitution." In 1999, twelve Democratic dissenters from the HJC majority report warned that the amendment's enactment "would open the door to government suppression of political protest, an activity that is central of our democratic process," and protested that it would protect the "symbol of free speech" by "diminishing free speech itself." Five Democratic dissenters from the 2000 SJC report termed the amendment a "wrong-headed response to a crisis that does not exist" and declared, "It would be the cruelest irony, if in a misguided effort to honor the symbol" of American liberties, "we were to undermine the most precious of our freedoms, the freedoms of the First Amendment. It would be an unprecedented limitation on the freedom Americans enjoy under the First Amendment and would do nothing to bolster respect for the flag." The SJC dissenters added, "If we want to stop people from burning the flag, the most effective way would be to stop daring them to do it. Passage of the proposed amendment—and the ensuing ratification debates—would do just the opposite."

Although the Clinton administration joined those expressing opposition to the amendment, it did so with arguments that placed little emphasis on free speech issues. Rather, Assistant Attorney General Walter Dellinger told the SJC in 1995, the administration opposed it because of a "traditional resistance" to "resorting to the amendment process," because of "the absence of any meaningful evidence that the flag is in danger of losing its symbolic value," especially given the lack of recent flag burnings, and because its text was too vague. Dellinger added that President Clinton felt that *Johnson* was "wrongly decided," had a personal "abhorrence" of "all forms of flag desecration," and "has a commitment to the protection of the flag."

According to White House and congressional sources interviewed in 1995, President Clinton personally vetted Dellinger's testimony and authorized wording that would avoid any inclination of sympathy for flag desecrators. According to virtually identical 1997, 1999, and 2000 White House statements that essentially reflected the "sacred" First Amendment position stressed by many amendment opponents in 1990, Clinton was "deeply committed to protection" of the flag and condemned "those who show it any form of disrespect," but believed that efforts to "limit the First Amendment to make a narrow exception for flag desecration are misguided" because "Congress should be deeply reluctant to tamper with the First Amendment which has never been amended since it was adopted 200 years ago." The White House also repeatedly, and bewilderingly, declared after 1994 that Clinton supported a "statutory" means of outlawing flag desecration, even though Dellinger, in his 1995 testimony, stated that Supreme Court rulings appeared to rule out "legislative efforts to prohibit flag burning." Although Republicans bitterly blamed Clinton's opposition to the amendment for the Senate's failure to endorse it in 1995, according to multiple White House and congressional sources interviewed that year, Clinton engaged in no personal lobbying whatsoever on the amendment.

Under the prodding of the CFA and the Republican congressional leadership, between 1995 and 1999 the HJC and SJC held a total of eight hearings on the amendment and repeatedly recommended its endorsement by their respective chambers. As Kevin Goldberg, a staff attorney for the antiamendment American Society of Newspaper Editors noted in 1998, one result was that "a lot of the arguments have been recycled for the last nine years," and much of the congressional proceedings were extraordinarily repetitious: for example, the 1997 and 1999 HJC majority reports supported the amendment with identical language. Dellinger's 1995 SJC testimony was repeated almost verbatim to the SJC in 1999 by Dellinger's replacement, Acting Assistant Attorney General Randolph Moss; Harvard law professor Parker submitted identical testimony backing the amendment to the SJC in 1998 and 1999; and Northwestern University law professor Presser presented substantially identical testimony on four separate occasions between 1995 and 1999. When CBS News correspondent Bob Schieffer reported on the June 24, 1999, House endorsement of the amendment, he declared "the arguments are always the same" and "it's the same old deal, literally," especially since with the amendment expected to go down to defeat in the Senate "it's all symbolism."

If the arguments and testimony largely remained the same, sometimes the witnesses varied. For example, a July 1998 SJC hearing featured, on behalf of the amendment, former *Dukes of Hazzard* television star John Schneider (whom SJC chairman Hatch congratulated for a "wonderful job" in recording Hatch's song, "I Love Old Glory") and Los Angeles Dodgers general manager Lasorda, who told the senators that "freedom of speech is when you talk." CFA-sponsored advertisements for the amendment in 1998 featured Lasorda, Schneider, football player Deion Sanders, and entertainers Wayne Newton and Pat Boone. In 1999, amendment backers brought before the SJC former Miss America Shawntel Smith, Senator John McCain, who had survived over five years as a prisoner of war in North Vietnam after his navy plane was shot down; and Senator Max Cleland, who had lost both legs and an arm in Vietnam. Opponents fired back with Senator Robert Kerrey, the only congressional recipient of the Medal of Honor, and former Senator Glenn, the first American astronaut to orbit Earth and a decorated marine fighter pilot in World War II and Korea, who had just become the oldest person to journey into space by blasting off for a space shuttle mission in late 1998 at age seventy-seven. McCain, who soon after gained enormous publicity during a brief, unsuccessful attempt to gain the 2000 Republican presidential nomination, told the SJC in 1999 that the nation should accord "some modicum of respect to the symbol of those precious freedoms for which so many our countrymen have laid down their lives" and that tolerating flag desecration would amount to "silent acquiescence to the degeneration of the broader values which sustain us as a free and democratic nation." However, Glenn warned his former colleagues that it would be a "hollow victory to protect the symbol while chipping away at the freedoms themselves that the flag represents" and declared that "those who have made the ultimate sacrifice . . . did not give up their lives for a red, white and blue piece of cloth" but rather "because of their allegiance to the values, the rights and principles represented by that flag."

In response to criticism of the 1989–1990 amendment's non-operative preamble, which had defined "physical desecration" as including "displaying the flag in a contemptuous manner," the 1995 amendment was stripped of the preamble, leaving only the operative text, which gave "Congress and the States" the "power to prohibit the physical desecration of the flag of the United States. After the House endorsed the amendment in 1995 but before the Senate voted that year, the reference to "the states" was deleted by amendment sponsors in an attempt to ward off the argument that the original text could lead to widely varying state laws.

On June 28, 1995, the House endorsed the amendment by 312 to 120, or 72 percent, well over the two-thirds majority required (an increase of fifty-eight votes and 13 percent over those voting in 1990). The House repeated its action by 310 to 114 (73 percent) on June 12, 1997, and again on June 24, 1999, by 305 to 124 (71 percent). However, throughout the 1995–2000 period, amendment proponents were unable to obtain similar victories in the Senate. On December 12, 1995, they fell three votes short of the required two-thirds Senate majority, despite a $1 million CFA television ad campaign aimed at a dozen supposedly wavering senators (although obtaining 63 out of 99 votes, a substantially larger majority than the 51 and 58 Senate votes respectively garnered in 1989 and 1990). The amendment was never debated in the Senate during the 1997–1998 congressional session: although the Republican leadership tentatively planned Senate floor debate for July 1998, CFA leaders, fearing that they were still short of votes, asked Senate Republican leader Trent Lott to postpone consideration of the amendment, and subsequently Democrats successfully objected to Lott's request, shortly before the Senate was scheduled to adjourn in October 1998, that it be considered with only two hours of debate. In a November 1998 interview, Steve Seale, chief counsel to Lott, said that other issues had "just overwhelmed us" in the press to adjournment after "the CFA and the American Legion asked us to withhold" the planned July consideration because "they were short of votes and they wanted extra time and thought it was better to have a vote closer to election day when it could have been an election issue, they thought, for those who were facing close votes." In March 2000, the Senate did debate the amendment once again—the timing was scheduled by the Republican leadership to coincide with a Washington national conference of the American Legion—but its backers fell four votes short of the needed two-thirds majority on March 29, obtaining 63 out of 100 votes.

The 2000 defeat was a severe blow to the CFA and its supporters, especially since they actually lost ground from the 1995 vote owing to the unexpected defection of two Democratic senators who had previously supported the amendment, Robert Byrd of West Virginia and Richard Bryan of Nevada. Byrd, generally regarded as the Senate's foremost historian and constitutional scholar, announced his change of mind in a March 28 speech to the Washington Legion conference in which he accepted an award for "distinguished public service." He declared that while the flag "symbolizes the nation," "we must love the Constitution more," as "it is not just a symbol; it is the thing itself." In an April 2000 interview, PAW public policy director Catherine Leroy characterized Byrd's speech to the Legion as "really going into the lion's den" and "a remarkable thing to do."

Foes of the amendment also especially hailed the public opposition voiced by two military heroes, Senator Charles Robb (D-VA), a decorated Marine Vietnam veteran, and retired general Colin Powell, chairman of the Joint Chiefs of Staff during the 1991 Persian Gulf War, who was generally viewed as an icon of level-headed American patriotism. Robb, who had previously voted against the amendment but was generally viewed as an uninspiring orator and had not been outspoken on the issue, delivered what was generally viewed as the most powerful antiamendment speech of the 2000 Senate debate. He declared that while two men had died in his arms in Vietnam, his comrades had "died fighting for all that our flag represents" but "did not die for a piece of cloth" that "eventually becomes worn and tattered." Robb added that "if we reach past our natural anger and disgust for a few publicity-hungry flag burners, we know in our hearts that a great nation like ours, a nation that defends liberty all over the world, should not imprison individuals who exercise their right to political dissent." Terming flag desecration "vulgar, crude, infantile, repulsive, ungrateful speech, but undeniably speech," Robb maintained that if "we seek to punish those who express views we don't share, then we—not the flag burners—begin to erode the very values, the very freedoms that make America the greatest democracy the world has ever known."

In a May 1999 letter to the SJC that became public only in March 2000, Powell declared that while he and other Americans were "rightfully outraged" in response to flag desecration, those who destroyed "a piece of cloth" did not damage "our system of freedom," whose First Amendment guarantees of freedom of expression applied "not just to that with which we agree or disagree, but also that which we find outrageous. I would not amend that great shield of democracy to hammer a few miscreants." Like the 1989–1990 opposition to the amendment by Senator Kerrey, the only sitting congressman who had received the Medal of Honor, and by former Vietnam prisoner of war John Warner, Powell's opposition was especially repeatedly cited by foes of the amendment because it undercut the suggestion that they might be unpatriotic: Powell's statement was quoted in full or part during the Senate debate by at least ten opponents of the amendment and was partly reprinted in a full-page ad in the March 27 issue of the nationally circulated newspaper *USA Today* paid for by PAW. PAW public policy director Leroy declared in an April 2000 interview, that "someone of Powell's stature and background came out so eloquently on the side of the First Amendment was really an important development" and "really puts an end" to allegations that opponents of the flag amendment love the country less than its proponents because Powell "is simply unimpeachable on this or virtually any other issue."

The 1995–2000 congressional votes reflected continuing sharp partisan divisions: in all three House votes, about 95 percent of Republicans voted for the amendment but only 50 percent or fewer of Democrats did so; in the two Senate votes, over 90 percent of Republicans, but only 30 percent of Democrats, voted "aye." The perception that Republican congressional election victories in 1994 and thereafter reflected a more conservative public sentiment that was presumably more favorable to the amendment

clearly affected the general congressional mood: in 1990, 37 percent of House Democrats supported the amendment, but in 1995
and 1997 Democratic backing increased to 47 percent and 50 percent, respectively, including votes from over a dozen Democrats
who had voted against the amendment in 1990. One of them,
Charles Stenholm of Texas, who had stunned his colleagues in
1990 by renouncing his sponsorship of the amendment because
"Americans do not try to silence those who are wrong or who disagree with us," because he loved the "ideals put into words by the
U.S. Constitution even more than the flag," and because flag burners "do not even deserve the time of day, much less a constitutional
amendment," was among those switching back in 1995, citing his
"deep concern about a growing, negative and disrespectful national
attitude."

What was particularly striking about the amendment's greater
success during 1995–2000 than in 1989–1990 was that, compared
to the earlier period, the entire controversy aroused far less press
coverage, public interest, and impassioned congressional debate,
and President Clinton opposed the amendment whereas Bush had
endorsed it. Moreover, the relatively few post-1990 flag desecration incidents and prosecutions rarely received more than local
attention, although the period between the 1989 and 1990 votes
had witnessed numerous and sometimes widely publicized flag
burnings and prosecutions, including especially those that culminated in *Eichman*. One clear reflection of the greatly lessened press
interest was that *Reader's Guide to Periodical Literature* listed thirty-
eight articles published about flag desecration in general interest
magazines in 1989 and twenty-two in 1990, but only six in 1995,
two in 1997, and none in 1998–1999. Newspaper and television
coverage similarly dropped off dramatically after 1990, even as the
amendment's prospect for passage markedly increased. A 1998 article in the Capitol Hill newspaper *Roll Call* noted that although the
media normally covered Washington developments "obsessively,"
the flag desecration story was "playing like a silent film." The
Washington Post, which normally assigns its own writers to micro-
scopically cover Congress, reported the 1997 House passage of the
amendment with a four-paragraph AP story buried in its inside

pages, and the *Los Angeles Times* similarly covered the House's 1999 endorsement. ABC and NBC each devoted three sentences to the 1999 House endorsement of the amendment on their evening news broadcasts.

The lessened press interest in the flag desecration issue after 1990 was accompanied by—and no doubt partly caused—a considerable diminishment in general public and political interest. Although the 1990 House and 1995 Senate votes had been conducted after extensive and impassioned debates held before packed chambers, the 1997 and 1999 House debates and the 2000 Senate discussion were much shorter, attracted virtually no congressional audience, and were conducted in a much calmer atmosphere, with increasingly fewer references to "30-second sound bites" or partisan motivations. Although CFA-sponsored national polls repeatedly indicated over 70 percent support for an amendment between 1995 and 1999—comparable to most 1989–1990 survey results— four other polls conducted between 1995 and 1999 by the *Washington Post*, the ABA, and the Freedom Forum found support from only about 50 percent or less of the public. In mid-1999, even John Smart, national commander-elect of the Veterans of Foreign Wars, which formally supported the amendment, termed it a huge distraction from more pressing issues such as the nation's "crisis-level" lack of funding for veterans' health care. Smart added, "This is not one of our top priorities. When was the last time you heard of a flag being burned? I'm surprised this is even still a major issue." Even in Indianapolis, the home of the CFA and the American Legion, only 150 people turned out in 1999 to celebrate Flag Day (June 14), "retire" a flag with a ceremonial burning, and urge passage of the amendment. Former congressman Andy Jacobs asked the gathering, in dismay, "Where is everybody?"

Reflective of the diminished flag fervor was that despite repeated threats by amendment proponents that congressional opponents would suffer severely politically (as in Senator Hatch's 1995 warning that "Those who don't vote for [the amendment] are going to be sorry"), the CFA almost completely failed in electoral efforts to defeat Democratic Senate amendment opponents, despite expensive television advertising campaigns directed against them. In 1998 interviews, a key Democratic SJC staffer who closely followed the flag desecration issue said, "I can't think of any [Senate Democrat] who saw a lot of political repercussions to voting against the amendment," and PAW senior staff attorney Larry Ottinger said there was "no evidence that the flag is a significant issue at all in any elections."

During the 1996 congressional elections, seven out of eight Democratic Senate candidates targeted by the CFA won reelection, and in 1998 three out of four CFA targets were victorious. Flag desecration did not become a significant issue in any of the 1996 races, and in the only 1998 race in which it became important, incumbent Senator Russ Feingold (D-WI) narrowly won reelection over Republican challenger Mark Neumann, despite numerous television ads run by Neumann that declared Feingold had looked "veterans in the eye and said it's OK to allow people to burn the American flag." In a 1998 interview, Feingold said he felt the flag issue was "decisive" for only a "relatively narrow group" of voters, but recalled that there was a "surprising amount" of intervention during the campaign by the CFA and other "out of state" groups that sought to make his opposition to the amendment an issue, including the circulation of "harsh and unfair" stories about him, such as "made up stories about my not having a flag in my office." He added that he was "just hopeful and somewhat confident that people know I had a strong record on veterans, especially veterans' health care, and that my reason for opposing the amendment was not that I didn't love the flag, but because I have a stronger passion for the Constitution and the Bill of Rights."

Amendment proponents had no greater luck in the 1996 presidential election, during which unsuccessful Republican candidate Robert Dole attacked President Clinton on numerous occasions for opposing the amendment. In a November 2 speech, for example, Dole declared that Clinton "didn't believe in serving his country [a reference to Clinton's efforts to escape conscription during the Vietnam War]; he doesn't believe in an amendment to protect the flag." In an earlier address to an American Legion convention, Dole declared that amendment proponents had narrowly been defeated in the Senate in 1995 because "the administration took the side" of the ACLU, but "next year we'll have a President who takes the side of the American Legion, and that would be a big, big change."

As press and public interest in the flag desecration controversy gradually evaporated after 1990, the far greater success of amendment proponents after 1994 was not only owing to the efforts of the CFA and the Republican congressional majority, but also to the disarray of amendment opponents, especially in Congress. In sharp contrast to 1989–1990, as one highly placed Senate Democratic source reported in a 1995 interview, after 1994 there was "no sort of organized, orderly campaign" by the Democratic congressional leadership against the amendment. Most striking, House Democratic leader Richard Gephardt (Foley's replacement), who was known to harbor presidential ambitions, abandoned his 1990 position and supported the amendment beginning in 1995. Gephardt never explained his switch, but, according to a 1995 interview with a Gephardt aide, he had hoped for a statutory "solution," but *Eichman* "in combination with an extreme public outcry in favor of the amendment led him to change his position." Senate Democratic leader Tom Daschle (who had replaced Mitchell) personally strongly opposed the amendment but refused to lobby his colleagues, because, according to a 1995 interview with his press aide Molly Rowley, he saw it as an issue of conscience and felt "that people should not be pressured to vote one way or another," a stance Rowley volunteered he had taken on only one other issue (lifting the arms embargo on Bosnia) during the previous year. According to a 1995 interview with PAW public policy director Leslie Harris, many Democrats, especially in the House, were shell-shocked in the aftermath of the 1994 Republican election triumphs, and "pulled their punches" because they felt they were faced with "a lot of speeding trains and that they couldn't stand in front of every one of them," and viewed the amendment's passage as a "fait accompli and saw voting against it as a suicide mission."

Especially in 1995, although less so thereafter, the civil liberties community also was significantly less organized than in 1990. A highly placed Senate Democratic staff aide reported in a 1995 interview that the role of the "public interest community" had been "non-existent" in 1995, and, combined with the lack of any organized Democratic opposition to the amendment, the result was that although "the CFA are no shrinking violets" there was "no push back." PAW public policy director Harris conceded in a 1995 interview that "We really deluded ourselves by having gone up against Goliath last time and prevailed [in 1990], and didn't realize it could come back and stomp us." When the issue re-emerged in 1995, Harris recounted, "I was stunned and couldn't believe it would happen again," especially because "nothing happened in [the] 1990 [elections] after all those threats and bravado." Even after the amendment began to move through Congress in early 1995, Harris continued, PAW was forced to fight many other battles, with the result that "resources have been spread very, very thin" and her organization had been "pulled in a million directions." Harris added that another reason for the greater success of the amendment forces in 1995 was "the failure of progressives to organize the grassroots across the board."

After 1995 PAW and the ACLU organized more effective opposition to the amendment and may have played a role in stemming the Senate tide. For example, in 1998, PAW sponsored television ads, costing about $100,000, in the states of several reportedly wavering senators, which featured former Vietnam prisoner of war and Reagan administration official John Warner declaring that he had "fought for the rights and freedoms" the flag represented and urging, "Don't let them burn our freedom." According to a 1998 interview with Catherine Leroy, the new PAW public policy director, PAW also concentrated on "garden variety retail lobbying," particularly focusing on senators "we know we need to hold onto and possibly identifying new ones whose minds might change, everything from grass roots organizing to finding out who their big donors are, trying to figure out their concerns and responding." She added, "With the margin of victory that close and the other side putting so many resources into it, we have to assume the worst and assume that every [Senate] vote was a potential switcher." Despite such efforts, by the late 1990s civil liberties groups were clearly suffering from a combination of flag desecration exhaustion and the need to constantly fight numerous other battles, and therefore could not match the concentrated attention or funding devoted by the CFA to the amendment. As Ed Hasbrouck, who was active in the defense of the 1989–1990 flag burners, told a reporter in 1999, "There's no parallel [to the CFA] on the other side. There's no Citizens Flagburning Alliance."

The Flag Desecration Controversy in the Galleries and the Streets, 1990–2000

Although about three dozen flag burnings had been reported in the press between October 1989 and June 1990, according to the Congressional Research Service only thirty-three flag desecration incidents of all kinds occurred between 1990 and 1994 (about six incidents per year), and even after the controversy began to attract more news coverage with the amendment's revival in 1995, fewer than forty-five incidents of flag desecration were reported between early 1995 and late 1998 (about eleven incidents per year). Nonetheless, many of these incidents led to (usually local) controversies, and in numerous cases alleged perpetrators were arrested. Frequently they were faced with charges such as arson, disturbing the peace, and inciting to riot, although their real "crime" appears to have been flag desecration. However, in numerous other instances, people were formally arrested under state flag desecration laws which had almost certainly been invalidated by *Johnson* and *Eichman*. In virtually all of these arrests, except where "content neutral" laws such as theft had clearly been violated, the charges were eventually either dropped or dismissed.

In a number of instances, controversies involved artistic depictions that were alleged to constitute flag desecration. For example, students at Elk Grove High School near Sacramento, California, had to go to court to win the right to paint a mural on the school's walls that included a depiction of a flag burning and textual information about the *Johnson* ruling in an attempt to celebrate American civil liberties. The controversy erupted after school officials invited student groups in the fall of 1991 to decorate the walls, but banned the proposed flag mural although approving other proposals that included controversial contents, such as one that portrayed black militants Malcolm X and Communist leader Angela Davis. After winning their battle in two different California courts and over two years of negotiations and litigation, however, the students lost the war when school officials voted in February 1994 to henceforth ban *all* permanent murals in an order to get rid of the flag mural, which the students had painted in September 1993 following their court victories. Subsequently, forty-seven students walked out of school in protest and were suspended for three days each, but the mural was painted over in August 1994. Elk Grove teacher Eleanor Kuechler-Van Acker lamented that the controversy would teach students to "follow the rules unless and until you lose, then change the rules" and that "the powerful always win."

Perhaps the most widely publicized flag desecration controversy of the post-*Eichman* era erupted in the spring of 1996 at the Phoenix Art Museum, where an exhibit of eighty artistic depictions of the flag provoked months of furious protests, including a demonstration that attracted about two thousand people on April 28. The special focus of the protests, which were spearheaded by the American Legion and the CFA, were displays that included a flag on the floor (a reinstallation of the exhibit by "Dread" Scott Tyler that had caused a furor when displayed in Chicago in 1989) and a flag draped over a toilet by artist Kate Millett titled "The American Dream Has Gone to Pot." Museum officials repeatedly rebuffed demands that the exhibit be closed on artistic and free speech grounds. Museum director Jim Ballinger declared, "What this exhibit celebrates is freedom in America. We have a story to tell and we're not going to take away a crucial part of the story." Although the exhibit ultimately proved by far the most popular in the museum's history, attracting almost fifty thousand visitors (as well as increased donations and museum memberships), by the time it closed on schedule in mid-June after thirteen weeks, the controversy led several museum corporate sponsors to disavow any connection with the show and led the largest Phoenix utility to cancel a planned $29,000 museum grant. Twenty-five Republican members of the Arizona legislature asked Phoenix officials to prosecute the museum for flag desecration, but were told by the city prosecutor that Supreme Court rulings had made clear that the exhibit was "constitutionally protected free speech." When the Arizona House passed its 1996 authorization bill for the Arizona Arts Endowment, it included an amendment banning the use of state money to finance art exhibits that desecrated American or Arizona flags. Representative Don Aldrige, one of the amendment's supporters, explained, "If these sleazeballs want to have an exhibit on their own, let them do it with their own money, not public money."

In numerous instances after *Eichman*, alleged flag desecrators faced a variety of legal penalties for their actions. RCP member Cheryl Lessin was sentenced to a year in jail for inciting to riot in Cleveland in August 1990 in connection with a flag burning protest against American foreign policy, after a trial in which a policeman testified that he had ordered her detention by saying, "She admitted burning the flag, arrest her." Lessin's conviction was overturned by the Ohio Supreme Court in 1993 on the grounds that the jury was not instructed that her "disgraceful and irreverent" burning of the flag was protected under the First Amendment and could not by itself be construed as proof of inciting violence. The U.S. Supreme Court refused in March 1994 to hear Ohio's request for an appeal and Cleveland officials subsequently decided not to exercise their option to retry her with amended jury instructions.

In February 1996, a fourteen-year old Green Bay, Wisconsin, student was suspended for three days and referred to juvenile authorities for possible prosecution for wearing to school a flag draped over his shoulder with the words "Star Spangled Lie" written on it. Further action was dropped after local officials declared, "We've got too many other cases that are more serious." In Galesburg, Illinois, two men were fined $300 each and ordered to serve forty hours of community service after pleading guilty to violating the town's open burning law by burning a flag in a street on July 4, 1996. After their sentencing, they ran out of the Knox County Courthouse to avoid being confronted by dozens of veterans and others who had jammed the small courtroom to witness the event.

In perhaps two dozen instances, individuals were arrested or prosecuted after June 1990 under flag desecration laws that were almost certainly invalidated by *Johnson/Eichman*, although generally these charges were eventually dropped or dismissed. In one of the most bizarre post-*Eichman* flag desecration prosecutions, Mark Cox was arrested in June 1991 in Youngsville, Pennsylvania, after a quarrel with his fiancée during which he allegedly tore down several American flags, threw them at her, and slapped a woman passerby who had chastised and slapped him for tossing the flags. After pleading guilty to charges of harassment of the passerby and insult to the flags, Cox was ordered in November 1991 by Warren County judge Robert Wolfe to pay a $500 fine, serve a jail term of nine to twenty-three and a half months, undergo alcohol counseling, and read and write a book report about *Man Without a Country*, the Civil War–era fictionalized account of a man required to spend the rest of his life without a homeland after denouncing the United States. Wolfe told Cox that he would read the book report to determine if writing it "rehabilitates your attitude towards the flag." Cox served almost four weeks in jail before being released on parole while appealing his sentence. Warren County officials eventually agreed to drop the flag insult allegations after an appeals court overturned Cox's convictions in late 1992 on the grounds that Cox had not been given adequate legal assistance at his trial.

In other post-*Eichman* flag desecration prosecutions, Barry Carpenter was convicted in connection with a 1991 Alabama protest against the Persian Gulf War, when police, who had originally arrested him for "littering" and "desecrating" a post office by chalking antiwar slogans on a nearby sidewalk, discovered a flag in his coat pocket that was allegedly soiled and in a "disorderly" and "wadded" condition. The charge was eventually thrown out of court after two appeals, on the grounds that the applicable state law required that flag desecration be performed in "public"; Carpenter won an out-of-court settlement after he sued local officials for false imprisonment and malicious prosecution. Another 1991 flag desecration prosecution, in Midland Country, Texas, involving the alleged writing and painting of obscenities and "satanic" symbols on Texas and American flags, was dismissed by a judge on the grounds that the 1989 Texas flag desecration law, modeled on the FPA, was unconstitutional. County district attorney Mark Dettman lost an appeal of the ruling in a state appellate court, and the Texas Court of Criminal Appeals and the U.S. Supreme Court both refused to hear further appeals. In Jacksonville, Florida, a homeless man was jailed for two days after he was sentenced in early 1999 for mutilating a flag and wearing it as a dress, but prosecutors later announced that the state law used against him was unconstitutional and voided the charges.

Local officials in Pennsylvania arrested four teenage boys for flag desecration in three separate incidents in 1998 and 1999 (with ultimate unknown results), but Dallas County, Texas, officials (who had brought the 1984 charges against Gregory Lee Johnson) refused to prosecute a man who had been arrested by police in the Dallas suburb of Richardson for flag desecration in late 1999 after he reportedly spray-painted flags and left them outside a church wrapped around dead rodents and excrement. According to a 1999 interview with Dallas County asssistant district attorney Mike Carnes, the decision was made after consultation with his colleague Kathi Drew—who had argued the *Johnson* case before the Supreme Court in 1989—because, in the light of *Johnson* and *Eichman*, "there's just no way that we could prosecute it and hope to sustain it," especially since "there was no way to get around that fact that [the arrested man] was trying to make some kind of statement." In late 1999, officials in Minnehaha County, South Dakota, lost twice in court before giving up attempts to prosecute for flag desecration Steven Knorr, nineteen, who had allegedly burned a flag when police broke up a large party. They maintained that Knorr was not engaged in political expression and therefore the prosecution was unaffected by *Johnson/Eichman*, which had explicitly struck down only flag desecration prosecutions brought against political protesters. However, a local magistrate and, subsequently (on appeal by the county), County Circuit judge William Srstka dismissed the prosecution as unconstituional under Supreme Court precedents after Knorr's lawyer maintained that Knorr had burned the flag to demonstrate "upset" and that although "his cause" was arguably "neither noble, well thought out, nor embraced by others," free expression "carries no such requirement." As he dismissed the case Judge Srstka declared, "Sometimes we have to make decisions we don't like" and verbally condemned Knorr for his conduct; according to a 1999 interview with Sioux Falls *Argus Leader* reporter Jennifer Gerrietts,

Srstka included in his remarks a lengthy recital of John Greenleaf Whittier's Civil War–era patriotic flag poem "Barbara Frietchie."

The most widely publicized post-*Eichman* flag desecration prosecution was brought in Appleton, Wisconsin, in 1997 in the wake of a series of flag stealing incidents reported in the area in mid-1996. On June 9, 1996, a flag that had been stolen from Reid Municipal Golf Course was discovered on the clubhouse steps with human waste on it. After another flag was stolen from the golf course on June 26, police discovered a note that declared, "The Anarchist Platoon has invaded Appleton" and intended "as long as you put flags up" to "burn them." After another flag was reported stolen from a private residence in Appleton, the police arrested Matthew Janssen, seventeen, and two companions on July 23 when they were found walking down a street with pieces of flags tied around their head and inside a duffel bag they were carrying. Janssen subsequently confessed to a rash of flag stealings and burnings and to what became known as the "flag defecation" incident, characterizing his acts as reflecting "antigovernment" views such as those earlier expressed in "songs for my band the Butt Ugly Bastards." Janssen added that the flag only represented "a piece of cloth" to him, and that the flag stealings and defecation were an attempt, by targeting the government-operated golf course, to "get the message across that there are people in America who disagree with the government" in the hope that "the media would jump on it" and "inform the masses" of "our message."

On March 10, 1997, Outagamie County Circuit Court judge John Des Jardins rejected the argument of county district attorney Vincent Biskupic that the flag defecation incident, which became the focus of a flag desecration charge brought against Janssen, had no element of "trying to make a political statement," instead reflecting mere "vandalism," especially since the incident occurred at night and was witnessed only by friends of Janssen. Des Jardins said that although Janssen's act would be considered "highly offensive and reprehensible" by the vast majority, he had to follow the clear guidelines of Supreme Court decisions by holding unconstitutional Wisconsin's 1919 flag desecration law, a felony statute that made it unlawful to "intentionally and publicly" mutilate, defile, or "cast contempt" on the flag. Des Jardins, a former prosecutor who exhibited American flags and military displays honoring two uncles killed as fighter pilots during World War II in his courtroom, was bitterly criticized for his ruling in a flood of virulent letters to the local newspaper, the Appleton *Post-Crescent*, as was Janssen and his attorney, public defender Brian Figy. In a 1997 interview Des Jardins described the reaction to his ruling as not "pleasant," but termed himself "duty-bound" to follow the "crystal clear rulings" and "marching orders" of the Supreme Court, as otherwise "I'm violating my oath of office."

Outagamie County officials appealed Des Jardins's dismissal of the flag desecration allegation and subsequently charged Janssen with thirty counts of flag theft. Janssen pleaded no contest to twenty counts in May 1997, and was sentenced to nine months in jail, three years of probation, and 350 hours of community service; the ten additional counts of flag theft were dropped as part of a plea agreement. Des Jardins's dismissal of the flag desecration charge was upheld by a state appeals court in September 1997 and by the Wisconsin Supreme Court in June 1998. In a unanimous ruling written with "personal anguish," Supreme Court justice Jon Wilcox termed Janssen's action "repugnant and devoid of any social value," but declared that the Wisconsin law was a "clear attempt to ban speech and conduct based on expressive content" and therefore violated the First Amendment. Wilcox added that "the facts of this case will remain a glowing ember of frustration in our hearts and minds," and, in what seemed to be an endorsement of a constitutional amendment, said that his court could not write "our private notions of policy into the Constitution, no matter how deeply we may cherish them" and that "if it is the will of the people in this country to amend the United States Constitution in order to protect our nation's symbols, it must be done through normal political channels."

Janssen told the *Post-Crescent* after the March 10 ruling (but before pleading guilty to the flag theft charges) that he had "made a mistake" in defecating on the flag to express his antigovernment message, but couldn't believe "people take the flag so seriously" and hoped someday to run for public office, including perhaps for mayor of Appleton, to help bring about needed change. However, he conceded it might be difficult to stay in Appleton, since "ten years from now, they'll probably still remember me as the one who defecated on the flag." In a 1997 interview and comments to the *Post-Crescent*, Figy said Janssen was "being shunned" by the community and appeared to be emotionally "overwhelmed" by the reaction to his case. Figy lamented that Janssen's "profuse" apologies had fallen on "deaf ears," and that "I don't think Matthew Janssen will ever be forgiven. I think it's fair to say this case has been a nightmare for Matthew and it has ruined his life. I think he's been branded with a great big X on his forehead that says flag desecrator and I think he'll carry that brand with him forever."

Figy stated that he took the case because he was the only public defender at his office when Janssen first came in asking for help and that it had turned into "the most notorious of my career, without a doubt" and a "wild, strange trip." According to Figy, who was an Air Force ROTC member at the University of Wisconsin, the case received far more local press coverage than was typical even for a homicide. He added, "I knew that it would be a controversial case, but I was not prepared for all of the hateful comments that my client, myself and Judge Des Jardins received as a result. I love America and I cherish the flag and it bothers me when people called in and questioned my patriotism when they don't know me." Figy termed his client's act a First Amendment–protected "means of expressing his dislike for the U.S. government and the American flag," albeit in a manner that was "highly unusual and highly primitive in nature."

The Wisconsin "flag defecation" case and its dismissal was repeatedly cited by the CFA and its supporters during the following three years—more often than any other flag desecration incident in American history—as clearly demonstrating the need for a flag desecration amendment. For example, American Legion National Adjutant Robert Spanogle, writing in the April 1997 edition of CFA's newsletter, termed Des Jardins's ruling another example of "the kind of twisted folly supporters of the flag protection amendment have been forced to deal with for years" and "of the erosion of decency and common respect for those values most

Americans hold dear." Representative Gerald Solomon told an April 1997 HJC hearing that the flag desecration amendment was designed to ban not only flag burning but also "the outrageous acts of people defecating on the flag" and "actually treating our flag like it was toilet paper." Vietnam veteran and Congressional Medal of Honor winner Gary Wetzel had the Wisconsin incident so much on his mind at a 1998 SJC hearing that he declared that "when we use the word 'desecration,' I think we are pertaining to one specific bodily function." CFA chairman Brady told the SJC in 1999 that the amendment would take power "over the flag back from the courts, who have declared that defecating on the flag is speech, and return that power to the people."

During the 2000 Senate debate on the constitutional amendment, leading sponsor and SJC chairman Hatch also repeatedly referred to the Janssen controversy, as he did during his brief, abortive effort to win the 2000 Republican presidential nomination, in which during a January 15 presidential debate he voiced his support for the amendment to "protect our flag from people urinating on it, defecating on it, tearing it and burning it with contempt."

———

As of early April 2000, there was no reason to expect the flag desecration controversy to disappear at any time in the foreseeable future. For example, it appeared possible that the amendment would become an issue during the 2000 presidential campaign, since the nominees-apparent, Republican Texas governor George W. Bush and Democratic vice president Al Gore, took opposing positions on it. Gore told reporters on Veterans' Day 1999 that he opposed the amendment because he agreed with Thomas Jefferson that "someone who expressed a view that is contrary to the view of the overwhelming majority should be allowed to stand undisturbed as a monument to our commitment to free speech." Bush, in a March 24, 2000, letter to the American Legion inserted into the *Congressional Record* during the 2000 Senate debate on the amendment, maintained it was needed to "honor our courageous veterans" who had "fought and died to protect the ideals of democracy that [the flag] represents" and "to send the unmistakable message that Old Glory is a sacred symbol of freedom to all Americans."

As the 2000 presidential race got under way and the Senate defeated the amendment on March 29, 2000, both flag burners and leading supporters of the flag desecration amendment made clear that their views had not changed and that they did not intend to go away. In a 1999 interview, "Dread" Scott Tyler, the center of the 1989 Chicago "flag on the floor" controversy and one of those prosecuted in *Eichman*, referring to the "fascist flag amendment," declared, "It was right for us to burn flags on the steps of the Capitol. It was right for people to protest the powers' efforts to make patriotism mandatory. It was right then, and it is right now." In 1999 comments to reporters, Gregory Lee Johnson, whose 1984 Dallas prosecution had touched off the entire post-1988 flag desecration controversy, maintained, "It's a myth that there's free speech in this country," and declared that if the amendment was enacted, "I hope people do find all kinds of ways to defy it. I know I will." He added, "It's not a big leap to say, 'You can't burn the flag' to saying 'You can't speak against the flag.'" The CFA and other backers of the amendment made clear that they intended to keep bringing it before Congress: thus in 1999 and 2000 comments, CFA chairman Brady said it was "just a matter of time" before the CFA triumphed; American Legion national commander Alan Lance declared that amendment supporters "will not go away" and "will not surrender"; SJC chairman Hatch told the Senate, "We are not going to quit until we win on this amendment" and "sooner or later we will get enough people here who feel strongly enough about this" to pass it; and CFA president Dan Wheeler declared, "I don't want to spend the rest of my life doing this. But if it comes down to that I will." As if in response to Wheeler, PAW public policy director Leroy declared in April 2000, "The flag amendment is a very high priority for our organization and we will continue to be there. This is not a fight we will be walking away from."

CHRONOLOGY

June 14, 1777	Continental Congress adopts the American flag
1812	Francis Scott Key writes "The Star Spangled Banner"
1840	Supporters of presidential candidate William Henry Harrison begin practice of inscribing politicians' names on the flag
1847	First private company manufacturing flags is established
July 4, 1858	Abolitionists in Boston drape flags in black to protest slavery
1861–1865	Civil War leads to massive boost of popularity of the flag in the North and incidents of flag desecration in the South
June 7, 1862	William Mumford hung in New Orleans for mistreatment of flag
1878	First bill introduced in Congress to prevent flag "desecration" in response to growing advertising use of flags
1890	House of Representatives passes flag "desecration" bill for the first time
1890s	Flag protection movement (FPM), led by Union veterans' groups and patriotic-hereditary groups, forms to fight use of flag for commercial and partisan political purposes; gradual adoption of flag rituals in schools begins
1896	Widespread use of flags for partisan purposes in presidential campaigns spurs FPM to demand that Congress and states pass flag desecration laws
1897	American Flag Association (AFA) formed to coordinate FPM
1897–1932	All states pass laws outlawing flag

	desecration, but FPM fails to obtain similar federal legislation
1907	Supreme Court upholds constitutionality of Nebraska flag desecration law in *Halter v. Nebraska*
1914–1920	Numerous prosecutions of perceived political dissidents for verbal and physical flag desecration during World War I reflects shift in FPM targets from "mainstream" commercial and political groups to perceived "un-Americans"
1931	Supreme Court strikes down attempts to ban peaceful display of red flags as unconstitutional under First Amendment in its first ruling protecting "symbolic speech," *Stromberg v. California*
1942	Congress enacts voluntary flag code, which recommends burning to retire worn flags
1943	Supreme Court strikes down compulsory flag salute and Pledge of Allegiance requirements for public school children as unconstitutional under First Amendment in *W. Virginia Board of Education v. Barnette*
1962	American Law Institute recommends dropping provisions related to commercial usage from state flag desecration laws as anachronistic
1966	National Conference of Commissioners on Uniform State Laws terms state flag desecration laws "obsolete"
1967	New York City flag burning to protest Vietnam War spurs Congress to debate federal flag desecration law, passed in 1968
1967–1975	Vietnam War era marked by hundreds of flag desecration prosecutions; Dallas teenager Gary Deeds receives four-year jail term for 1970 burning of flag bunting
1969	Supreme Court strikes down "verbal" flag

　　{ *Flag Burning and Free Speech* }

	desecration provisions of state laws as unconstitutional under First Amendment in *Street v. New York*
1974	Supreme Court strikes down two state flag desecration convictions on narrow grounds that avoid issue of fundamental constitutionality of laws that ban physical flag desecration in *Smith v. Goguen* and *Spence v. Washington*
1979–1984	Revolutionary Communist Party (RCP) organizes series of flag burnings to protest American foreign policy and attract attention
August 22, 1984	Dallas flag burning during protest against Republican renomination of Ronald Reagan leads to arrest of Gregory Lee Johnson, member of RCP youth group, for flag burning alleged to violate 1973 Texas venerated objects law
December 13, 1984	Johnson convicted and sentenced to maximum year in jail and $2,000 fine by Dallas jury
January 23, 1986	Johnson conviction upheld by Texas Court of Appeals
April 20, 1988	Johnson prosecution overturned on First Amendment grounds by Texas Court of Criminal Appeals
Fall 1988	Pledge of Allegiance becomes major issue in 1988 presidential campaign
October 17, 1988	Supreme Court announces it will hear appeal in *Johnson* case
Winter 1989	Major controversy in Chicago over "flag on floor" art exhibit
June 21, 1989	Supreme Court decision in *Texas v. Johnson* upholding Texas ruling that political dissidents cannot be prosecuted for flag desecration under the First Amendment triggers political uproar

{ *Chronology* }

June 27, 1989	President Bush endorses a constitutional amendment to overturn *Johnson*
Summer 1989	Congress holds hearings on possible responses to *Johnson*
Fall 1989	Congress passes Flag Protection Act (FPA) in attempt to circumvent *Johnson* by statute; Senate defeats proposed constitutional amendment on October 19
October 1989	FPA becomes law and is quickly violated by flag burners in Seattle and Washington, D.C., triggering federal prosecutions
Winter 1990	Federal district courts in Seattle and Washington, D.C., hold FPA unconstitutional under First Amendment and *Johnson* as applied to political protesters, triggering appeals to Supreme Court
June 11, 1990	Supreme Court upholds district court rulings striking down FPA as applied to political protesters in *U.S. v. Eichman*
June 21, 1990	Despite renewed call by President Bush for a flag desecration constitutional amendment, House defeats amendment
1994	American Legion forms Citizens Flag Alliance (CFA) to renew demands for constitutional amendment
June 28, 1995	House of Representatives endorses amendment 312 to 120
December 12, 1995	Amendment falls three votes short of needed two-thirds in Senate, 63 to 36
June 12, 1997	House of Representatives again endorses amendment, 310 to 114, but Senate fails to consider amendment in either 1997 or 1998
June 24, 1999	House of Representatives once more endorses amendment, 305 to 124
March 29, 2000	Amendment falls four votes short of needed two-thirds in Senate, 63 to 37

BIBLIOGRAPHICAL ESSAY

Note from the Series Editors: The following bibliographical essay contains the major primary and secondary sources the author consulted for this volume. We have asked all authors in the series to omit formal citations in order to make our volumes more readable, inexpensive, and appealing for students and general readers. In adopting this format, Landmark Law Cases and American Society follows the precedent of a number of highly regarded and widely consulted series.

The primary sources for this book are the legal briefs, transcripts, and decisions of the Supreme Court and the Texas and federal district courts that considered *Texas v. Johnson* and *U.S. v. Eichman* between 1984 and 1990, plus congressional hearings, reports, and debate concerning the flag desecration controversy, especially during 1989 and thereafter. I also had limited access to some documents from the Bush presidential library and from two deceased Supreme Court justices, although much other material from these sources is still not publicly available. Houston attorney Charles Spain acted as my eyes and hands in obtaining Bush library materials. I have previously published an edited and annotated collection of the most important such documents, including vital unpublished material such as the 1984 Dallas trial transcript in the original flag burning prosecution of Gregory Lee Johnson, in Robert Justin Goldstein, ed., *Desecrating the American Flag: Key Documents of the Controversy from the Civil War to 1995* (Syracuse: Syracuse University Press, 1996). A much more massive but unedited and unannotated collection of documents, totaling thousands of pages concerning the flag desecration controversy (although limited to published material), is Marlyn Robinson and Christopher Simoni, compilers, *The Flag and the Law: A Documentary History of the Treatment of the American Flag by the Supreme Court and Congress* (Buffalo: W. S. Hein, 1993). The *Johnson* and *Eichman* Supreme Court briefs and rulings can be conveniently accessed in Philip Kurland and Gerhard Caspers, eds., *Landmark Briefs and Arguments of the Supreme Court of the United States: Constitutional Law*, vols. 190 and 194 (Bethesda, Md.: University Publications of America, 1990 and 1991). A tape recording and transcript of portions of the Supreme Court oral argument in *Texas v. Johnson* is available in Peter Irons and Stephanie Guitton, eds., *May It Please the Court: The Most Significant Oral Arguments Made Before the Supreme Court Since 1955* (New York: The New Press, 1993). A collection of numerous law journals articles about *Johnson* and *Eichman* can be found in Michael Curtis, ed., *The Constitution and the Flag*, vol. 2: *The Flag Burning Cases* (New York: Garland, 1993). Although Congress has held about a dozen hearings on the flag desecration controversy since *Johnson*, by far the most important of them are House Judiciary Commitee, *Statutory and Constitutional Responses to the Supreme Court Decision in Texas v. Johnson*, 101st Congress, First Session, Serial no. 24 (1989); and Senate Judiciary Committee, *Hearings on Measures to Protect the Physical Integrity of the American Flag*, 101st Congress, First Session (1989).

Beyond the documentary published record, I have relied most heavily on newspaper and magazine articles and on interviews with over one hundred key actors in the 1989–1990 flag desecration controversy, including flag burners Gregory Lee Johnson and "Dread" Scott Tyler; lawyers on both sides, including former solicitor general Kenneth Starr, the late William Kunstler, David Cole, and Kathi Drew; the original *Johnson* trial court judge, John Hendrik, and the author of the Texas Court of Criminal Appeals ruling that first overturned Johnson's conviction, Judge Charles Campbell; leading consitutional law professors, including Laurence Tribe and Walter Dellinger; congressmen on both sides of the issue, including former House Republican leader Robert Michel and assistant Democratic House leader David Bonior; numerous congressional staff and Supreme Court clerks, most of whom requested anonymity; and journalists, such as Cokie Roberts and Lyle Denniston. Unfortunately, other important sources have consistently refused to be interviewed, including President Bush and his top advisers, such as Chief of Staff John Sununu, White House counsel Boyden Gray, and Attorney General Richard Thornburgh, as well as former Senate leaders Robert Dole and George Mitchell, Dallas District Attorney John Vance and University of Michigan president Lee Bollinger.

I have previously published a far longer and footnoted account of *Texas v. Johnson*: Robert Justin Goldstein, *Burning the Flag: The Great 1989–90 American Flag Desecration Controversy* (Kent, Ohio: Kent State University Press, 1996). There is a useful account of *Johnson* by

James Simon in *The Center Holds: The Power Struggle Inside the Rehnquist Court* (New York: Touchstone, 1995); I am indebted to Simon for allowing me to access a 1991 interview he conducted with William Kunstler. For a recent biography of Kunstler with some information about the flag burning cases, see David Langum, *William M. Kunstler, the Most Hated Lawyer in America* (New York: New York University Press, 1999). David Baum, *The Supreme Court* (Washington, D.C.: Congressional Quarterly, 1998) is an excellent short introduction to the workings of that body. For a good "inside" account of the workings of the Court in 1988–1989 by a former Court clerk, see Edward Lazarus, *Closed Chambers: The Rise, Fall and Future of the Modern Supreme Court* (New York: Penguin, 1999); for biographical essays on the nine justices who heard *Johnson* and *Eichman*, see *Eight Men and a Lady: Profiles of the Justices of the Supreme Court* (Bethesda, Md.: National Press, 1990). Nat Hentoff, "Profiles: The Constitutionalist," *The New Yorker,* March 12, 1990, 45–70, is an excellent short profile of Justice Brennan, the author of the two opinions.

For general background to the flag desecration controversy, stressing the period before 1989, see Robert Justin Goldstein, *Saving 'Old Glory': The History of the American Flag Desecration Controversy* (Boulder, Colo.: Westview, 1996). An excellent account of early cultural attitudes toward the flag is contained in Scot Guenter, *The American Flag: Cultural Shifts from Creation to Codification* (Rutherford, N.J.: Fairleigh Dickinson University Press, 1990). Much useful information on this topic can also be found scattered through Cecilia O'Leary, *To Die for: The Paradox of American Patriotism* (Princeton, N.J.: Princeton University Press, 1999); John Bodnar, ed., *Bonds of Affection: Americans Define Their Patriotism* (Princeton, N.J.: Princeton University Press, 1996); and Wallace Davies, *Patriotism on Parade: The Story of Veterans' and Hereditary Organizations in America, 1783–1900* (Cambridge, Mass.: Harvard University Press, 1955).

For specialized accounts of flag controversies in recent years, see Whitney Smith, "The American Flag in the 1988 Presidential Campaign," *Flag Bulletin* 128 (1988), 176–95; on the 1989 Chicago "flag on the floor" controversy, Steven Dubin, *Arresting Images: Impolitic Art and Uncivil Actions* (New York: Routledge, 1992), 102–34; and several articles by Robert Justin Goldstein: "This Flag is Not for Burning," *The Nation,* July 18, 1994, 84–86; "The Revolutionary Communist

Party and Burning the Flag During its Forgotten Years, 1974–1989," *The Raven* 6 (1999), 19–40; "Whatever Happened to the Great 1989–90 American Flag Desecration Uproar?" *The Raven* 2 (1995), 1–32; and "The American Flag Desecration Controversy: Its Current Status and Legal Background," *Free Speech Yearbook* 35 (1997), 27–44. Carolyn Marvin and David Ingle, *Blood Sacrifice and the Nation: Totem Rituals and the American Flag* (Cambridge, England: Cambridge University Press, 1999), appeared too late for me to use.

Current developments involving the flag desecration amendment and the flag burning controversy in general can be followed on several Internet sites. The Freedom Forum of the First Amendment Center at Vanderbilt University offers comprehensive reporting at www.free-domforum.org. The leading proamendment organization, the Citizens Flag Alliance, has a site at www.cfa-inc.org, and a leading antiamendment group, People for the American Way, maintains a site devoted to the amendment controversy at www.flagamendment.org. The "flag burning page" includes a variety of information about the controversy, primarily from an antiamendment standpoint, as well as the opportunity to "virtually" burn a flag: www.esquilax.com/flag.